Siegel's

CONSTITUTIONAL LAW

Essay and Multiple-Choice Questions and Answers

Fifth Edition

BRIAN N. SIEGEL
J.D., Columbia Law School

Revised by

Ronald J. Krotoszynski, Jr.
John S. Stone Chair,
Director of Faculty Research, and
Professor of Law
The University of Alabama School of Law

Wolters Kluwer
Law & Business

Published by Wolters Kluwer Law & Business in New York.

Wolters Kluwer Law & Business serves customers worldwide with CCH, Aspen Publishers, and Kluwer Law International products. (www.wolterskluwerlb.com)

To contact Customer Care, e-mail customer.service@wolterskluwer.com, call 1-800-234-1660, fax 1-800-901-9075, or mail correspondence to:

> Wolters Kluwer Law & Business
> Attn: Order Department
> PO Box 990
> Frederick, MD 21705

The authors gratefully acknowledge the assistance of the California Committee of Bar Examiners, which provided access to questions on which many of the essay questions in this book are based.

Printed in the United States of America.

1 2 3 4 5 6 7 8 9 0

ISBN 978-1-4548-0925-8

About Wolters Kluwer Law & Business

Wolters Kluwer Law & Business is a leading global provider of intelligent information and digital solutions for legal and business professionals in key specialty areas, and respected educational resources for professors and law students. Wolters Kluwer Law & Business connects legal and business professionals as well as those in the education market with timely, specialized authoritative content and information-enabled solutions to support success through productivity, accuracy and mobility.

Serving customers worldwide, Wolters Kluwer Law & Business products include those under the Aspen Publishers, CCH, Kluwer Law International, Loislaw, Best Case, ftwilliam.com and MediRegs family of products.

CCH products have been a trusted resource since 1913, and are highly regarded resources for legal, securities, antitrust and trade regulation, government contracting, banking, pension, payroll, employment and labor, and healthcare reimbursement and compliance professionals.

Aspen Publishers products provide essential information to attorneys, business professionals and law students. Written by preeminent authorities, the product line offers analytical and practical information in a range of specialty practice areas from securities law and intellectual property to mergers and acquisitions and pension/benefits. Aspen's trusted legal education resources provide professors and students with high-quality, up-to-date and effective resources for successful instruction and study in all areas of the law.

Kluwer Law International products provide the global business community with reliable international legal information in English. Legal practitioners, corporate counsel and business executives around the world rely on Kluwer Law journals, looseleafs, books, and electronic products for comprehensive information in many areas of international legal practice.

Loislaw is a comprehensive online legal research product providing legal content to law firm practitioners of various specializations. Loislaw provides attorneys with the ability to quickly and efficiently find the necessary legal information they need, when and where they need it, by facilitating access to primary law as well as state-specific law, records, forms and treatises.

Best Case Solutions is the leading bankruptcy software product to the bankruptcy industry. It provides software and workflow tools to flawlessly streamline petition preparation and the electronic filing process, while timely incorporating ever-changing court requirements.

ftwilliam.com offers employee benefits professionals the highest quality plan documents (retirement, welfare and non-qualified) and government forms (5500/PBGC, 1099 and IRS) software at highly competitive prices.

MediRegs products provide integrated health care compliance content and software solutions for professionals in healthcare, higher education and life sciences, including professionals in accounting, law and consulting.

Wolters Kluwer Law & Business, a division of Wolters Kluwer, is headquartered in New York. Wolters Kluwer is a market-leading global information services company focused on professionals.

Introduction

Although law school grades are a significant factor in obtaining a summer internship or entry position at a law firm, no formalized preparation for finals is offered at most law schools. For the most part, students are expected to fend for themselves in learning how to take a law school exam. Ironically, law school exams may bear little correspondence to the teaching methods used by professors during the school year. At least in the first year, professors require you to spend most of your time briefing cases. This is probably not great preparation for issue-spotting on exams. In briefing cases, you are made to focus on one or two principles of law at a time; thus, you don't get practice in relating one issue to another or in developing a picture of an entire problem or the entire course. When exams finally come, you're forced to make an abrupt 180-degree turn. Suddenly, you are asked to recognize, define, and discuss a variety of issues buried within a single multi-issue fact pattern. Alternately, you may be asked to select among a number of possible answers, all of which look inviting but only one of which is right.

The comprehensive course outline you've created so diligently, and with such pain, means little if you're unable to apply its contents on your final exams. There is a vast difference between reading opinions in which the legal principles are clearly stated and applying those same principles to hypothetical essay exams and multiple-choice questions.

The purpose of this book is to help you bridge the gap between memorizing a rule of law and ***understanding how to use it*** in an exam. After an initial overview describing the exam-writing process, you see a large number of hypotheticals that test your ability to write analytical essays and to pick the right answers to multiple-choice questions. ***Read them—all of them!*** Then review the suggested answers that follow. You'll find that the key to superior grades lies in applying your knowledge through questions and answers, not through rote memory.

GOOD LUCK!

Table of Contents

Preparing Effectively for Essay Examinations

Essay Questions

Essay Answers

Multiple-Choice Questions

Multiple-Choice Answers

Table and Index

Preparing Effectively for Essay Examinations

To achieve superior scores on essay exams, a law student must (1) learn and understand "blackletter" principles and rules of law for each subject, (2) analyze how those principles of law arise within a test fact pattern, and (3) clearly and succinctly discuss each principle and how it relates to the facts. One of the most common misconceptions about law school is that you must memorize each word on every page of your casebooks or outlines to do well on exams. The reality is that you can commit an entire casebook to memory and still do poorly on an exam. Our review of hundreds of student answers has shown us that most students know most of the rules. Students who do **best** on exams are able to analyze how the rules relate to the facts in the questions, and they are able to communicate their analysis to the grader. You also should note that, although some essay questions have discrete "right" and "wrong" answers, law professors often will devise exam questions that simply do not have a definitive answer precisely to see how effectively a student can apply rules to facts that could relate to more than one legal rule or produce more than one possible result. Thus, the ability to correctly state a rule is only the first step to an excellent answer — you must be able to apply the rule persuasively as well. The following pages cover what you need to know to achieve superior scores on your law school essay exams.

The "ERC" Process

To study effectively for law school exams you must be able to "ERC" (*E*lementize, *R*ecognize, and *C*onceptualize) each legal principle covered in your casebooks, class discussions and course outlines. *Elementizing* means reducing each legal theory and rule you learn to a concise, straightforward statement of its essential elements. Without knowledge of these elements, it's difficult to see all the issues as they arise.

For example, if you are asked, "May Congress, under the Commerce Clause power, require individuals to purchase health insurance from a private company?" it is **not** enough to say, "Congress can regulate economic and business activity under the Constitution." This educated layperson description would leave a grader wondering if you actually know the relevant legal doctrines that define the precise metes and bounds of Congress's Commerce Clause power. An accurate statement of the commerce power would go something like this: "Since 1937, the Supreme Court has held that, pursuant to the Commerce Clause, Congress may regulate

(1) the instrumentalities of interstate commerce (including roads, navigable waterways, and the means used to travel among the states and across national borders), (2) goods, services, and people moving in the channels of interstate commerce (i.e., things that are moving, or have moved, across a state or national boundary), and (3) economic or commercial activity that, aggregated across the national economy, substantially affects in-state commerce. *U.S. v. Morrison.* Moreover, a strong answer would note that in the cases decided since 1937, the commercial or economic activity aggregated when applying the substantial effects test has involved activity of some sort, rather than the failure to engage in activity (like buying health insurance).

Recognizing means perceiving or anticipating which words or ideas within a legal principle are likely to be the source of issues and how those issues are likely to arise within a given hypothetical fact pattern. With respect to commerce power question, there are at least two **potential** issues. First, does the failure to buy health insurance fall within one of the three strands of the Commerce Clause power? If the answer is no, then the analysis is at an end. However, if doubt exists regarding strength of a conclusion, that is, is it **certain** that Congress could not invoke any of the three aspects of the commerce power?, then you should proceed to a second level of analysis, namely, does an **argument** in favor of Congress having such authority exist under the modern test? If the answer is yes, then you should explain the source of your uncertainty, making the best arguments **in favor and also *against* the proposition**. Here, the question asks about regulating "inactivity" rather than "activity," which provides a possible basis for a federal court to find that the commerce power does not support the legislation. Because Congress has never before tried to regulate the failure to engage in interstate commerce, some doubt exists about the ability of Congress to invoke the commerce power on these facts. Good arguments exist in favor of extending the commerce power on these facts, but so do arguments in favor of finding that the existing precedents do not go far enough to support mandating that individuals engage in an economic transaction. To obtain a good grade on an examination in Constitutional Law, the key is to state the governing test but to note any complications that might exist in applying the test to the facts given in the call of the question.

Conceptualizing means imagining situations in which each element of a rule of law can give rise to factual issues. ***When you can imagine or construct an application of each element of a rule, you will truly understand*** *the rule!* The inability to conjure up hypothetical fact patterns or stories involving particular rules of law foretells a likelihood that you will miss issues involving those rules on an exam. It's **crucial** (1) to **recognize** that issues result from the interaction of facts with the words defining a rule of law and (2) to develop the ability to **conceptualize** or **imagine** fact patterns using the words or concepts within the rule. Thus, it's not enough simply to know and state a potentially governing standard of review, you must be able to apply it to relevant facts and also make arguments by analogy in favor of—or opposing—extending the rule to reach different (or distinguishable) facts.

For example, a set of facts illustrating the intentional discrimination requirement of an Equal Protection Clause claim involving heightened judicial scrutiny could be the following:

> The Avalon city council adopts a new standardized test and requires all would-be municipal employees to score at least 70 (of 100) points in order to be considered for a position with the city. The city council, at the time it adopts the new policy, states that "[w]e believe municipal employees should have strong abilities in math, English, and science in order to best meet the needs of the city." After a few months of using the test, it appears that women consistently score higher than men and that Latino test takers substantially outperform all other racial and ethnic groups. Thus, the use of the test has the effect of substantially boosting the number of Latino women eligible for employment with the city and decreasing the number of men and non-Latino applicants eligible for employment.

An illustration of how the intentional discrimination requirement for an Equal Protection Clause claim may be met through indirect forms of proof might generate an issue is the following:

> The County of Eden (Eden) uses voter registration rolls to select the members of the petit jury pools. Eden has a population that is 40 percent Caucasian, 35 percent African American, and 25 percent Latino. For the last two years, the petit jury pool has been 75 percent Caucasian, 15 percent Latino, and 10 percent African American. The population of *registered voters* in Eden is 50 percent Caucasian, 30 percent African American, and 20 percent Latino. Suppose that a defendant objects to the composition of the petit jury pool and alleges that its composition violates the Equal Protection Clause. What standard of review should a reviewing court apply to such a claim?

A fact pattern involving the rule that a classification established for race neutral reasons may trigger heightened judicial scrutiny when a jurisdiction chooses to retain the rule **because of,** rather than despite, its discriminatory effects might be the following:

> The City of Anywhere (Anywhere) establishes a system of at-large elec-
> tions for members of the city council in 1892, during a time when only
> Caucasian citizens were permitted to register and vote in Anywhere. In
> 1982, after large numbers of African-American and Latino residents have
> successfully registered to vote, Anywhere considers changing its election
> process to use districts to select city council members. Without any public
> explanation, however, the city council votes to retain the at-large system
> of electing members of the city council. The local newspaper reports the
> contents of a secret memorandum prepared by the city attorney that says
> "[t]he city will no longer have a white majority on the city council if we
> alter the city's election procedures to use districts."

Carefully considering the legal effects of particular fact patterns such as
these is simply *critical* to successfully answering essay questions in constitutional law. You must consider and apply every possible permutation of
the governing legal standard (in the above examples, the intentionality or
purposeful discrimination rule for successfully invoking heightened scrutiny to a facially neutral statute or regulation, see *Washington v. Davis*) to
obtain the best possible grade.

Issue-Spotting

One of the keys to doing well on an essay examination is issue-spotting. In
fact, issue-spotting is the most important skill you will learn in law school.
In practice, if you recognize a legal issue, you can find the applicable rule of
law (if there is one) by researching the issue. But if you fail to see the issues,
you will serve your clients badly. In law school exams, it is important to
remember that (1) an issue is a question to be decided by the judge or jury
and (2) a question is "in issue" when it can be disputed or argued about at
trial. The bottom line is that *if you don't spot an issue, you can't raise it
or discuss it*.

The key to issue-spotting is to learn to approach a problem in the same
way an attorney does. Let's assume you've been admitted to practice and a
client enters your office with a legal problem involving a dispute. He or she
will recite his facts to you and give you any documents that may be pertinent. The client will then want to know if he or she can sue (or be sued,
if your client seeks to avoid liability). To answer your client's questions
intelligently, you will have to decide the following: (1) what principles or
rules can possibly be asserted by your client, (2) what defense or defenses
can possibly be raised to these principles, (3) what issues may arise if these
defenses are asserted, (4) what arguments each side can make to persuade
the fact finder to resolve the issue in the client's favor, and finally, (5) what

the *likely* outcome of each issue will be. *All the issues that can possibly arise at trial will be relevant to your answers.*

How to Discuss an Issue

Keep in mind **that *rules of law are the guides to issues*** (i.e., an issue arises where there is a question whether the facts do, or do not, satisfy an element of a rule); a rule of law **cannot dispose of an issue** unless the rule can reasonably be **applied to the facts.**

A good way to learn how to discuss an issue is to study the following mini-hypothetical and the two student responses that follow it.

Mini-Hypothetical

Elementary School Principal (P) fires Teacher (T) after a parent complains to P of "inappropriate behavior and methods" by T. After receiving the complaint and without any prior notice, P sends T a note stating simply "You are hereby immediately relieved of your teaching duties, effective immediately. Please clean out your desk and do not return to work after the close of business today." You work as a lawyer in the same community. T approaches you and seeks legal advice regarding her rights, if any, to a pretermination hearing and reinstatement to her job..

Discuss any potential constitutional claims by T against P and the school district.

Pertinent Principles of Law:

1. The first and most important consideration will be whether T can claim either a property or liberty interest in continued employment as a public school teacher. *Perry v. Sindermann*; *Board of Regents v. Roth*. In general, a government employee does not have any right to keep her job. In order to claim protection, the employee must establish more than a unilateral wish to remain employed—she must establish that she possesses "a legitimate claim of entitlement" to her job. This can be established under a state law or regulation, a local school district regulation, or even an employee handbook adopted and distributed by the government employer.

2. *If* T can first establish a protected libery or property interest in her job, an open-ended balancing test will govern how much process must be provided and when the process must be provided by the school district.. Under *Mathews v. Eldridge*, a reviewing court must consider (1) the nature of the private interest, (2) the process that the government

observed, the risk of error associated with this process, and the probability that additional process would reduce the risk of error, and (3) the nature of the government's interest. In general, some sort of predeprivation process usually must be provided absent good reason. *Goss v. Lopez.*

First Student Answer

Did T have a right to process before being fired?

Employment is a very important interest, and the government should not be permitted to fire an otherwise well-performing employee without providing advance notice. T's interest in her job plainly constitutes a kind of property interest that triggers procedural due process rights. Moreover, T also possesses an interest in liberty because her reputation will be harmed by virtue of the summary firing by P. Because T can invoke both property and liberty interests, P and the school district must provide T with notice and an opportunity to be heard.

Did P and the school district provide sufficient process?

On these facts, P summarily fired T without any prior notice or opportunity to be heard. T's interest in her job plainly should control on these facts, and P and the school district have violated her right to procedural due process. The government's interest here is weak, T's interest is quite strong, and there is a *huge* risk of error. In sum, T should prevail against P and the school district if she were to file a procedural due process claim.

Second Student Answer

Government Employment and Procedural Due Process:

The facts do not provide sufficient information to determine whether or not T has a valid property interest in her employment. In order to have a valid property interest in government employment, T would have to show that she possesses a "legitimate claim of entitlement" to her job. For example, if she had been granted formal tenure or a long-term contract, a legitimate claim of entitlement would exist. The facts do not specify whether T has tenure or even an informal guarantee of continued employment. Assuming however, that T has tenure or even a contract for the current school year that P summarily terminated, T would be able to establish a legitimate claim of entitlement to her job and procedural due process rights would apply. Liberty is not likely at issue in this case. Liberty interests can arise through judicial recognition or through operation of positive state or federal law. Although T's reputation could be harmed as a result of the discharge, reputation, standing alone, is not a protected liberty interest. *Paul v. Davis.* The strongest claim for procedural due process rights would arise from successfully claiming a legitimate claim of entitlement to continued employment (whether for the balance of the school year or for a longer period).

It is Unclear if Predeprivation Process Would Be Due

Normally, the existence of a protected property interest would require the government to provide some type of pre-deprivation notice and hearing. However, the rule is not inexorable and if the government possesses a good reason for terminating employment before providing either notice or a hearing, the government could prevail. On the facts provided, it is simply not possible to know whether or not T's discharge was consistent with procedural due process).

Under *Mathews* balancing, a reviewing court considers the nature of the private interest, the nature of the government's interest, and the risk of error associated with the procedure provided, in conjunction with the probability that additional process would, in fact, reduce the risk of an erroneous decision. Here, T would claim an interest in continued employment, which is certainly an important property interest. The government's claim would depend on the nature of the complaint raised by the parent (the facts do not specify it). If the complaint related to something minor, such as a poor grade received by the parent's child in T's class, the government interest would be negligible. On the other hand, if the parent complained about something more serious, such as sexual abuse or drug use, P could probably prevail in discharging T without providing any significant notice or predeprivation process. Thus, in order to apply *Mathews*, more facts are needed to ascertain the strength of the government's interest in immediately removing T from her classroom.

If the parent's complaint did not involve alleged conduct by T that would present an immediate and palpable risk to the health or well-being of T's students, however, it is almost certain that T would prevail against P and the school district on a procedural due process claim. Here, T received no notice or process before P fired her. T had, quite literally, no opportunity to know the nature of the charges or to respond to them. Moreover, without even an informal give-and-take between T and P, a simple error could occur that leads to P firing the wrong person (suppose an assistant wrote down the wrong teacher's name when the parent called the school). The Supreme Court has held that even a very brief suspension from a public high school requires at least some opportunity to be heard before the suspension is imposed and enforced. *Goss v. Lopez*. Surely at least this sort of informal predeprivation hearing should also have been provided here, unless the basis for the discharge involves an immediate and serious threat to the students. Clearly, the absence of any process creates a significant risk of error, so the burden in this case will rest squarely on the government to show that a need for speed and expeditious action existed. It is unlikely that the government will be able to carry this burden, but it would not be impossible. Accordingly, in order to predict with confidence the likely outcome of a lawsuit by T against P and the school district alleging a denial of procedural due process, I would need to have additional facts regarding the exact basis of the parent's complaint against T.

Finally, regardless of the outcome of the *Mathews* balancing test with respect to *pretermination* process, T surely has a right to some sort of *postdeprivation* hearing (again assuming that T can establish a legitimate claim of entitlement to continued employment). Even when the government can establish an exigency sufficient to justify waiving any predeprivation process, it must still provide postdeprivation process. *North American Cold Storage Co. v. Chicago.*

Critique

Let's start by examining the First Student Answer. It mistakenly states the governing standard—in fact, it never actually states the controlling legal standard (a procedural due process plaintiff must show a "legitimate claim of entitlement" in a property interest in order to claim procedural due process rights). The assertion of a liberty interest in reputation is also incorrect. It states a naked conclusion without providing the governing legal standard or the facts that arguably meet it. Even worse, the first student answer *assumes facts not given!* The facts do not state whether T had a contract or tenure, or some other basis for claiming a legitimate claim of entitlement to continued employment at the public school. **Never** assume facts not provided when answering a law school exam question. In all probability, the instructor is looking to see if you will recognize that information essential to analyzing the problem correctly is absent.

The same two mistakes also exist in the second paragraph of the First Atudent Answer. The First Student Answer once again fails to state and apply the governing standard of review (*Mathews* balancing). A professor grading this answer will have serious doubts about whether this student knows and understands the governing standard of review. In this paragraph as well, the First Student Answer foolishly assumes facts not given and does not even state that an assumption is being made: The facts do not state, at all, the basis of the parent's complaint to P. The nature of the government's interest to act quickly depends entirely on the nature of the complaint. This is a catastrophic error that only compounds the prior (repeated) error of not clearly stating the governing legal standard applicable to a particular constitutional claim.

The second student answer is *much better* than the first student answer. First, this answer clearly identifies critical facts not given that are essential to correctly analyzing the claim. This answer demonstrates that the student recognizes that information essential to answering the question correctly has not been provided. Second, the Second Student Answer clearly states—and then applies—the governing legal standards for determining whether a procedural due process claim exists and then, if one does, whether additional procedures not provided were constitutionally requisite. Also, this answer states a clear conclusion if one assumes that a critical fact favors T over P (that the parent's complaint would not be sufficient to justify immediately discharging T). Finally, the Second Student Answer correctly notes that even if the facts support the government's denial of pretermination process, this would not excuse the absence of some sort of posttermination hearing.

Structuring Your Answer

Graders will give high marks to a clearly written, well-structured answer. Each issue you discuss should follow a specific and consistent structure that a grader can easily follow.

The Second Student Answer basically utilizes the *I-R-A-A-O format* with respect to each issue. In this format, the *I* stands for *Issue*; the *R* for *Rule of law*, the first *A* for *one side's Argument*, the second *A* for *the other party's rebuttal Argument*, and the *O* for your *Opinion as to how the issue would be resolved*. The *I-R-A-A-O* format emphasizes the importance of (1) discussing *both* sides of an issue and (2) communicating to the grader that, where an issue arises, an attorney can only advise her client as to the *probable* decision on that issue.

A somewhat different format for analyzing each issue is the *I-R-A-C format*. Here, the *I* stands for *Issue*, the *R* for *Rule of law*, the *A* for *Application of the facts to the rule of law*, and the *C* for *Conclusion*. *I-R-A-C* is a legitimate approach to the discussion of a particular issue, within the time constraints imposed by the question. The *I-R-A-C format* must be applied to each issue in the question; it is not the solution to the entire answer. If there are six issues in a question, for example, you should offer six separate, independent *I-R-A-C* analyses.

In general, the *I-R-A-C* approach is preferable to the *I-R-A-O* formula. However, either can be used to analyze and organize essay exam answers. Whatever format you choose, however, you should be consistent throughout the exam and remember the following rules:

First, *analyze all of the relevant facts*. Facts have significance in a particular case *only as they come under the applicable rules of law*. The facts presented must be analyzed and examined to see if they do or do not satisfy one element or another of the applicable rules, and the essential facts and rules must be stated and argued in your analysis.

Second, you must communicate to the grader the *precise rule of law* controlling the facts. Because of eagerness to start their arguments, some students fail to state the applicable rule of law first. Remember, the *R* in either format stands for *rule of law*. Defining the rule of law *before* an analysis of the facts is essential in order to allow the grader to follow your reasoning.

Third, it is important to treat *each side of an issue with equal detail*. If a hypothetical describes how an elderly man was killed when he ventured upon the land of a huge power company to obtain a better view of a nuclear reactor, your sympathies might understandably fall on the side of the old man. The grader will nevertheless expect you to see and make every possible argument for the other side. Don't permit your personal viewpoint to affect your answer, and don't assume you are supposed to present an analysis from the point of view of the plaintiff. When discussing an issue, always state the arguments for each side unless the question gives you specific directions to assume a particular role.

Finally, remember to *state your opinion or conclusion* on each issue. Keep in mind, however, that your opinion or conclusion is probably the *least* important part of an exam answer. Why? Because your professor knows that no attorney can tell his or her client exactly how a judge or jury will decide a particular issue. By definition, an issue is a legal dispute that can go either way. An attorney, therefore, can offer the client only his or her best opinion about the likelihood of victory or defeat on an issue. Because the decision on any issue lies with the judge or jury, no attorney can ever be absolutely certain of the resolution. Also take care to avoid undue certainty in your conclusion when a reviewing court could reasonably decide the question either way. At the same time, also avoid being unduly tentative if the question has a clear answer. Professors write essay questions that have clear answers, but they also write questions that involve situations in which a court could plausibly decide in favor of either party. Recognizing the probability of an outcome can help to demonstrate your mastery of the materials. For example, if a question asks whether someone 18 years old may constitutionally serve as president, the Constitution itself provides a clear answer ("no": *see* Article II, §1, cl. 4). On the other hand, if an exam question asks whether the president must obtain a declaration of war before committing armed forces abroad, it is almost certain that no clear answer would exist given the inherent conflict between the Congress's power to declare war and the president's power to act as commander-in-chief.

Discuss All Possible Issues

As we've noted, a student should draw *some* type of conclusion or opinion for each issue raised. Whatever your conclusion on a particular issue, it is essential to anticipate and discuss *all of the issues* that would arise if the question were actually tried in court. In this respect, it might be wise to reread a question before beginning your answer. You must make sure you have identified all the relevant issues; if you do not read a question carefully, you run a serious risk of missing issues. Also consider outlining your answer, briefly, before writing the full answer. Doing this can help you to identify issues and also to organize a coherent, logical answer to the question.

Let's assume that a First Amendment hypothetical involves a government regulation limiting public protests on local city streets, sidewalks, and parks, to between the hours of 10 A.M. and 4 P.M. daily for "antigovernment" protests. Under *Ward*, a time, place, and manner regulation must be "content neutral." If the regulation is *not* content neutral, strict judicial scrutiny applies, and the regulation is likely unconstitutional. Even so, however, and even if you feel *very* strongly that the defendant will lose the case because restricting "antigovernment" protests clearly constitutes a content-based speech regulation, you should still state and apply the other elements of the *Ward* test, namely that time, place, and manner regulations must advance a significant government interest, be narrowly tailored, and leave open ample alternative channels of communication. Thus, you *must* go on to discuss all of the other potential issues as well (whether the city's ordinance advances a significant interest, is narrowly tailored, and will leave open ample alternative channels of communication). If you were to terminate your answer after a discussion of the content neutrality element only, you'd probably receive an inferior grade. At the same time, however, it would be entirely appropriate to flag the content neutrality requirement as probably controlling the outcome of the case and stating a strong position that a city ordinance prohibiting "antigovernment" speech is *not* content neutral.

Why should you have to discuss every possible issue if you are relatively certain that the outcome of a particular issue would be dispositive of the entire case? Because at the commencement of litigation, neither party can be **absolutely positive** about which issues he or she will prevail upon at trial. We can state with confidence that every attorney with some degree of experience has won issues he or she thought he or she would lose and has lost issues on which victory seemed assured. Because one can never be absolutely certain how a factual issue will be resolved by the fact finder, a good attorney (and exam writer) will consider **all** possible issues. There is also the question of establishing that you know the governing legal test and also can apply it persuasively; if you simply identify one element of a four-part test and then ignore the other elements, the instructor will likely wonder whether you actually know the governing law and can apply it to the facts presented by the question. As in your high school geometry class, you cannot simply offer naked conclusions (even if they are correct); instead, you must show your proofs.

To understand the importance of discussing all of the potential issues, you should reflect on what you will do in the actual practice of law. If you represent the defendant, for example, it is your job to raise every possible defense. If there are five potential defenses and your pleadings only rely on three of them (because you're sure you will win on all three), and the plaintiff is somehow successful on all three issues, your client may well sue you for malpractice. Your client's contention would be that you should be liable because if you had only raised the two additional issues, you might have prevailed on at least one of them, and therefore liability would have been avoided. It is an attorney's duty to raise **all** legitimate issues. A similar philosophy should be followed when taking essay exams.

What exactly do you say when you've resolved the initial issue in favor of the defendant, and discussion of any additional issues would seem to be moot? You should begin the discussion of the next issue with something like, "Assuming, however, the plaintiff prevailed on the foregoing issue, the next issue would be . . . . " The grader will understand and appreciate what you have done.

The corollary to the importance of raising all potential issues is that you should avoid discussion of obvious nonissues. Raising nonissues is detrimental in three ways: First, you waste precious time; second, you usually receive absolutely no points for discussing an issue that the grader deems extraneous; and third, it suggests to the grader that you lack the ability to distinguish the significant from the trivial. The best guideline for avoiding the discussion of a nonissue is to ask yourself, "Would I, as an attorney, feel comfortable bringing that issue to the attention of a judge or one of the lawyers working with me or against me in a case?"

Delineate the Transition from One Issue to the Next

It's a good idea to make it easy for the grader to see the issues you've found. One way to accomplish this is to cover only one issue per paragraph. Another way is to underline each issue statement. Provided that time permits, we recommend that you use both techniques. The essay answers in this book contain numerous illustrations of these suggestions.

One frequent student error is to write two separate paragraphs in which all of the arguments for one side are made in the initial paragraph, and all of the rebuttal arguments by the other side are made in the next paragraph. This organization is *a bad idea*. It obliges the grader to reconstruct the exam answer in his or her mind several times to determine whether all possible issues have been discussed by both sides. It will also cause you to state the same rule of law more than once. A better-organized answer presents a given argument by one side and follows that immediately in the same paragraph with the other side's rebuttal to that argument.

Understanding the "Call" of a Question

The statement *at the end* of an essay question or of the fact pattern in a multiple-choice question is sometimes referred to as the "call" of the question. It usually asks you to do something specific such as "discuss," "discuss the rights of the parties," "list X's rights," "advise X," "give the best grounds on which to find the statute unconstitutional," "state what D can be convicted of," "recommend how the estate should be distributed," and so forth. You should read the call of the question carefully because it tells you exactly what you're expected to do. If a question asks, "What are X's rights against Y?" or "What is X liable to Y for?" it would be a mistake to write about Y's rights against Z. You will usually receive absolutely no credit for discussing issues or facts that are not required by the call. On the other hand, if the call of an essay question is simply "discuss" or "discuss the rights of the parties," then *all* foreseeable issues must be covered by your answer.

Students are often led astray by an essay question's call. For example, if you are asked for "X's rights against Y" or to "advise X," you may think you may limit yourself to X's viewpoint with respect to the issues. This is *not correct*! You cannot resolve one party's rights against another party without considering the issues that would arise (and the arguments the other side would assert) if litigation occurred. In short, although the call of the question may appear to focus on the rights of one of the parties to the litigation, a superior answer will cover all the issues and arguments that that person might **encounter** (not just the arguments he or she would **make**) in attempting to pursue his or her rights against the other side.

Be sure to answer the question from the perspective that your professor has asked you to assume. Thus, if an essay question states that you work for the state attorney general's office and are defending a state law in federal court, your answer should put forth best arguments in favor of sustaining the statute against a constitutional challenge (regardless of whether this is the strongest argument). That said, however, a good lawyer always advises her client about the possibility of an adverse outcome. Keep in mind that assuming an advocacy role **does not** mean that you should ignore problems or shortcomings in your client's best argument(s). The key, however, is to assume the role that the question tells you to take. More often than not, you will be asked to evaluate a problem either from an advocate's point of view or from a reviewing court's point of view. Make sure that your answer adopts the proper perspective. If a question does not specify a perspective from which to analyze the problem, assume one of neutrality (i.e., what is the best answer?).

Finally, avoid the temptation to prove all that you have learned by writing a historical overview of an area of constitutional law. Instead, **answer the question that your professor has asked**. For example, if a question implicates the Commerce Clause, do not start with *Gibbons v. Ogden* unless that case has some particular relevance. Survey courses often cover the development of legal doctrine over time, but when writing an examination answer, you should apply the currently controlling legal test or standard. Similarly, answer the question that your professor has asked, not the question that you wish she had asked. For example, if standing could preclude a federal court from reaching the merits, you should discuss standing in your answer. On the other hand, if the plaintiff in an essay question plainly possesses standing, you should avoid the temptation to start your answer with an analysis of the requirements of Article III standing (unless the question specifically asks you to address standing).

The Importance of Analyzing the Question Carefully Before Writing

The overriding **time pressure** of an essay exam is probably a major reason why many students fail to analyze a question carefully before writing. Five minutes into the allocated time for a particular question, you may notice that the person next to you is writing furiously. This thought then flashes through your mind: "Oh my goodness, he's putting down more words on the paper than I am, and therefore he's bound to get a better grade." The *unequivocal* truth: There is no necessary correlation between the number of words on your exam paper and the grade you'll receive! Students who begin their answer after only five minutes of analysis have probably seen only the most obvious issues and missed many, if not most, of the subtle ones. They are also likely to be less well organized.

Opinions differ as to how much time you should spend analyzing and outlining a question before you actually write the answer. We believe that you should spend about 15 minutes analyzing, organizing, and outlining a one-hour question before writing your answer. This will usually provide sufficient time to analyze and organize the question thoroughly *and* enough time to write a relatively complete answer. Remember that each word of the question must be scrutinized to determine if it (1) suggests an issue under the operative rules of law or (2) can be used in making an argument for the resolution of an issue. Because you can't receive points for an issue you don't spot, it is usually wise to read a question *twice* before starting your outline.

When to Make an Assumption

The instructions for a question may tell you to *assume* facts that are necessary to the answer. Even when these instructions are *not* given, you may be obliged to make certain assumptions about missing facts in order to write a thorough answer. Assumptions should be made only when you are told or when you, as the attorney for one of the parties described in the question, would be obliged to solicit additional information from your client. On the other hand, assumptions should *never be used to change or alter the question*. Don't ever write something like "if the facts in the question were . . . , instead of . . . , then . . . would result." If you do this, you are wasting time on facts that are extraneous to the problem before you. Professors want you to deal with *their* fact patterns, not your own.

Students sometimes try to "write around" information they think is missing. They assume that their professor has failed to include every piece of data necessary for a thorough answer. This is generally *wrong*. The professor may have omitted some facts deliberately to see if the student *can figure out what to do* under the circumstances. However, in some instances, the professor may have omitted them inadvertently (even law professors are sometimes human).

The way to deal with the omission of essential information is to describe (1) what fact (or facts) appears to be missing and (2) why that information is important. As an example, go back to the "arbitrarily fired public school teacher" hypothetical discussed earlier in this section. In that fact pattern, there was no mention of either the terms and basis of the teacher's employment *or* the precise allegation raised in the parent's complaint to the school's principal. The first missing fact is essential to whether any procedural due process protections apply *at all*. Absent a "legitimate claim of entitlement," the school district could fire the teacher without providing *any* pre- or postdeprivation process. So, this fact is crucial to the viability of the relevant constitutional claim. So, too, the precise reason for the principal's decision to fire the teacher will weigh heavily in determining the strength of the government's interest. If the complaint involved activities or behaviors that are harmful to children, such as sexual abuse or drug use, the government's interest could be quite compelling. Conversely, if the parent complained about another student's book report on a *Harry Potter* novel (perhaps because the book series touches on themes involving witchcraft and occult), the government's interest would be considerably weaker and the teacher's claim to predeprivation process significantly more compelling.

Assumptions should be made in a manner that keeps the other issues open (i.e., they lead to a discussion of all other possible issues). Don't assume facts that would virtually dispose of the entire hypothetical in a few sentences. For example, suppose that A called B a "convicted felon" (a statement that is inherently defamatory—that is, a statement that tends to subject the plaintiff to hatred, contempt, or ridicule). If A's statement is true, he has a complete defense to B's action for defamation. If the facts don't tell whether A's statement was true or not, it would *not* be wise to write something like, "We'll assume that A's statement about B is accurate, and therefore B cannot successfully sue A for defamation." So facile an approach would rarely be appreciated by the grader. The proper way to handle this situation would be to state, "If we assume that A's statement about B is not correct, A cannot raise the defense of truth." You've communicated to the grader that you recognize the need to assume an essential fact and that you've assumed it in a way that enables you to proceed to discuss all other issues.

Case Names

In most courses, a law student is *not* expected to recall case names on an exam. The professor knows that you have read several hundred cases for each course and that you would have to be a memory expert to have all of the names at your fingertips. That said, however, constitutional law is simply different in this regard—the selective and thoughtful use of case names can help convey that you have mastery of the material. For example, in discussing abortion regulations, noting the controlling "undue burden" test is the most important element of a good answer. But, it will likely help to also add a notation to *Casey* after stating the applicable rule; stating the case name demonstrates knowledge and facility with controlling legal precedents. Constitutional law relies on landmark precedents for establishing rules to a degree that goes well beyond the importance of case law in courses like criminal law and contracts, which feature codes (the MPC in one case, the UCC in the other) that provide the relevant rules of decision. In general, you will do yourself more good than harm by noting the names of landmark case in constitutional law. ***NOTE If your constitutional law professor specifically instructs you to use or refrain from using case names in your answers, be sure to follow her instructions on this question, rather than this general advice.***

If you confront a fact pattern that seems similar to a case you have reviewed (but you cannot recall its name), it is perfectly permissible simply to write something like, "One case we've read held that . . . " or "It has been held that . . . . " In this manner, you have informed the grader that you are relying on a case that contained a fact pattern similar to the question at issue. However, if you are discussing a landmark case, you should try to identify the case with particularity if you can do so.

How to Handle Time Pressures

What do you do when there are five minutes left in the exam and you have only written two-thirds of your answer? One thing ***not*** to do is write something like, "No time left!" or "Not enough time!" This gets you nothing but the satisfaction of knowing you have communicated your personal frustrations to the grader. Another thing ***not*** to do is type a brief list of topics you meant to cover but didn't have time to write about. Professors will rarely look at these.

First of all, it is not necessarily a bad thing to be pressed for time. The person who finishes five minutes early has very possibly missed some important issues. The more proficient you become in knowing what is expected of you on an exam, the greater difficulty you may experience in staying within the time limits. Second, remember that (at least to some extent) you're graded against your classmates' answers and they're under exactly the same time pressure as you. In short, don't panic if you can't write the "perfect" answer in the allotted time. Nobody does!

The best hedge against time management problems is to *review as many old exams as possible*. These exercises will give you a familiarity with the process of organizing and writing an exam answer, which, in turn, should result in an enhanced ability to stay within the time boundaries. If you nevertheless find that you have about 15 minutes of writing to do and 5 minutes to do it in, write a paragraph that names the remaining issues or arguments you would discuss if time permitted and says one cogent thing about each of those points. As long as you indicate that you're aware of the remaining legal issues and can connect them to the problem, you'll probably receive some credit.

Formatting Your Answer

Make sure your answer presents your analysis in the best possible light. Use many paragraphs instead of just creating a document in which all of your ideas are merged into a single lengthy paragraph. Remember, your professor may have a hundred or more exams to grade. If your answer is difficult to read, you will rarely be given the benefit of the doubt. On the other hand, an answer that is easy to read creates a very positive impression on the professor.

The Importance of Reviewing Prior Exams

As we've mentioned, it is *extremely important to review old exams*. The transition from blackletter law to essay exam can be a difficult experience if the process has not been practiced. Although this book provides a large number of essay and multiple-choice questions, *don't stop here*! Most law schools have recent tests online or on file in the library, by course. If they are available only in the library, we strongly suggest that you make a copy of every old exam you can obtain (especially those given by your professors) at the beginning of each semester. The demand for these documents usually increases dramatically as "finals time" draws closer.

The exams for each course should be scrutinized *throughout the semester*. They should be reviewed as you complete each chapter in your casebook. Sometimes the order of exam questions follows the sequence of the materials in your casebook. Thus, the first question on a law school test may involve the initial three chapters of the casebook; the second question may pertain to the fourth and fifth chapters; and so forth. In any event, *don't wait* until the semester is nearly over to begin reviewing old exams.

Keep in mind that no one is born with the ability to analyze questions and write superior answers to law school exams. Like any other skill, it is developed and perfected only through application. If you don't take the time to analyze numerous examinations from prior years, this evolutionary process just won't occur. Don't just **think about** the answers to past exam questions; take the time to **write the answers down.** It's also wise to look back at an answer a day or two after you've written it. You will invariably see (1) ways to improve your organizational skills and (2) arguments you missed.

As you practice spotting issues on past exams, you will see how rules of law become the sources of issues on finals. As we've already noted, if you don't **understand** how rules of law translate into issues, you won't be able to achieve superior grades on your exams. Reviewing exams from prior years also should reveal that certain issues tend to be lumped together in the same question. For instance, where a fact pattern involves a false statement made by one person about another, three potential theories of liability are often present—defamation, invasion of privacy (false, public light), and intentional infliction of severe emotional distress. You will need to see if any or all of these legal remedies apply to the facts.

Finally, one of the best means of evaluating if you understand a subject (or a particular area within a subject) is to attempt to create a hypothetical exam for that subject. Your exam should contain as many issues as possible. If you can write an issue-packed exam, you probably know that subject well. If you can't, then you probably haven't yet acquired an adequate understanding of how the principles of law in that subject can spawn issues.

As Always, a Caveat

The suggestions and advice offered in this book represent the product of many years of experience in the field of legal education. We are confident that the techniques and concepts described in these pages will help you prepare for, and succeed at, your exams. Nevertheless, particular professors sometimes have a preference for exam-writing techniques that are not stressed in this book. Some instructors expect at least a nominal reference to the **prima facie** elements of all pertinent legal theories (even though one or more of those principles are **not** placed into issue). Other professors want their students to emphasize public policy considerations in the arguments they make on a particular issue. Because this book is intended for nationwide consumption, these individualized preferences have **not** been stressed. The best way to find out whether your professor has a penchant for a particular writing approach is to ask him or her to provide you with a model answer to a previous exam. If a model answer is not available, speak to second- or third-year students who received a superior grade in that professor's class.

One final point. Although the rules of law stated in the answers to the questions in this book have been drawn from commonly used sources (casebooks, hornbooks, etc.), it is still conceivable that they may be slightly at odds with those taught by your professor. In instances in which a conflict exists between our formulation of a legal principle and the one taught by your professor, ***follow the latter!*** Because your grade is determined by your professor, his or her views should always supersede the views contained in this book.

Essay Questions

Question 1

Following several highly public incidents involving the deaths caused by firearms, and particularly small handguns, the state of Avalon adopts a statute that bans "the sale, possession, or use of a handgun." The law also provides that "violations are punishable by a fine of up to $20,000 and by imprisonment for not more than five years." Jane Doe (JD), a resident of Avalon, owns several small handguns, which she keeps in her home for personal protection in the event of a break in or burglary. JD initiates a law suit in the local federal district court seeking a declaratory judgment that the ban on possession of handguns violates the Constitution. How should the district court rule and why?

Question 2

Margaret Chase (MC) is elected to the U.S. House of Representatives from a congressional district located in the state of Cascadia (C). MC is 32 years old, a natural born citizen of the United States, and a resident of C at the time of her election. The following January, the U.S. House of Representatives refuses to seat MC, noting that she has previously been convicted of a violating state laws against disorderly conduct and criminal trespass. (These charges arose from anti-war protest activity that MC participated in while a college student some ten years earlier.) The House votes to exclude MC from membership, notwithstanding the fact that she possesses an otherwise valid certificate of election from the appropriate state officials. MC immediately initiates a lawsuit against the Speaker of the House, seeking a writ of mandamus ordering her seated. How should the district court rule and why?

Question 3

The state of Beta, citing public health and safety concerns, enacts a statute that "prohibits the use of coffins or caskets purchased out of state from use for either a human burial or cremation in the state of Beta." Susan Jones (SJ), a resident of Beta, purchases a coffin on the Internet from a supplier in Gamma, a neighboring state that borders Beta, for use in the burial of her recently deceased husband, Fred Jones. However, the local funeral director handling the burial services, citing the state law, refuses to receive or otherwise make use of the coffin purchased in Gamma for a burial in Beta. SJ contacts you, a local lawyer licensed to practice law in Beta, seeking legal advice on the validity of the law prohibiting the use of imported out-of-state coffins or caskets in Beta. Specifically, SJ wishes to know if any valid constitutional objection or objections exist to the new law. How do you advise her?

Question 4

The state of Acadiana (A) enacts a new state personal income tax credit program that permits residents to deduct up to $2,000 per year in K-12 education expenses against their state income taxes. The credit is available for expenses associated with a dependent minor child attending a public, private, or parochial/religiously affiliated school located within A, provided that the school has been properly accredited by the state. Mary and Joseph Smith (MJS), residents of A, are committed and evangelical atheists. They object strongly to the use of so-called "tax expenditures" to subsidize pervasively sectarian education. MJS file a lawsuit arguing that the tax credit program violates the Establishment Clause of the U.S. Constitution. A immediately moves to dismiss the suit, arguing in support of its motion that MJS lack standing to bring this challenge. How should the federal district court rule on the motion to dismiss?

Question 5

City, a municipality in state X, has a permit ordinance that prohibits making speeches in City-owned parks without first obtaining a permit from City's police chief. The ordinance authorizes the police chief to establish permit application procedures and to grant or deny permits based on the chief's "overall assessment of the good of the community." The ordinance also provides that denial of a permit may be appealed to the city council.

On Tuesday, Tom applied to Dan, City's police chief, for a permit to speak in the city park the following Saturday. Tom gave Dan his name and local address, but Dan denied Tom's application for a permit because Tom refused Dan's request for a summary of what he intended to say in his speech. When Tom told Dan that he intended to make his speech anyway, Dan immediately gave Tom's name and address to the city attorney.

The city attorney did nothing about the matter until Friday, when, without notice to Tom, he made application on behalf of City to a state X court of general jurisdiction for a temporary restraining order preventing Tom from speaking in the city park without a permit. The state X court issued an *ex parte* temporary restraining order and an order to show cause, answerable in five days, directed to Tom. The orders were served on Tom in the city park on Saturday, as he was about to speak. Despite the temporary restraining order, Tom spoke to about 20 mildly interested persons who were then in the park for various other reasons.

The essence of Tom's speech was that the federal government, "aided and abetted" by City's government, was "leading America to destruction" and that "those who survive will eventually have to fight in the streets of City to regain their liberties." Tom urged the audience to "stockpile weapons" and to "start thinking about forming guerrilla units to take back freedom from the government."

Tom was arrested and charged in the state X court that had issued the temporary restraining order with (1) speaking in the city park without a permit, a misdemeanor; (2) contempt of court for violating the temporary restraining order; and (3) violation of the state X criminal advocacy statute prohibiting "advocating insurrection against the local, state, or federal government," a felony.

Five years ago, the state X Supreme Court construed the criminal advocacy statute as applying only to advocacy that is not protected by the U.S. Constitution.

A week after Tom's speech, in a case unrelated to the charges against Tom, the state X Supreme Court construed City's permit ordinance as authorizing City's police chief to consider "only the time, place, and manner of the proposed speech and not its content" in passing upon permit applications.

What rights guaranteed by the U.S. Constitution should Tom assert in defense to the charges brought against him, and how should the court rule? Discuss.

Question 6

Paul was born in the United States. After voluntarily serving in the Canadian army for several years, he returned to his home state and became employed as a meter reader by the City Water Department, a municipal agency. In the performance of his job, Paul enters private residences and commercial buildings in City to read water meters.

No regulations governing the dress or appearance of Water Department employees existed when Paul was hired. Subsequently, City enacted a dress code ordinance that stated: "All City Water Department employees shall wear a uniform supplied by City when engaged in their employment, and no such employee may wear a beard while so engaged." Paul wore a beard when first employed. Although requested by the head of the Water Department to shave off his beard and wear the uniform provided, Paul refused to do either.

Shortly thereafter, a city election occurred. The incumbent Water Department head was replaced. Paul was a registered voter in the same political party as the unsuccessful incumbent, but took no active part in the election campaign. Immediately upon taking office, the newly elected Water Department head, who was a member of a different political party, notified Paul that he was terminated because he was "registered in the wrong political party and for several other reasons."

After unsuccessfully appealing his dismissal in administrative proceedings with the Water Department and City, Paul filed suit in state court against City, asking for a judgment ordering that his discharge be declared void and that he be reinstated in his job. City's answer alleged that the termination of Paul's employment was proper because (1) Paul had violated City's dress code ordinances for Water Department employees; and (2) a state statute requires that "all state and municipal employees must be citizens of the United States," and a federal statute provides that the U.S. citizenship of any person who voluntarily serves in the armed forces of a foreign country is deemed surrendered.

What issues under the U.S. Constitution are raised by Paul's suit against City and by City's defenses, and how should each of them be decided? Discuss.

Question 7

The Mayo Christian Church (Church) is located in the city of Mayo in state X. The governing body of Church established the Lawyers Society (Society) as a state X nonprofit corporation to increase the participation of Church in Mayo's community problems. Society is composed exclusively of Church members who are lawyers licensed to practice in state X, all of whom have agreed to work for Society without compensation. Society offers free legal services to residents of Mayo who are "victims of racial or religious discrimination." Society is financially supported by both Church funds and a grant of funds from Agency, which administers a state X program providing public funds to legal-aid organizations.

Soon after its establishment, Society "targeted" certain apparent instances of discrimination in Mayo as appropriate objectives for its services. Society members have directly approached Mayo residents who appeared to be victims of discrimination, explained their legal rights, and then offered them free legal assistance in commencing litigation aimed at redressing the apparent discrimination.

However, Society has begun to have legal problems of its own:

1. An organization called "Mayo Taxpayers for Separation of Church and State" (Taxpayers), consisting of state X taxpayers who are residents of Mayo, has brought an action in federal court in state X against Church, Society, and Agency. The complaint challenges the propriety of the use of public funds by a church-sponsored organization and seeks a judgment prohibiting Agency from granting funds to Society.

2. Jay, a lawyer admitted to practice in state X, volunteered to join and work for Society without compensation. He was rejected because he was not a Church member. Jay has brought an action in federal court in state X against Church, Society, and Agency, seeking a judgment requiring Society to admit him to membership. He alleges that his exclusion from membership in Society as an organization supported by public funds constitutes unlawful discrimination in violation of the U.S. Constitution.

3. The state X Bar Association (Bar), which is responsible for the enforcement of state X law regulating the practice of law, has charged that Society's solicitation practices violate the state X attorneys' professional disciplinary code, which prohibits "direct solicitation" of clients

and legal work by lawyers. Bar has instituted an action in state X court against Society and its members, seeking an injunction prohibiting any further "solicitation" activity by Society members.

What issues arising under the U.S. Constitution are involved in these three cases, and how should each issue be decided? Discuss.

Question 8

Five years ago, City adopted a municipal ordinance prohibiting the placing of "commercial" signs on rooftops within city limits. The stated purpose of the ordinance was "improving the quality of life within City by emphasizing and protecting aesthetic values." The ordinance also provided that all signs in place on the date of its adoption in violation of its terms must be removed within five years.

Three years ago, Rugged Cross Church (Church), with its church building situated within City's limits, placed a 20-foot blue neon-lighted sign in the shape of a cross on its church roof, with the message "Join and Support Our Church" in white neon lights inside the blue neon borders of the cross.

After the Church sign was in place, various citizens of City urged that the sign ordinance be amended to include all rooftop signs in City. Other citizens complained to City officials that Church's sign, in particular, was "an eyesore."

Effective two months ago, City amended its sign ordinance by deleting the word "commercial." City then notified Church that its rooftop sign would have to be removed within five years.

Church has brought suit against City in a state trial court of proper jurisdiction, claiming that the amended City sign ordinance is invalid under the U.S. Constitution, both (1) by its terms and general application and (2) as City seeks to apply it to Church.

How should the court rule on each of Church's claims? Discuss.

Question 9

Students Against Defense Spending (SADS), a national college student organization, decided to conduct a campaign protesting government defense spending. SADS members at a university in City planned to distribute campaign literature within City to motorists stopped at major intersections and to patrons at a shopping center owned by Owen.

For years, community service organizations have distributed literature in City to motorists stopped at intersections. There were several accidents causing serious injuries to persons engaged in such practices. For that reason, the city council had been considering for several months a proposed ordinance that would prohibit pedestrians from approaching motorists stopped at intersections within City. Immediately after the SADS distribution plan was publicly announced, the proposed ordinance was passed out of committee and unanimously enacted by the city council. SADS members have not yet attempted to deliver literature to motorists.

City has a municipal ordinance making it a misdemeanor to trespass on private property, including shopping centers. Owen's shopping center is posted with signs stating that no tenant or visitor may distribute on the premises literature not directly related to the commercial purposes of businesses in the center and that violators are subject to removal by the center's security guards and prosecution under the antitrespass ordinance.

SADS has filed two actions in the appropriate federal district court. One action is against City, seeking a declaratory judgment that the recently enacted ordinance violates the rights of SADS members under the U.S. Constitution. The other action is against Owen, seeking a declaratory judgment that any action by Owen or his employees to stop SADS members from distributing campaign literature at his shopping center would violate the rights of free speech of SADS members under the U.S. Constitution.

No SADS campaign literature has yet been distributed at Owen's shopping center, and no threat has been made to remove SADS members from the center or to have them prosecuted under the antitrespassing ordinance if they attempt to distribute their literature on the center premises.

City has filed its answer to the complaint in the first action, and that case is set for trial.

Owen has moved to dismiss the second action on the grounds that (1) the action is not ripe, and (2) the complaint fails to state a claim for relief because SADS members have no constitutionally protected right to distribute the campaign literature on private property.

1. What arguments should SADS make in support of its claim against City, and how should the court decide that claim? Discuss.

2. How should the court rule on Owen's motions? Discuss.

Question 10

Acme Brothers (Acme) operates a men's clothing store in a shopping center it owns in City, state X. Acme embarked on an advertising campaign that has been criticized by a feminist coalition as sexist. In its store windows, Acme has life-size posters of a young woman wearing a bikini. The posters' captions portray her as saying things such as, "I like to be treated rough by a man in an Acme suit." The coalition concedes that the posters are not legally obscene.

Members of the feminist coalition in City attempted to picket on the privately owned sidewalk in front of the Acme store to protest these posters. They were told by Acme's private security guards that the shopping center was private property and that the picketers were trespassing. Acme's security guards then physically removed all picketers from the shopping center premises.

The Acme store is part of a 16-store chain of Acme outlets located in 4 states. Acme's advertising campaigns are planned in the home office in another state and are sent to stores such as that in City. The stores have no choice under company policy but to use the advertising.

After removal of the picketers, the city council of City adopted an ordinance that provides in part:

> It shall be unlawful to display for commercial purposes any picture, or to use any other advertising material, that portrays any individual in a demeaning or sexist fashion.

Violation of this section of the ordinance was made a misdemeanor punishable by a fine of up to $500.

The ordinance also provides:

> The right to picket peacefully, with due regard to pedestrian and vehicular traffic and the rights of all other citizens, shall remain inviolate. Such right shall extend to shopping centers and other areas, where the title to sidewalks is privately owned but open to the public for access to retail sales outlets.

Since the adoption of the City ordinance, picketers have appeared in front of the Acme store during business hours. When asked to leave by the Acme store manager, the picketers have shown him a copy of the City ordinance and have threatened to sue Acme if its security guards attempt to remove them physically.

City has filed a criminal complaint in the appropriate state X court, charging that Acme's continuing display of the posters violates the "sexist advertising" section of the ordinance. Acme also has filed suit in a state X court against City, seeking a declaratory judgment that the picketing section of the ordinance is unconstitutional.

What issues arising under the U.S. Constitution are raised by (1) City's prosecution of Acme under the ordinance and (2) Acme's action against City for declaratory relief? How should each be decided? Discuss.

Question 11

A statute in state A levies an "obscene publication tax" of $1 a copy "on the publication of each copy of any lewd, lascivious, or obscene material." The publisher must pay the tax within 30 days of publication. If the tax is not paid, state A revenue agents finding such material in state A are authorized to seize and destroy it.

Price is a book publisher in state B. Price published 1,000 copies of a book of questionable taste and sold half of them to independent "adult book-stores" in state A. Price had received these orders for the books by tele-phone as a consequence of a promotional flyer that he had sent to the purchasers. Price shipped the books by parcel service.

Price has failed to pay any "obscene publication tax" to state A.

1. Is the statute valid? Discuss.

2. May state A revenue agents seize and destroy copies of the books in state A? Discuss.

Question 12

County School Board (Board) canceled the remedial reading program in County's public schools. At the same time, Board increased funding for dramatic-arts workshops provided for seniors in the public high schools of County. Such increased funding is about 15 percent of the cost of the remedial reading program.

Racial minorities comprise 10 percent of County's population, and their children comprise 50 percent of the students enrolled in County's remedial reading program. AB is an organization consisting of the parents of these minority students.

Some students are enrolled in the remedial reading program because of learning disabilities or other disabilities adversely affecting reading skills. CD is an organization of the parents of these students.

AB objected to the cancellation of the remedial reading program on the ground that the program's termination would disproportionately affect their children adversely. CD objected to the program's termination on the ground that it would effectively end public education for their children.

In recommending termination of the program, Board's director had stated: "This action is a necessary economic measure. We have other programs, such as pre-college math, which are educationally more important. Disabled students will simply have to be served sometime in the future when we again have sufficient financial resources. We will, even then, have to target the program so that it helps disabled children, not children of racial minorities who just need to improve their English language skills." Board's actions were based on its director's recommendations.

AB and CD filed suit against Board in federal court, asserting that termination of the remedial reading program violated the constitutional rights of the parents and the children represented by the organizations and asking that Board be ordered to reinstate the program. While the suit was pending, Congress enacted a federal statute requiring school boards of all state political subdivisions to provide remedial reading courses. In passing this legislation, Congress relied on findings derived through congressional hearings that adults without reading skills inhibit production, sales, and travel in interstate commerce.

Assume that both AB and CD have standing to assert their claims.

1. Is the federal statute constitutional? Discuss.

2. If the court rules that the federal statute is unconstitutional:

   a. What issues under the U.S. Constitution should AB raise against the actions of Board? How should they be decided? Discuss.

   b. What issues under the U.S. Constitution should CD raise against the actions of Board? How should they be decided? Discuss.

Question 13

Three student groups, each consisting of ten adult students, protested against X State University's (University's) decision to cease dormitory construction.

Group A placed advertisements in the local newspapers, charging that University's decision resulted from "political pressure exerted by State Senator X, who owns several private apartments that compete with the dormitories." Each member of Group A was convicted of "criminal libel," defined by state law as "publishing any false statements exposing another to public hatred, contempt, or ridicule." The convictions were supported by evidence that Group A's statement (1) was false because Senator X had secretly sold his apartments before he took a position on the issue of the new dormitories and (2) had severely damaged the senator's public reputation.

Group B, all carrying "WE WANT DORMS!" signs, paraded along the sidewalk facing University's administration building. They attracted few spectators and carefully avoided blocking sidewalk traffic, but street traffic was delayed by curious drivers who slowed down as they drove past. Each member of Group B was convicted under a "breach of the peace" statute prohibiting "the congregation of persons upon a public sidewalk under circumstances tending to disrupt public order or tranquility."

Group C was invited to a discussion with University's president in his office. Although subsequently asked to leave, Group C remained in his office as a protest gesture. Each member was convicted under a newly adopted criminal trespass law proscribing "entry upon lands of another after receiving notice prohibiting such entry."

Assume that (1) all of the convictions have been upheld by the highest state X court, and (2) all constitutional issues were raised and diligently pursued throughout the proceedings.

Should the convictions of the members of Groups A, B, and C be reversed by the U.S. Supreme Court? Discuss.

Question 14

D, a state X corporation, maintains a vessel that transports cargo among several states on the Great Lakes. The vessel, equipped with hand-fired coal boilers, emits smoke of a density and duration that exceed the limits imposed by the Smoke Abatement Code of Lakeport, a city in state X. Violations are punishable by a $100 fine, 30 days' imprisonment, or both. No such code exists in other ports visited by the vessel. Pursuant to a comprehensive federal statute governing seagoing safety, the Coast Guard has inspected, approved, and licensed D's vessels (including boilers and fuel).

D's vessel enters state X's ports for occasional refueling and repairs. Loading and unloading are carried out at main terminals located in other states. State X has levied its personal property tax on the full value of D's vessel, and no such tax is imposed by the other states visited.

After trials in state X courts, D is convicted of violating Lakeport's Smoke Abatement Code and is found liable for the state X property tax. State X's highest court has affirmed both decisions, and the U.S. Supreme Court has granted review. How should the Supreme Court decide these two issues? Discuss.

Question 15

Doe is the leader of a tenant association in a housing project owned and operated by state X. On May 1, Doe issued a public statement condemning the poor judgment of the housing director in recommending increased rents to the state X agency that oversees these projects. The director then informed Doe that the project "didn't need troublemakers" and that Doe's lease would not be renewed upon its expiration on June 1. Doe challenged the director's decision in the proper state X court, but lost. The court held that applicable state X law did not recognize the retaliatory eviction doctrine, and therefore Doe had no right to be a tenant once the lease expired.

Doe then announced a large protest rally of 200 tenants to be held on June 2 in a small park, capable of holding approximately 100 persons, adjoining the project. On May 5, the director obtained an *ex parte* order enjoining Doe from "holding any mass rally in the park." Doe did not challenge the order, but went ahead with the June 2 rally.

The rally was conducted peacefully, although the overflow blocked all traffic entering the housing project for about 20 minutes. Doe was subsequently charged with criminal contempt. The court refused to consider Doe's constitutional objections to the injunction, holding that she should have raised such objections by available state procedure prior to the demonstration. Doe was found guilty and sentenced to a jail term.

The U.S. Supreme Court has accepted review of both the original action challenging Doe's eviction and the contempt conviction. What result? Discuss.

Question 16

The legislature of state A recently passed a law requiring drivers of trucks carrying explosives on roads in state A to have "special driving permits." These permits are to be issued only after rigorous physical examinations and driving tests. The state A law also provides that only permits issued by state A are acceptable for truck drivers; permits issued by certain other states, all of which have less stringent requirements, are not acceptable. Under the state A law, permits cannot be issued to persons under 30 or over 60 years of age because statistical studies have shown that drivers in these categories have higher rates of accidents.

Assume that a federal law prohibits employers from discriminating against employees on the basis of age.

Ned, who is 62 years old, is a driver for Ajax, a trucking company engaged in the interstate transportation of dynamite for construction projects in various states, including state A. Ned would normally be assigned to drive dynamite shipments from Ajax's headquarters in state B into state A, but he cannot obtain a special driving permit from state A. Ned would be able to satisfy both the physical examination and the driving test requirements of the state A law, but is barred solely because of his age. Ned has a driver's permit issued by state B, qualifying him to drive trucks carrying explosives. As a consequence of the state A law, Ajax has been obliged to revise its normal driver assignment policy to schedule Ned on routes that do not require ingress into state A.

Ajax and Ned have brought suit in the U.S. district court in state A against the appropriate state A officials, seeking to have the state A law declared invalid. The defendants have moved to have the case dismissed on the grounds that (1) the plaintiffs lack standing, and (2) state A courts have not yet ruled on the validity of the new law.

1. How should the court rule on the motion for dismissal? Discuss.

2. Assume the motion for dismissal is denied. What rights arising under the U.S. Constitution should Ajax and Ned urge in support of their claims that the state A law is invalid, and what result should follow? Discuss.

Question 17

The Pacific state legislature enacted the Pacific Home Television Movie Control Act in response to numerous demands by parents of young children. The act provides the following:

1. It is unlawful for any person or enterprise to transmit motion pictures via a cable television system to a home television receiver in the state of Pacific in violation of this Act.
2. No motion picture rated by the National Motion Picture Association Rating Board as "R" (restricted, to be viewed when accompanied by an adult only) or "NC-17" (adults only) shall be transmitted to any household in Pacific, except between 12:01 A.M. and 4:30 A.M. local time.
3. Any person or enterprise that violates this Act is subject to a fine of not less than $100 and not more than $500 per household in Pacific that subscribes to the violator's transmission system.
4. This Act does not apply to any cable television system owned and operated by a governmental subdivision of Pacific.

Martha, the president of Microsystem (Micro), a company that owns and operates a cable television system in Pacific, has retained you to consider bringing a suit challenging the validity of the act. She claims that enforcement of the act by Pacific will bankrupt her company. Both market studies and practical experience in the cable television industry have confirmed that R- and NC-17-rated movies are a significant revenue source for Micro in Pacific. Micro shows R-rated motion pictures starting at 8:00 P.M., and it shows NC-17-rated motion pictures starting at 10:00 P.M. R- and NC-17-rated motion pictures were described as "lewd" and "violent" by some legislators as reasons for adoption of the act. Micro has successfully marketed its cable television motion picture service to over 20,000 subscribers in households in Pacific, most of whom subscribe to Micro's special R and NC-17 channels at an additional charge of $25 per month, per household.

You contemplate filing an action for declaratory relief for Micro as the plaintiff in federal court in Pacific against the Pacific Department of Justice (DJ), which is charged under applicable state law with enforcement of the act, as the defendant.

What arguments under the U.S. Constitution should you make against the validity of the act, what defenses would you expect DJ to assert as to each argument, and how should the federal court decide these contentions? Discuss.

Question 18

Arrow, a retail toy seller, is a state of Hio corporation with all of its facilities and employees located in Hio. Arrow owns most of its equipment, but leases packaging machines from the U.S. government. Arrow specializes in mail-order sales solicited solely through catalogs mailed throughout the country. Orders are prepaid and are subject to acceptance by Arrow. Toys ordinarily are shipped by return mail, with the purchaser paying mailing costs. However, each year, several large orders are delivered in Arrow's own trucks to state of Penn purchasers.

The following taxes have been imposed on Arrow:

1. The state of Ut imposes a use tax on Ut residents making mail-order purchases. Ut law places the burden of collection on the seller, and the failure to collect makes the seller directly liable to Ut.

2. Penn requires a highway use fee of "$20 per truck regularly used" in that state. This standard fee applies irrespective of the degree of vehicle use within the state.

3. Hio imposes an *ad valorem* property tax based on the value of all equipment owned by Arrow, including the trucks. The property tax does not apply to property leased from any governmental agency. A "leasehold value" tax — applying the same rate to one-half of the value of leased property — is imposed on the lessee in lieu of the property tax. Property leased from Hio, however, is exempted from both the property and the leasehold taxes.

Can these taxes and obligations constitutionally be imposed on Arrow? Discuss.

Question 19

U, a large state university with insufficient dormitory space, maintains a housing bureau to assist its students in obtaining off-campus housing. At the request of private homeowners in the area and to save students possible embarrassment, the housing bureau has compiled two different lists. One lists the persons who will rent only to Caucasian students. This list is not given to African American students. U is internationally known for its excellent programs for foreign students and has no ascertainable policy of racial or religious discrimination. No federal or state statutes require licenses for, or otherwise regulate, the rental of rooms in private homes.

The National Association for the Advancement of Colored People (NAACP) has publicly proclaimed that U's housing policy is both morally and legally wrong. It recently sought to publicize this position by picketing the main administration building on U's campus. Campus police informed the 50 picketers that their conduct was prohibited by a university rule forbidding any on-campus activity that disturbed the free flow of traffic or the ability of university officials to carry out their normal functions. Before the campus police acted, a large crowd of opposing students had assembled in the surrounding quadrangle, some with signs supporting U and asserting that the picketers should be concerned with finals (rather than racism). As a consequence of the activities of both groups, some students had difficulty moving around the picketers and their opposition and getting to their next classes on time. After futile efforts to persuade the picketers to leave, state officers (summoned by the campus police) arrested the picketers.

U obtained a restraining order from a state court that enjoined further picketing at U and, after a full hearing, a permanent injunction that is currently pending on appeal to the highest state court. Meanwhile, the NAACP, joined by three African American students of U, has sought, in the appropriate U.S. district court, a declaratory judgment and injunction against U's listing of any housing facilities that discriminate against persons based on race.

As to both proceedings, what result and why?

Question 20

Smith is a lawfully-present permanent resident alien who has been employed as a temporary science teacher at Centerville High School, a public school. When his term of employment expired, Smith applied to the Centerville School Board for the vacant job of full-time science teacher, but he was not hired. After requesting a public hearing before the board on the rejection of his application, Smith received the following letter from the school board, signed by the board chairman:

> Dear Mr. Smith:
>
> The School Board wishes to inform you that it will not grant you a hearing of any kind on your application for full-time employment. The Board has decided to hire another teacher for the position.
>
> Your recent verbal attacks on our other teachers for teaching what you called "evolutionary heresy" have been so strong that we do not believe you could faithfully teach the scientifically accepted doctrines of evolution in the classroom.
>
> Further, your continuing insistence that you be allowed to take meditation periods from 10 to 11 A.M. and 2 to 3 P.M. each day, although based on your religious or metaphysical beliefs, so conflicts with the ordinary classroom work schedule from 9:00 A.M. to 3:30 P.M. as to make your employment quite impossible.
>
> Finally, in light of the present high level of unemployment among locally educated science teachers, the Board would prefer to hire an American citizen who has had teacher training in Centerville State College, rather than a foreigner like yourself who received teacher training elsewhere in the United States.

Assuming that the facts recited in the letter from the board are true and that Smith has a teacher's certificate from the state education department, has the board deprived Smith of his rights under the U.S. Constitution? Discuss.

Question 21

Powerco, a private company, generates electric power at a plant in the state of Orange. It transmits that power over its own lines to public utilities in Orange, selling the power to these utilities at wholesale prices. The plant in Orange includes several gas-fired generators and one atomic reactor generator.

The atomic reactor is operated under a permit obtained from the Atomic Energy Commission (AEC). The Atomic Energy Act of 1954 authorized the AEC to license the commercial use of atomic reactors and to regulate the emission of radioactive waste. Section 1(a) of the act declares as its policy: "The development, use, and control of atomic energy shall be directed so as to make the maximum contribution to the general welfare, subject at all times to the paramount objective of contributing to the common defense and security."

Powerco has been operating its atomic reactor generator for several years. In response to recent public concern about nuclear reactors (precipitated by a minor accident at a nuclear plant in a nearby state), the legislature of Orange has recently enacted two laws:

1. the State Pollution Control Law (Pollution Law), prohibiting any person or firm within the state from emitting radioactive waste in excess of a prescribed level (which is lower than that permitted by the AEC)
2. the State Power Revenue Law (Revenue Law), levying an annual license tax of $500,000 on every atomic reactor within the state and imposing a 2 percent gross-receipts tax on the proceeds from "all electric power generated within the state"

Powerco's atomic reactor emits relatively minimal amounts of radioactive waste, which are well within the limits established by the AEC. Powerco claims it would be very expensive to comply with the Orange emission standards and has developed substantial evidence in support of its claim.

May Powerco lawfully continue to use the reactor without modification? Must it pay either of the Orange taxes? Discuss.

Question 22

A statute of state X concerning the adoption of children states that (1) only agencies licensed by the state may place children for adoption; and (2) the primary duty of such adoption agencies shall be to promote the best interests of the child, including her moral and spiritual well-being. Another section of the statute provides: "The race and religious affiliation of the adoptive parents shall be the same as that of the natural parents, or in the case of children born to unmarried biological parents, that of the mother."

Husband (H) and Wife (W) applied to Agency, a private, nonprofit corporation licensed by state X to place children for adoption, to adopt the next available Hispanic child born to unmarried biological parents. H is Hispanic, W is white, and both are professed agnostics. Their application was rejected after an investigation by Agency. In a letter to H and W, Agency stated, "Although our investigator found you both highly qualified to be adoptive parents, in other respects we must reject your application because the social problems created by the difference in your ethnic backgrounds and your lack of religious affiliation combine to indicate that the requested adoption would not be in the best interests of the child."

H and W filed suit in the appropriate state X court, seeking both a declaratory judgment that the quoted requirements of the statute are unconstitutional and an order compelling Agency to process and approve their application. The state X trial court denied relief, and the state X Supreme Court affirmed. Assuming all questions are properly preserved, discuss the issues that are likely to arise on review by the U.S. Supreme Court and how they should be resolved.

Question 23

The president of the United States issued an executive order authorizing the Federal Bureau of Investigation (FBI), without first obtaining a search warrant, to tap the telephones of aliens in cases of suspected espionage or subversion by foreign powers.

Congress subsequently passed a bill prohibiting all wiretaps without a warrant, but the president vetoed the bill and Congress was unable to override the veto. Congress then passed a concurrent resolution (which does not require presidential approval) stating that the sense of the Congress is that no warrantless wiretaps should be permitted within the United States. Congress, over the president's veto, passed a statute permitting any federal taxpayer to bring suit in a federal district court to contest the validity of the president's executive order. No other statute affects the subject.

An action was later filed in federal district court by Jones, a U.S. citizen and taxpayer. Jones contested the validity of the executive order on constitutional grounds and sought to show at the trial that the FBI had, in fact, tapped telephones in the United States without a warrant and that some telephones of U.S. citizens had been tapped. Jones caused an FBI agent to be subpoenaed to testify and produce records regarding the telephone taps in issue, but the president claimed executive privilege and the agent neither appeared nor produced any records.

The federal district and appellate courts ruled against Jones, and the Supreme Court has granted review.

What result on all of the constitutional issues? Discuss.

Question 24

Suburban Primary School (Suburban) is a public school supported entirely by local property taxes and federal grants. The Parent Teacher Association (PTA) is an unincorporated association consisting of parents of some of the students at Suburban. The PTA decided to institute an extracurricular program for the school's students, in which the PTA would sponsor four courses, each to be held once a week, after regular hours. Certain PTA members would voluntarily serve as teachers for the courses. After such classes, participating students would be allowed to take the "late" school bus home. The Suburban principal has agreed to let the PTA use the school premises and bus for the program.

The PTA determined that, because of possible behavior problems, none of the courses would be coeducational.

Each parent was to register his child, in person, at 8:45 A.M. on the opening day of the program. Classes were to be filled on a "first come, first served" basis. Before the program began, it was described in a pamphlet given to each child attending Suburban to take home. The available courses were described as follows.

1. Embroidery—8 girls, fifth and sixth grades, $300
2. Creative Crafts—10 boys, second grade, $400
3. Baseball Practice—10 boys, fifth and sixth grades, $200
4. Bible Studies—12 girls, no fee/free

Mother (M), who is not a PTA member, did not arrive at school on the prescribed day until 9:15 A.M. because of a flat tire on her car. M attempted to enroll her son, Harold (H), a second-grader at Suburban, in Creative Crafts, but was told that the course was filled. She also tried to enroll her daughter, Alice (A), a sixth-grader at Suburban, in Baseball Practice, but was refused (although several vacancies were left).

M has sued the PTA in the appropriate U.S. district court to compel enrollment of H in Creative Crafts and of A in Baseball Practice. Two other parents who are not members of PTA, but who are taxpayers residing in the school district with children attending Suburban, have sued to enjoin continuation of the entire program. Both suits rely exclusively on rights guaranteed to the plaintiffs under the U.S. Constitution.

Assume that all proper defendants have been joined in both actions.

What constitutional issues are raised by the suits, and how should they be decided? Discuss.

Question 25

Three years ago, the United States completed construction of a dam on a large river, creating a navigable lake in state X. Regulatory control of the lake as a fishery was granted by the United States to state X, "subject to all constitutional provisions."

One year ago, at its own expense, state X stocked the lake with an imported fish species, the river salmon, which grew to spectacular size because of the unique physical and chemical properties of the lake. On weekends and holidays, anglers from all over the United States came to the lake to catch the large fish as trophies.

Six months ago, realizing the lake was rapidly being depleted of river salmon, state X enacted the following statute:

> §1. A special license shall be required to fish for river salmon in this state. The license fee for residents shall be $10, and the license fee for nonresidents shall be $100.
>
> §2. No river salmon shall be transported out of state X.
>
> §3. No one shall fish for river salmon in this state unless such person is accompanied by a guide licensed by this state for that purpose, and only residents of this state are eligible to apply for, or to hold, such guide licenses.

Guy had been a state X resident and held a license to guide on the lake for the purpose of fishing for river salmon. On most weekends and holidays, Guy would guide a small boatload of persons desiring to fish on the lake. Two years ago, Guy moved his domicile from state X to adjoining state Y. Solely because he had become a nonresident, Guy's annual application for renewal of his license was recently refused.

Guy commenced a suit in state X, contending that the entire state X statute is unconstitutional. He has been unsuccessful in the state courts, and his case is now before the U.S. Supreme Court for decision on the merits. Assume Guy has preserved all constitutional claims.

1. Does Guy have standing to assert claims of the unconstitutionality of §§1 and 2 of the state X statute? Discuss.

2. Assuming that Guy has standing, what claims of unconstitutionality might Guy reasonably assert with respect to the entire act, and how should they be resolved? Discuss.

Question 26

State X requires that every person teaching in public or private schools be certified by the state. Legislatively established grounds for denial of certification include the following:

§1. Knowing membership in any Fascist, Nazi, or Communist Party, or any other organization that advocates or teaches the propriety of overthrowing the government by force or violence.

§2. Failure to provide the certification committee with complete answers to questions seeking legally relevant information.

John Doe sought certification in order to take a job with a private secondary school. In checking his references, state investigators were told that Doe was a member of the American Nazi Party. Doe was informed of this charge, and the state scheduled a hearing on the matter.

Doe attended the hearing, but stated at the outset that he would not answer any questions concerning his alleged membership in the Nazi Party. Doe claimed that to compel answers to such questions constituted a denial of his "right of privacy as guaranteed by the Fifth Amendment." He did not offer any further explanation of his refusal, and he was not asked to do so. The committee then announced that Doe's application was denied.

Doe has now brought suit in federal court attacking the constitutionality of the committee's action. What result? Discuss.

Question 27

The County Board of Education (Board) seeks your advice as Board's legal counsel regarding two current problems:

1. The public high school in County District (District) has scheduled graduation ceremonies for a Saturday morning, as has been the custom for all schools in District. This year's senior class valedictorian, Val, holds religious beliefs that prevent her from attending the graduation ceremony because Saturday is the Sabbath day observed by her religion. Val has requested that Board reschedule the graduation so she can attend and deliver the traditional valedictory address.

2. Board has had a policy of permitting community groups to use the high school auditorium for evening and weekend meetings at a modest rental fee. Now NFO, a local organization that advocates racial and religious discrimination, has applied for use of the auditorium for a major recruiting meeting on April 20. Persons and groups opposed to what they characterize as the "extremist" views of NFO are demanding that Board reject the application "out of hand, without giving it serious consideration." The local police chief also opposes the application on the basis of "hard intelligence" that some militant "antifascists" plan to remove NFO members from the school auditorium by physical force if the meeting takes place.

Val and NFO have each delivered letters to Board invoking "rights under the U.S. Constitution" in support of their respective demands and applications.

What issues arising under the U.S. Constitution are presented by the following:

1. Val's demand? Discuss.

2. NFO's application? Discuss.

Question 28

The *National Explorer*, a tabloid newspaper based in New York City, famous for its coverage of alien baby sightings on New York City subways, publishes a story alleging that Susie Boole, a Welsh singing sensation made famous on YouTube and the British television show *Shocking Singing Sensations!* suffers from a serious heroin addiction. The story also suggests that Ms. Boole has regularly given heroin to her beloved housecat, Miss Pickles. The *National Explorer*'s source for the story is Harry "Sweet Stuff" Gibbons, a homeless man with a long criminal record who currently lives under an expressway overpass near Ms. Boole's hometown of Cardiff, Wales. Gibbons gave an "exclusive" interview to the *National Explorer*, which then broke the story in its pages. Following publication of the story, General Foods drops an endorsement deal with Boole, as does the Walt Disney Company. Both corporations cite the *National Explorer* news story as the reason for the termination of the endorsement contract. Both contracts contain clauses that expressly permit termination of the relationship if "adverse publicity occurs that relates either to criminal acts or acts of moral turpitude on the part of Ms. Boole."

Boole promptly files a lawsuit for libel against the *National Explorer* in the U.S. District Court for the Southern District of New York (based on diversity of citizenship), seeking both compensatory and punitive damages. The *National Explorer* denies the allegations and files a motion to dismiss Boole's suit, arguing that the plaintiff has failed to state a claim upon which relief may be granted.

You work as a law clerk to the U.S. district judge deciding whether to grant or deny the defendant's motion to dismiss. How should your boss rule? Why?

Question 29

The Mississippi legislature, meeting in emergency session after Hurricane Blanche delivers a crippling blow to the state, enacts the Emergency Relief Act (ERA). The ERA provides a variety of benefits to persons living in counties "within the Hurricane Blanche impact zone." One of the benefits includes a "temporary moratorium" on mortgage foreclosures and evictions of tenants from residential or business rental properties. Section 9 of the ERA provides, in relevant part, that "[n]o person shall be subject to foreclosure for nonpayment of a mortgage associated with residential or business real property located in the Hurricane Blanche impact zone for 12 months from the date of the hurricane's landfall in Mississippi. All rights of foreclosure and eviction are hereby suspended for 12 months." Section 10 of the ERA provides, in relevant part, that "[n]o person renting real property located in the Hurricane Blanche impact zone, whether for a residential or business purpose, shall be evicted from such premises earlier than 12 months after the date Blanche made landfall in Mississippi or until the expiration of the existing lease, whichever first occurs." The law does not permanently cancel any financial obligation arising under either a mortgage or a real estate lease agreement.

You serve as general counsel for Magnolia Properties, an integrated real estate and mortgage finance company doing business on the Mississippi Gulf Coast. Section 9 of the ERA will preclude Magnolia Properties from foreclosing on preexisting mortgages, regardless of the payment history, for the 12 months immediately following the landfall of Hurricane Blanche; §10 of the ERA will preclude Magnolia Properties from evicting tenants in company-owned rental properties until the expiration of the existing lease agreement or for a 12-month period following the landfall of Hurricane Blanche (depending on which occurs first).

Leona Trumpette, president and CEO of Magnolia Properties, e-mails you, seeking advice on how the company should respond to the new law. Specifically, Trumpette wishes to know whether any viable constitutional challenges to §§9 and 10 of the ERA exist. How do you advise Ms. Trumpette?

Question 30

Congress has been increasingly concerned about the health effects associated with the consumption of all forms of tobacco products. You work as a legislative aide to Senator Bill Smythe, who asks you to determine whether Congress could constitutionally ban the transportation, sale, possession, and/or consumption of tobacco products. How do you advise him? Under what constitutional powers, if any, could Congress enact a comprehensive ban on all tobacco products?

Senator Smythe, anticipating that the tobacco industry would likely challenge such legislation, if Congress were to enact it, also asks you to advise him as to the best arguments *against* the constitutionality of such a statute. In particular, he wishes to know whether, if Congress enacted a ban on tobacco products and a proper constitutional challenge to the law came before the Supreme Court of the United States, the current Supreme Court would be likely to sustain or invalidate the law.

How do you advise Senator Smythe? Why?

Question 31

The North Dakota state legislature, alarmed at the growing and persistent depopulation problem currently facing the state, enacts the "Re-Populate North Dakota Now! Act," and the governor signs the bill into law. The act imposes a tax of $5 per condom or other one-time-use birth control device, a tax of $10 per birth control pill prescription, and a tax of $100 on the sale of intrauterine devices (IUDs) and diaphragms; the tax is payable by any and all persons or entities offering either birth control devices or prescription medications in the state. The monies collected under the act will be used to pay for prenatal and postnatal care for indigent women in North Dakota.

Planned Parenthood of North Dakota operates two family-planning clinics in North Dakota that offer comprehensive medical counseling and access to birth control and abortion services, with locations in Bismarck and Fargo. Planned Parenthood files suit in federal district court in Bismarck, North Dakota, seeking invalidation of the act as a violation of the constitutional right of privacy. The suit includes as plaintiffs Planned Parenthood, its officers, and individual clients, both in their individual capacity and as class representatives. North Dakota's attorney general files a motion to dismiss, arguing that the plaintiffs lack standing to challenge the act. In addition, the state's brief argues that the act does not violate the Fourteenth Amendment and, accordingly, that the plaintiffs have failed to raise a claim for which relief may be granted. Planned Parenthood opposes this motion and also files a cross-motion for summary judgment. You work as a law clerk to the federal district judge charged with hearing the case. How do you advise her to rule on the state's motion to dismiss and Planned Parenthood's cross-motion for summary judgment?

Question 32

Congress, responding to public controversy associated with the content of certain violent video games popular with teenagers, enacts the "Child Violent Video Game Protection Act," (Act) which prohibits the "sale, distribution, or dissemination, whether or not for a commercial purpose, to minors of computer games that feature unduly violent content or themes." The Act includes a definitions provision that defines "unduly violent content or themes" as "comprising material that features, as a dominant characteristic, a morbid and pervasive focus on graphic and offensive depictions of violence, including but not limited to criminal activity, such as murder, rape, or assault, depictions of human or animal torture, and other depictions of cruel and sadistic behavior." Softco (S) develops and sells computer games designed to appeal to teenagers; the company's primary market demographic consists of boys aged 12 to 15. S titles include a highly popular series entitled "Sociopath Killer" in which players role play a psychotic criminal engaged in various forms of sadistic criminal behavior. Since enactment of the Act, orders for S's products, and the "Sociopath Killer" series titles in particular, have fallen more than 50 percent. S brings an action in a federal district court, arguing that the Act violates the First Amendment. How should the district court rule on the merits of this claim?

Essay
Answers

Answer to Question 1

1. Possible constitutional claims that JD could assert:

JD could assert a number of constitutional claims, including claims sounding in equal protection (A permits the ownership and possession of guns other than handguns), due process (one could assert a fundamental liberty interest in gun ownership), or even under the Takings Clause (e.g., JD owns "several guns" that she may no longer legally possess, depriving the guns of all economic value and arguably constituting a regulatory taking). By far the most promising claim, however, is Second Amendment claim. Although the facts do not expressly state the claims that JD has asserted in her suit against A, I will assume for purposes of this answer that her primary/principal claim rests on the Second Amendment.

2. Second Amendment analysis:

The Supreme Court squarely has held that the Second Amendment creates a personal right to keep and bear firearms, including handguns, at least for the purpose of personal self-defense. *District of Columbia v. Heller.* Moreover, the Justices also have held that this personal right to keep and bear arms applies with full force against state and local governments because it is incorporated through the Due Process Clause of the Fourteenth Amendment. *McDonald v. City of Chicago.*

Unfortunately, however, in both *Heller* and *McDonald*, the majority failed to specify the standard of review that governs Second Amendment claims. In *Heller*, Justice Scalia, writing for the majority, explained that "[u]nder any of the standards of scrutiny that we have applied to enumerated constitutional rights, banning from the home the most preferred firearm in the nation to 'keep' and use for protection of one's home and family [fails to pass] constitutional muster." It bears noting that in *Heller*, the District of Columbia had completely **banned** handguns and also required that other guns be kept in an inoperable condition. Both regulations were held inconsistent with the Second Amendment's personal right to keep and bear arms "for the purpose of immediate self-defense."

In *McDonald*, the majority found that the right to keep and bear arms for personal self-defense was incorporated against the states via the Due Process Clause of the Fourteenth Amendment (because it is deeply rooted in the Anglo-American legal tradition and enjoys the strong imprimatur of history). However, the *McDonald* Court also failed to specify the governing standard of review applicable to such claims; instead, Justice Alito simply cited and applied *Heller* to Chicago's ban on handgun ownership.

Thus, although "[t]he Second Amendment right is fully applicable against the States," *McDonald*, the precise contours of the right, and the governing standard of review remain opaque. It bears noting, however, that *McDonald*, like *Heller*, involved a flat ban on handgun ownership.

Given that both *Heller* and *McDonald* found that a flat ban on handgun ownership violates the Second Amendment, the district court should hold that A's identical statute violates the personal right to keep and bear arms unless A can offer a justification for its law not presented by Chicago or Washington, D.C. The facts indicate, however, that A adopted the handgun ban for reasons largely *identical* to the justifications offered by Chicago and Washington, D.C. in defense of their handgun bans. Accordingly, the outcome in this case should be the same—that is, the flat ban is unconstitutional on Second Amendment grounds. Finally, it bears noting that states are probably free to adopt less burdensome regulations of gun ownership, such as registration requirements (upheld in *Heller*) and perhaps even mandatory gun safety courses. However, a flat ban on commonly owned firearms, such as handguns, is unconstitutional.

3. Conclusion:
The district court should rule in favor of JD and against A based on the Second Amendment. *McDonald*; *Heller*.

Answer to Question 2

1. Does MC have a justiciable claim?

The first question that the district court would have to determine involves the justiciability of MC's claim. In general, the federal courts will not second guess the determinations of a coordinate branch of the federal government when the Constitution contains a demonstrable textual commitment of a particular power or responsibility to Congress or the president. *Baker v. Carr.* In this case, the Constitution squarely states that "[e]ach House shall be the Judge of the Elections, Returns, and Qualifications of its own Members." U.S. Const., art. I, §5. At least arguably, this language grants the House unreviewable power to determine whether a person seeking admission has been properly elected and meets the qualifications for member in the House. To serve in the House, a person must be at least 25 years old, a citizen of the U.S. for not less than seven years, and an "inhabitant" of the state from which she was elected. U.S. Const., art. I, §2, cl. 1. Given the demonstrable textual commitment to the House to ascertain the qualifications of its members, it seems doubtful that a federal court would superintend the House's exercise of this power. *Nixon v. United States.*

On the other hand, in *Powell v. McCormack,* the Supreme Court found that if the House attempted to add qualifications for office to the age, citizenship, and residency requirements set forth in Article I, a person "excluded" from Congress based on an additional de facto qualification presented a justiciable claim. And, in fact, the Supreme Court reached the merits of Adam Clayton Powell, Jr.'s claim in *McCormack.*

It would seem that the controlling factor is whether, in a given case, the House is simply *applying* the existing qualifications for membership in the House or, alternatively, trying to alter or amend these qualifications. Here, the facts state that MC has been denied her seat based on alleged prior criminal convictions. The Constitution does not require that a person not have been convicted of a felony in state court in order to serve in the House. Because the House is *augmenting* the qualifications for membership in the House, the district court should hold that MC's claim is justiciable.

2. May the House constitutionally exclude MC from her seat?

Moving on to the merits, MC should prevail in her suit against the Speaker of the House. In *McCormack,* the Supreme Court held that although the House has the power to ascertain whether a person has satisfied the constitutional requirements for membership in the House, it lacks the power to change or augment those requirements (again, age, citizenship, and residency). The Supreme Court also had held that states may not alter or augment the qualifications for service in the Congress, whether it does so directly via a statewide constitutional referendum, *U.S. Terms Limits, Inc. v. Thornton*, or indirectly by imposing unfavorable ballot access conditions, *Cook v. Gralike*. In *Thornton*, the Supreme Court explained that the Framers established nationally uniform standards for membership in the House and Senate, and that modification of these requirements would require a federal constitutional amendment. Based on *McCormack* and *Thornton*, it seems clear that the House may not create additional requirements for membership—including a ban on permitting persons previously convicted of a crime from serving in the body.

If the House had seated MC and then subsequently voted to expel her, the question would be closer because of the uncertain justiciability of a claim challenging the legality of a vote to *expel* a member of the House. The Constitution provides that "[e]ach House may . . . with the Concurrence of two thirds, expel a Member." In *McCormack*, the majority carefully distinguished a vote to *exclude* a member (which the House had taken) from a vote to *expel* a member. Because the Constitution seems to vest the House with unlimited discretion to expel members, provided that two thirds of the voting members support the action, it is unlikely that a federal court would intervene; the decision to *expel* a member would probably constitute a nonjusticiable political question, for the reasons discussed above. MC is in luck, however, because the facts plainly state that she was denied her seat (excluded), and not admitted to her seat and then removed (expelled).

Finally, I should note that a federal court would probably pause and consider carefully the implications of ordering the Speaker (and by implication the House of Representatives) to seat a member through a writ of mandamus. Serious and important separation of powers issues would arise from a federal court taking such an action. However, the Supreme Court found that Speaker McCormack could be required to seat Congressman Powell (and to pay damages for the period for which he was excluded), and so, although the question is not free from doubt, it seems likely that the same result would obtain in MC's case. Moreover, the Supreme Court squarely held that mandamus could be used against high ranking executive branch officials in *Marbury v. Madison*; if the judiciary has the power to subject the Secretary of State to a writ of mandamus, it stands to reason that it possesses the same power with respect to the Speaker of the House.

3. Conclusion:

MC has presented a justiciable claim, and the district court should reach the merits of her suit. On the merits, based on *McCormack*, the district court should hold that the House cannot constitutionally add additional qualifications (such as never having been convicted of a crime) for serving in the House beyond those expressly set forth in the Constitution.

Answer to Question 3

1. SJ's potential constitutional claims:

SJ could bring several constitutional claims. For example, the Equal Protection and Due Process Clauses of the Fourteenth Amendment require that all state laws meet a requirement of minimum rationality; economic and social legislation is unconstitutional if a plaintiff can show that it lacks a rational relationship to a legitimate state interest. *Williamson v. Lee Optical Co.* A flat ban on coffins and caskets purchased outside of the state comes very close to being "irrational." Moreover, the Supreme Court has applied the rationality test more aggressively in cases where a state attempts to favor its own economic interests by imposing direct burdens on out-of-state competitors. *Metropolitan Life Insurance Co. v. Ward.*

The Privileges and Immunities Clause of Article IV, §2, cl. 1 might also support a claim on these facts. It prohibits a state from denying nonresidents the rights and privileges afforded to its own residents, at least when the right at issue is "fundamental" to national comity; in general, the right to pursue a lawful trade, including the sales of goods and services, constitutes a fundamental interest for purposes of this clause. However, the Privileges and Immunities Clause is facially limited to "citizens," as opposed to corporations, and most of the lost sales in question might well take place outside of Beta. In fact, it's not clear from the facts whether an out-of-state seller could evade the ban through the simple expedient of opening a store within the state to service residents of Beta. If the purchase technically occurs within Beta, arguably the citizenship of the seller is irrelevant. In sum, these issues would augur against making an argument premised on the Privileges and Immunities Clause (particularly when a *much* strong argument, see below, exists).

The strongest possible argument would be to assert that the ban violates the dormant aspect of the Commerce Clause (also commonly called the "negative" aspect of the Commerce Clause). Art. I, §8, cl. 3; *Dean Milk Co. v. Madison.* In fact, because SJ has such a strong case under the dormant Commerce Clause, a claim that is much stronger, in fact, than under any other possible constitutional claims (including those discussed above), she should probably focus on this claim to the exclusion of the other potential claims.

2. Does SJ have standing to bring a Commerce Clause challenge to the Beta statute?

Before proceeding to an analysis of SJ's potential dormant Commerce Clause claim, the preliminary issue of standing merits *brief* mention. In order to litigate a claim in the federal courts, a plaintiff must show injury in fact, traceability, and redressability. *Lujan v. Defenders of Wildlife*. Based on the facts presented, SJ has standing to litigate a dormant Commerce Clause claim in federal court. She has purchased a coffin from an out-of-state supplier located in Gamma, which she now cannot use to bury her deceased husband in Beta. Her inability to use the coffin stems directly from the state law banning the use of imported coffins (traceability exists) and a judicial ruling in her favor invalidating the law would permit her to make use of the coffin (redressability exists). Accordingly, SJ has standing to litigate a Commerce Clause challenge to the ban.

3. The Beta ban on the use of out-of-state coffins and caskets violates the Dormant Commerce Clause:

The Supreme Court has articulated a rule of almost *per se* invalidity for state laws that facially discriminate against interstate commerce. *New Energy Co. v. Limbach*. In order to sustain this law, the burden would rest on Beta to show that (1) the ban on out-of-state coffins and caskets advances a legitimate government interest and (2) no less discriminatory means exist to advance the state's objective. *Maine v. Taylor*. Here, the asserted legitimate purpose appears to be entirely pretextual. However, for purposes of analysis, even if one assumes that Beta can successfully assert a legitimate interest in the ban, there are plainly less discriminatory means of advancing whatever health or safety concerns motivated the state legislature to enact the statute. For example, Beta could adopt neutral regulations that govern the construction of coffins and caskets; provided that such regulations apply to all sellers (both in-state and out-of-state) and do not unduly burden the flow of interstate commerce relative to the local health, safety, and welfare benefits, such a law would not transgress the dormant Commerce Clause. *Pike v. Bruce Church, Inc.*

It also bears noting that the Supreme Court has systematically invalidated state attempts to trap or capture beneficial economic activity within its borders, for example by requiring that private power companies purchase minimum amounts of coal produced in state, *Wyoming v. Oklahoma*, or by requiring private in-state producers of a commodity, such as natural gas, to favor in-state consumers over potential out-of-state buyers. *Pennsylvania v. West Virginia*. Here, the Beta law appears to have the purpose and effect of trapping local demand for coffins and caskets for the exclusive benefit of local, in-state retailers of these products. Attempting to capture the market in this way for the benefit of local in-state interests constitutes precisely the sort of parochial protectionism that the dormant Commerce Clause doctrine exists to prevent.

4. Conclusion:

SJ has standing to bring a legal challenge premised on the dormant Commerce Clause against the statute. Because the Beta law facially discriminates against interstate commerce by banning out-of-state sellers of coffins and caskets from selling an otherwise lawful product to in-state buyers based solely on their out-of-state status, a reviewing court should hold the law unconstitutional on dormant Commerce Clause grounds.

Answer to Question 4

1. The Standing Doctrine's general requirements:

In order to challenge the tuition tax credit program's aid to religiously affiliated schools in federal court, MJS must establish that they possess constitutional standing. This consists of showing injury in fact, traceability, and redressability. *Bennett v. Spear*. On the facts presented, the injury in fact requirement will present the most difficult question for MJS—obviously, the injury (assuming it is cognizable) is traceable to the statute and, were a reviewing court to invalidate the tuition credit program on Establishment Clause grounds, the injury would be redressed. These two aspects of standing are not really at issue. For the reasons discussed below, however, the injury requirement appears to be absent.

2. The general rule against taxpayer standing:

As noted above, a plaintiff must establish that she has constitutional "standing" to pursue litigation in federal court. U.S. Const., art. III, §2, limits the federal judicial power to "cases" and "controversies." The Supreme Court has explained that consistent with this requirement, the federal courts may not render "advisory" opinions in cases that lack a genuine and ongoing dispute between truly adversarial litigants. *Correspondence of the Justices*; *Hayburn's Case*. Moreover, the Court has expressly disallowed so-called "taxpayer" standing because a person's mere status as a taxpayer does not provide a sufficiently "concrete and particularized" injury to support the existence of a live case or controversy. *Frothingham v. Mellon*. Thus, under the general rule, MJS would lack standing to bring a challenge to the tuition credit program if their only claim of an injury relates to their status as taxpayers.

3. The exception to the general rule for Establishment Clause cases:

Nevertheless, the Supreme Court has held that an exception to the general rule against the existence of standing based on one's status as a taxpayer exists with respect to claims grounded on Establishment Clause violations. Citing Madison's remonstrance that "not three pence" of government money should be spent to support a religious establishment over a citizen's objection, the Supreme Court held in *Flast v. Cohen* that even a nominal financial injury was sufficient to establish the required "injury in fact" in this particular circumstance. This is so because a plausible nexus exists between a would-be plaintiff's status as a taxpayer and the specific constitutional right that the plaintiff seeks to vindicate in federal court. As the *Flast* Court explained, the Establishment Clause "is a specific constitutional limitation on the exercise by Congress of the taxing and spending power under Art. I, §8."

Under the logic of *Flast*, then, MJS should have standing to challenge A's new tuition program, at least insofar as the program provides financial benefits to religiously affiliated schools. Unfortunately, the question is more complicated because the Supreme Court has not consistently followed the logic of *Flast* in subsequent cases.

4. The Supreme Court has severely limited Flast in recent holdings:

MSJ face a serious problem, however, in that the Supreme Court has repeatedly limited the scope of *Flast*, although it has never squarely overruled the case. For example, the Justices declined to apply *Flast* to a subsequent case involving the gift of government *property* to a religiously affiliated college, holding that the nexus between a would-be plaintiff's taxpayer status and the gift of government-owned property was insufficient to establish the required injury in fact. *Valley Forge Christian College v. Americans United for Separation of Church and State.* More recently still, the Supreme Court refused to apply *Flast* when a general appropriation was used to sponsor government activities that benefit religious organizations, such as conferences and meetings on "charitable choice" programs that rely on religious groups to provide social services. *Hein v. Freedom From Religion Foundation, Inc.* Most recently, the Supreme Court has held that tax expenditures, as opposed to direct financial subsidies, will not support taxpayer standing, even though the underlying claim arises under the Establishment Clause. *Arizona Christian School Tuition Org. v. Winn.*

The *Winn* case, in particular, would seem to foreclose a court from finding that MJS have standing in this instance. Because the Supreme Court has distinguished *tax credits* from *direct expenditures* for purposes of applying *Flast*, MJS will be unable to rely on *Flast* to escape the general rule that taxpayer status is not sufficient to support constitutional standing (and, in particular, the injury in fact requirement). The distinction rests on the idea that, under a tax credit, individual citizens choose to spend their own money to support religiously affiliated schools, whereas with a direct state financial subsidy, the government spends money collected from taxpayers within the jurisdiction. According to the *Winn* majority, because the subsidy under a tax credit is the product of private choice, and only indirectly and remotely funded by the government, the necessary nexus between taxpayer status and the Establishment Clause is absent.

5. Conclusion:

Unless MJS can establish an injury in fact based on a more particularized claim of injury, the district court should dismiss the case on standing grounds. Thus, absent facts not provided, the state's motion to dismiss for lack of standing should be ***granted*** because MSJ cannot successfully invoke taxpayer standing.

Answer to Question 5

1. The misdemeanor charge:

Tom (T) could initially contend that the misdemeanor charge should be dismissed because it was based on a statute that was overly broad (i.e., the entity charged with enforcing the law had virtually total discretion in determining whether it should be applied to a particular situation). Such broad enactments cannot serve as the basis for governmental action. *Lovell v. Griffin.* Because the statutory standard to be used in granting or refusing licenses is highly subjective in nature (i.e., the "overall community good"), T would argue that it was constitutionally defective. Although it would be difficult for City to argue that the test for determining if licenses should be granted is adequate, it could assert that where the defendant should have anticipated a constitutionally curative construction, an overly broad enactment may serve as the basis for governmental action. *Shuttlesworth v. Birmingham.* Because the state X Supreme Court had made a proper narrowing interpretation of the criminal advocacy statute five years earlier, T should have foreseen that a constitutionally proper interpretation of the misdemeanor statute would also be rendered upon judicial review.

T could respond, however, that he could **not** foresee a constitutionally curative interpretation of the licensing ordinance because it appeared to be plain on its face (i.e., it would have been very difficult to anticipate that the requirement for speaking would be almost completely repudiated and the factors of time, place, and manner of speech substituted in lieu thereof).

Alternatively, T could argue that, even if a proper narrowing interpretation could have been anticipated, a law that is unconstitutionally applied (i.e., the permit was rejected for T's failure to disclose the content, not for time, place, or manner considerations) cannot serve as the basis for a criminal conviction where there is no adequate opportunity for review. T would assert that this standard was satisfied because (1) there was no provision for independent review by a judicial body (any appeal was to be heard by the city council, presumably the same entity that enacted the law), and (2) the facts are unclear as to how often the city council met (if it was not until after T's projected speaking date, no timely appeal to that body could possibly be taken). Although City could rebut that T waived any potential constitutional defect in the prescribed review by neglecting to contest the police chief's denial of T's permit request before the city council, this procedure requiring appeal to a legislative branch of local government is probably inadequate. In summary, the prosecution of T for violation of the licensing ordinance will probably **not** be successful.

2. The contempt-of-court decree:

Ex parte orders are ordinarily not appropriate unless there is a need to act immediately and there is no opportunity to give the opposing party notice. Because the attorney for City was apparently aware of T's prospective speech on Tuesday (the facts indicate that Dan "immediately" gave City's attorney T's name and address), T probably should have been given an opportunity to contest the injunction. Although even an improper court order must ordinarily be obeyed, where an *ex parte* injunction is deliberately sought and served in such a manner as to preclude effective judicial review (here, City's attorney served the order upon T just as he was beginning to speak), it may be attackable in a subsequent proceeding. *Walker v. Birmingham.*

3. The felony charge:

Although the First Amendment (applicable to the states via the Due Process Clause of the Fourteenth Amendment) protects the advocacy of ideas, speech that is made for the purpose of inciting immediate unlawful conduct and that is likely to incite such action may be proscribed. *Brandenburg v. Ohio.* T could contend that the felony charges must be dismissed because (1) the statute in question is too vague (i.e., a person of ordinary intelligence could not determine what constitutes "advocating insurrection"); and (2) alternatively, the above-cited standard is not satisfied in this instance because (i) although he advocated that the listeners "stockpile weapons," he never suggested doing so illegally (in most states, various types of firearms can be purchased in a lawful manner); (ii) even if his words could be construed as urging illegal conduct, the conduct would not be imminent (i.e., it would take time to aggregate these weapons); and (iii) it was unlikely that the listeners would respond to T's speech because they were (a) in the park for "various other reasons" and (b) only "mildly interested" in T's speech. Finally, T's comment to "begin thinking about forming guerrilla units" obviously does not contemplate immediate unlawful conduct (it merely suggests "thinking").

City could respond to T's vagueness assertion by pointing out that the statute had received a constitutionally curative interpretation. Even so, there appears to be no successful rebuttal to T's argument that the *Brandenburg* test is not met. Thus, the felony charge should be dismissed.

Answer to Question 6

Because City (C) did not put into issue the "wrong party" statement of the newly elected department head, this assertion is presumably not in question.

Can C exclude Paul (P) because he is purportedly not a U.S. citizen?

P could attack this ground for dismissal in three ways. He could contend that (1) the U.S. statute is unconstitutional, (2) the state statute requiring municipal employees to be U.S. citizens is unconstitutional, and (3) the state statute forbidding beards and requiring uniforms is also unconstitutional.

Is the U.S. statute constitutional?

(If not, then P was technically still a citizen, and the state statute requiring municipal employees to be citizens would be satisfied.)

P would probably initially contend that the federal statute is unconstitutional because he did not consent to forfeit his citizenship. *Afroyim v. Rusk.* Although C might argue in rebuttal that a citizen is presumed to know the law, and therefore P voluntarily forfeited his citizenship, P should prevail on this point because there are no facts that indicate P knowingly consented to a loss of U.S. citizenship.

Is the state statute requiring municipal employees to be U.S. citizens constitutional?

Assuming, however, that the federal statute was valid, P would argue that the state statute requiring municipal employees to be U.S. citizens is invalid. Aliens are ordinarily regarded as a "suspect" classification, unless involved in a "basic" or "political" governmental function. *Foley v. Connelie.* Reading water meters would probably not be regarded as such because this task is not critical to the effective functioning of local government. A meter reader seems clearly distinguishable from a police officer, a parole officer, and a schoolteacher, the three vocations that the Supreme Court has held that states may limit to citizens. *Ambach v. Norwick.* The controlling test is whether a particular government job involves a high degree of responsibility and discretion in the fulfillment of a basic governmental obligation; P's duties do not seem to meet either condition. Thus, C will have to show that a compelling interest is served by restricting meter readers to U.S. citizens and that there is no less burdensome means of accomplishing that objective. C could contend that there is a compelling interest in having only U.S. citizens work as meter readers because persons would be reluctant to let someone into their homes and businesses if he could not speak English clearly. However, a less burdensome means of satisfying the state's concern would be to require each applicant for this position to pass a fluency test that demonstrates his ability to respond to customers' questions. Thus, P probably could **not** be constitutionally discharged on the basis that he was **not** a U.S. citizen.

Is the state statute forbidding beards and requiring uniforms constitutional?

First, it is assumed that the "no beard" and uniform requirements have been enforced against all employees, so P cannot contend that the statute is being applied unequally (thereby violating his rights under the Equal Protection Clause of the Fourteenth Amendment).

The constitutionality of legislation pertaining to the health, safety, and welfare of a state's citizens is ordinarily judged by the rational-relationship test (i.e., provided that a reviewing court could posit even a merely theoretical rational relationship between a legitimate state interest and the statute's attempt to further that interest, the legislation is constitutional against substantive due process or equal protection objections). *Williamson v. Lee Optical Co.* Although P could argue that a beard and lack of a uniform bear no relationship to one's capability for meter reading, C could probably successfully contend in rebuttal that customers are more likely to permit meter readers into their homes and stores if they are (1) clean shaven and (2) have an identifying characteristic (i.e., a specifically designated uniform).

P might next argue that the right to dress and groom as one desires is a fundamental right (similar to the rights of privacy found within the penumbra of the Bill of Rights). However, C could probably successfully contend in rebuttal that due-process rights of privacy have not been extended to grooming and dress requirements at work (i.e., they have been limited to an individual's home or body). *Kelly v. Johnson.*

P might finally contend that because the "no beard" and uniform requirements were not promulgated until **after** his employment with C had commenced, the state's action constituted an impairment of an existing contractual relationship. U.S. Const. art. I, §10. However, C could probably successfully argue in rebuttal that (1) there was no agreement that measures reasonably necessary to make performance of the job more efficient would not be undertaken; and (2) in any event, the beard and uniform requirements are an inconsequential modification of the employment arrangement (i.e., P has not been asked to accept major modifications, such as reduced compensation or reassignment to a different geographical area).

Note that no viable Free Exercise Clause claim appears to exist on these facts. First, P does not claim that wearing a beard constitutes a form of religious practice, a necessary component of a valid free-exercise claim. Second, even if it did, nothing in the facts suggests that the "no beard" rule reflects anything other than a neutral rule of general application, which would not trigger strict scrutiny under the Free Exercise Clause in any event. *Employment Division v. Smith.*

Because an independent, constitutional basis for P's dismissal existed, his lawsuit against C probably would *not* be successful.

Answer to Question 7

1. Taxpayers v. Church, Society, and Agency:

Do Taxpayers have standing?

The defendants' initial contention would be that Taxpayers lack standing to pursue this lawsuit. However, because the state X spending program whereby Agency provides funds to legal-aid organizations was created through a state (as opposed to a federal) statute, the criterion for standing is simply: "Does the state action involve measurable expenditures?" Because the amounts expended on the legal-aid program are easily calculable, Taxpayers would appear to have standing. *Flast v. Cohen.*

Is there state action?

The Establishment Clause (applicable to the states via the Fourteenth Amendment) pertains only to governmental action. Taxpayers could contend that there is significant governmental involvement in the program because it is funded by a state agency. *Norwood v. Harrison.* Although the defendants could argue in rebuttal that mere governmental funding should not constitute state participation (the facts are silent as to the extent of the funding provided to Society by Agency), the government's decision to fund Agency unquestionably constitutes state action and is subject to constitutional attack. Whether Agency itself is a state actor presents a much harder question. *Blum v. Yaretsky.* The outcome would turn on the degree of "entwinement" that exists between the state and Agency. *Brentwood Academy v. TSSAA.*

Does the legislation violate the Establishment Clause?

Pursuant to the Establishment Clause, legislation that impacts upon religion is invalid unless (1) it has a secular purpose, (2) its primary effect is neither to advance nor to inhibit religion, and (3) it does not produce excessive entanglement between religion and the state. *Lemon v. Kurtzman.* The program arguably has a secular purpose because it assists the victims of discrimination in vindicating their legal rights. It does not appear to advance or inhibit religion because preventing discrimination against someone for racial or religious reasons appears to be neutral in its impact. (Although taxpayers might contend that assisting the victims of religious discrimination promotes religion, this contention should fail because protecting the right to practice religion is a neutral governmental function.) Finally, although monitoring the use of funds would arguably create an excessive governmental entanglement because state officials would have to constantly monitor Society to make certain that preference was not given to cases affecting Church members, the U.S. Supreme Court has rejected this argument in a factually similar context (grants to family-planning centers). *Bowen v. Kendrick.*

If the state provided grants to individuals to defray the cost of obtaining legal services through a voucher system, it would be even more likely to pass constitutional muster. *Zelman v. Simmons-Harris.* The facts make clear that the grants at issue here were paid directly to Agency; accordingly, the *Zelman* rule would not apply.

2. Jay v. Church, Society, and Agency:
Does Jay have standing?

To have standing in federal court, the plaintiff must ordinarily demonstrate a direct and immediate personal injury resulting from the allegedly unconstitutional action. The defendants could contend that because Society members work gratuitously, there is no significant injury to Jay (they are refusing only to let him work without pay). Although Jay could argue in rebuttal that participation in Society might enhance his professional reputation and possibly lead to referrals, these gains are extremely speculative, so the defendants should prevail.

Assuming, however, that there was standing and state action (discussed above), there seems to be little doubt that Society's refusal of admittance to Jay would violate both the Equal Protection Clause of the Fourteenth Amendment (there is no rational relationship between practicing law for a particular entity and not being a member of a specific religious sect) and the Establishment Clause (an arrangement whereby only members of a particular religious sect can obtain a particular governmental position).

3. Bar v. Society:
Does Bar have standing?

An association has standing to assert the rights of its members where (1) one or more of its members would have standing, (2) the interest asserted is pertinent to the association's purpose, and (3) the claim asserted and relief requested do not require that individual members participate in the suit. Because (1) Bar is presumably concerned with practices that would diminish its credibility and public esteem, and (2) these requisites would seem to be satisfied in this instance, Bar would probably have standing.

Does the state X disciplinary code violate the First Amendment?

Although "legitimate" commercial speech has been held to be within the First Amendment, Bar could contend in rebuttal that in-person solicitations (which raise the potential of overreaching and the initiation of frivolous litigation) can be restricted. However, Society can probably successfully argue in rebuttal that because it was offering its services gratuitously, the application of this situation to Bar's code violates Society's First Amendment rights. *In re Primus.*

Answer to Question 8

Church will probably raise the following contentions with respect to its assertion that the amended statute is invalid.

Is the statute a valid exercise of the police power?

Church (C) will initially contend that, pursuant to the Tenth Amendment, the state is allowed to legislate for the health, welfare, and safety of its citizens. Because the acknowledged purpose of the ordinance was primarily aesthetic in nature (i.e., to enhance the appearance of City), the applicable standard is *not* satisfied. However, City could argue in rebuttal that (1) improving the physical look of an area is a valid general-welfare purpose, and (2) another possible purpose of the law might have been to diminish visual distractions and thereby reduce vehicular accidents. *Railway Express Agency v. New York.* Thus, the law is probably valid.

Does the statute violate C's First Amendment right of freedom of speech?

C could next contend that the statute violates its First Amendment right of freedom of speech (applicable to the states via the Fourteenth Amendment) because the sign law prohibits C from communicating its message to the public. C could argue that a private means of communication to the public (rooftop billboards) may not be foreclosed entirely. *Metromedia, Inc. v. San Diego*; *Members of the City Council of the City of Los Angeles v. Taxpayers for Vincent.* In the latter case, an ordinance prohibited the posting of flyers on utility poles in Los Angeles. The city justified the law on purely aesthetic grounds. Citing *Metromedia*, the majority sustained the ban against a First Amendment challenge, holding that the city could legitimately restrict outdoor advertising (whether of a commercial or noncommercial character) to combat "visual blight."

The majority's conclusion also rested on the fact that the Los Angeles ban was content and viewpoint neutral and left open ample alternative channels of communication. The facts in this case should bring it within the rule of *Taxpayers for Vincent.*

Does the ordinance constitute an unconstitutional taking?

C could contend that (1) requiring it to dismantle the sign constitutes a governmental "taking" under the Fourteenth Amendment; and (2) because it does not provide for compensation, the ordinance is unconstitutional. First, City could argue in rebuttal that no "regulatory taking" has occurred because, although the ordinance diminishes the value of the sign, the five-year phaseout period (probably) fairly correlates to the useful life of the sign, and therefore the effect on the value of C's property is not great.

Second, C did not have any reasonable, "investment-backed expectations" that the sign would be extant forever. Third (and finally), the character of the government's action, in this case a traditional zoning rule designed to enhance local aesthetics, is plainly **not** of the sort that the federal courts routinely find to be unfair or unjust. Thus, City should prevail on all three prongs of the *Penn Central* test; prevailing on just one would probably be sufficient to defeat C's claim. *Eastern Enterprises v. Apfel*; *Penn Central Transportation Co. v. New York City*. City also is not seeking to possess or use for its own purposes either the sign or the rooftop; on these facts, neither a taking by occupation nor a taking by exaction would exist. *Dolan v. City of Tigard.* Again, City should prevail.

Does the ordinance violate C's First Amendment right to freedom of religion?

Legislation (1) that does not have a secular purpose (i.e., was aimed at inhibiting the practice of a particular religion) and (2) whose primary effect is to inhibit religion is unconstitutional under the Establishment Clause of the First Amendment. *Church of the Lukumi Babalu Aye v. City of Hialeah.* C could argue that because City responded to the complaints of individuals who wanted C's sign removed, City's action was done with the basic purpose and primary effect of impeding C's religious views. However, City could probably successfully contend in rebuttal that (1) there is no indication that the persons complaining about C's sign (or the members of City's council who enacted the ordinance) were motivated by antireligious feelings toward C; and (2) the ordinance had, at most, only an incidental effect upon C's ability to function.

Indeed, even under the pre-*Smith* strict-scrutiny regime of *Sherbert* and *Yoder*, plaintiffs making a free-exercise claim had to show that their religious beliefs precluded compliance with the regulation at issue in a direct, rather than indirect, way. In this case, C would need to show that its religious beliefs mandated the placement of the sign on the building's roof, a contention that the facts do not support. *Jimmy Swaggert Ministries v. Board of Equalization.* By way of contrast, under *Smith*, a viable free-exercise claim would require that C prove discriminatory intent by City. Neither test appears to be met here. Accordingly, the ordinance probably did **not** violate C's First Amendment right to freedom of religion.

Does the ordinance violate C's equal-protection rights?

Finally, C might argue that the ordinance violates its equal-protection rights because it is irrational and arbitrary to prohibit only rooftop signs.

If City's concern is the distraction of drivers and aesthetics, it should also preclude other highly visible forms of advertising (i.e., billboards, signs painted on the sides of buildings, etc.). However, it is well established that a legislative body can elect to deal with one aspect of a problem at a time. *Williamson v. Lee Optical Co.* Thus, City would prevail on this issue.

Summary:
Because all of C's arguments would probably be unsuccessful, the ordinance is valid.

Answer to Question 9

1. Arguments of SADS against City (C):

SADS would initially contend that an association has standing to assert the rights of its members where (1) one or more of its members would have standing, (2) the interest sought to be protected is pertinent to the association's purpose, and (3) neither the claim nor the relief requested require that individual members participate in the suit. Because (1) the rights of SADS members to convey their message are proscribed by the C ordinance, (2) the extent of government spending on defense is an issue about which college students are appropriately concerned, and (3) it is unnecessary that any particular individual member of SADS participate in the suit, the requisites of "organizational" standing appear to be satisfied.

SADS should next be able to successfully claim that this is not an appropriate situation for federal court abstention because (1) the statute, being clear on its face, would not be susceptible to a constitutionally curative interpretation by a state court; and (2) the case involves a First Amendment (applicable to the states via the Fourteenth Amendment) question.

Substantively, SADS could claim that the streets are a traditional public forum, and the government may not completely proscribe speech in such an area. Because the ordinance limits use of part of the public streets for speech, it is arguably unconstitutional. C could contend in rebuttal, however, that public safety constitutes a sufficiently significant state interest (especially where there have already been several accidents resulting in serious injuries as a consequence of the means of communication sought to be utilized by SADS). The ban is also completely viewpoint and content neutral; it applies to everyone regardless of message. Additionally, only a complete ban on this type of activity could accomplish the governmental objectives sought to be achieved; it would be too difficult for C to legislate or supervise a more limited ban.

Whether SADS's contention will be successful probably depends on whether other means of distribution of its message are readily available. Assuming SADS may still hold rallies in parks, distribute literature on sidewalks, and hold marches in the streets during low traffic-density periods, the total closure of distribution to momentarily stopped motor vehicles is probably constitutionally permissible. Thus, C should prevail if adequate alternative channels of communication exist and would be available to SADS. *Ward v. Rock Against Racism.*

SADS could alternatively contend that the statute is violative of its equal-protection rights because its enactment was hastened when the council learned of SADS's distribution plan. Where a statute appears to be speech neutral upon its face, but was enacted with the intention of discouraging speech with a particular content, its enforcement violates the First Amendment. However, C could probably successfully contend in rebuttal that the ordinance was being considered prior to SADS's decision to protest and that it was the possibility of additional injuries (rather than the message sought to be conveyed by SADS) that prompted the council's action.

2. Owen's (O's) motions:

a. Ripeness:

Article III, §2, of the U.S. Constitution limits federal court jurisdiction to actual "cases or controversies." O could therefore contend that SADS's action is not ripe (i.e., there is no real and immediate danger to SADS members) because (1) no SADS member has actually attempted to publicize her message at O's shopping center, and (2) O has not tried to remove SADS members or have them prosecuted under the antitrespass ordinance. However, SADS could successfully argue in rebuttal that its members should not have to be exposed to (1) physical harm (i.e., there is always the possibility that a protestor could be injured while being removed from the shopping center) or (2) criminal sanctions (i.e., if O desired to file a trespassing complaint against those persons distributing literature on his property, the leafletters would presumably be arrested by the police and subsequently prosecuted by the local district attorney's office) to vindicate their First Amendment right of free speech. So SADS's action is probably ripe.

b. SADS's right to distribute campaign literature on private property:

In *Hudgens v. National Labor Relations Board*, the Supreme Court held that there is no First Amendment right to access a private shopping center for the purpose of engaging in free speech activities, unless the area at issue was owned and controlled by a private entity that had assumed responsibilities for otherwise exclusive government functions such as fire protection, policing, and other essential and exclusive government activities (i.e., the shopping center was, in effect, a company-owned town). *Marsh v. Alabama*. Because the facts fail to indicate that O had undertaken all the functions of a municipal government, SADS has no constitutionally protected right to distribute its literature at the shopping center.

In *Pruneyard Shopping Center v. Robins*, the Supreme Court held that where a ***state constitution*** had been interpreted by the highest court of that jurisdiction to permit reasonable access to a privately owned shopping center to disseminate information of public concern, the property owner's due-process and First Amendment rights were not violated. Assuming, however, there has been no similar interpretation of this state's constitution or corresponding legislative enactment, SADS would have no constitutional right to protest upon O's property.

Answer to Question 10
Criminal prosecution of Acme (A):
Because a city is a subdivision of a state, the ordinance must be analyzed as "state" action. A would contend that the statute is unconstitutional upon each of the following independent grounds.

Impermissible viewpoint- and content-based regulation:
Although City can regulate speech under some circumstances, it cannot do so through viewpoint- or content-based regulations, absent the most compelling reasons and a lack of any less restrictive means of achieving its objectives. Here, the regulation proscribes speech based on its content and viewpoint. The U.S. Supreme Court has summarily affirmed a court of appeals decision invalidating a nearly identical ordinance. *American Booksellers Assn. v. Hudnut.* This ordinance is virtually identical to the ordinance in *Hudnut* and is also invalid.

Moreover, even if the ordinance related solely to proscribable forms of speech (such as obscenity, fighting words, and true threats), it would not be constitutional because the government cannot selectively punish otherwise proscribable speech based on viewpoint. *RAV v. City of St. Paul.* The speech at issue, however, is not within an unprotected class.

Discrimination against commercial speech:
Commercial speech enjoys full First Amendment protection, and the government may not subject it to regulations not generally applicable to all forms of speech, unless commercial speech contributes to the creation of a problem in a unique and distinctive way. *City of Cincinnati v. Discovery Network.* Here, there is no evidence suggesting that commercial speech in this context creates problems that identical noncommercial speech would not. Because the ordinance singles out commercial speech for adverse treatment while permitting identical noncommercial speech, it violates the Free Speech Clause of the First Amendment.

Overbreadth:
Initially, one should note that, although the statute is limited to commercial and advertising materials, such speech is nevertheless entitled to constitutional protection. *Central Hudson Gas & Electric v. Public Service Commn.*

A statute is overly broad where it can be interpreted as circumscribing constitutionally protected conduct or speech. Although obscene literature may be constitutionally restricted, the facts stipulate that the allegedly "demeaning" and "sexist" pictures are not obscene. Although City presumably has an interest in not having its citizens view individuals portrayed in a "demeaning" or "sexist" fashion (these portrayals arguably engender degrading and sexist conduct), it is unlikely that this relatively vague objective would overcome A's First Amendment free-speech rights (applicable to the states via the Fourteenth Amendment). In summary, the statute is overly broad. *American Booksellers Assn. v. Hudnut.*

Vagueness:

A statute is unconstitutionally vague when a person of ordinary intelligence would not, even though aware of the law, know if his conduct was illegal. A would contend that the words "demeaning," "sexist," and "advertising material" are too vague. Given that two people can look at the same picture (e.g., a beauty contest participant dressed in a skimpy bathing suit) and have dramatically different views of the portrayal (one might think it demeaning and sexist, and another might feel there is absolutely nothing wrong with the portrayal), A should prevail on this argument as well. *Coates v. Cincinnati.*

Equal protection:

Finally, A would probably also assert that the ordinance violates its equal-protection rights because similar displays for noncommercial purposes are not proscribed. However, general-welfare legislation such as the type in question must satisfy only a legitimate state objective (in this instance, it is probably aimed at preventing the debasement of City citizens). Legislation need not address every possible evil within the area covered by a law. *Railway Express Agency, Inc. v. New York.* Thus, City should prevail on this contention.

Summary:

In summary, because the statute is a viewpoint- and content-based speech restriction and discriminates against commercial speech without a sufficient predicate, it will not survive constitutional review. Moreover, it is probably overly broad and vague. Accordingly, it cannot serve as the basis for a criminal prosecution of A. Thus, City's prosecution of A should fail.

A's declaratory judgment action:

There does not appear to be much question that the statute is valid (i.e., it serves a legitimate constitutional purpose by assuring and promoting citizens' free-expression rights). Moreover, the Supreme Court has sustained a similar rule derived from a state constitution's free-speech guarantee. *Pruneyard Shopping Center v. Robins.*

Ripeness:

City might initially contend that because A has not attempted to remove any of the picketers, the case is not ripe. However, A could probably successfully argue in rebuttal that (1) injury to its business is presently occurring (the picketers are on A's land and presumably have discouraged at least some persons from entering A's premises), and (2) A should not have to risk criminal and civil liability (i.e., by physically ejecting the picketers) to determine if the picketers' actions are lawful.

Vagueness:

The statute apparently fails to define the terms "shopping center" and "retail sales outlet." Is a "shopping center" two or more stores with common, private parking facilities or does it include any physically connected series of retail store outlets under a common landlord? Is a "retail sales outlet" a place that sells only to the ultimate consumer or does it also include a business that sometimes acts as a distributor (i.e., some sales are made to the public, although larger-volume transactions are entered into with other retail entities)? City could contend in rebuttal that (1) a shopping center is a series of business establishments with common, private parking facilities; and (2) *any* sales to an ultimate consumer would make a business establishment a "retail sales outlet" for purposes of the ordinance. This is a close question, but City would probably prevail.

Deprivation of property/First Amendment:

Pursuant to the Fourteenth Amendment, a state may not deprive persons of "property" without due process of law. A could contend that the picketing ordinance is unconstitutional because it permits the public to use private property without compensation to the landowner (i.e., authorizing the picketing constitutes a "taking" of a portion of A's property interest in its business premises). A could also argue that its First Amendment rights are violated by the ordinance because persons going to the shopping center might presume that the picketers had been authorized by the owner of the shopping center (and their views shared by the owner). However, the Supreme Court rejected similar claims in *Pruneyard Shopping Center v. Robins*. The question would turn on the relative burden placed on A's property; on the facts presented, the burden does not seem more excessive than in *Pruneyard*, and so this case would probably govern the outcome. Thus, City would prevail on these issues.

Equal protection:

A might also contend that its equal-protection rights are being violated by the picketing ordinance because only shopping centers are covered by the statute (leaving all other types of commercial and business establishments unaffected). Again, however, assuming the legislation has a constitutional purpose (which it does), it is not necessary that all of the potential problems in the field be cured in a single instance. Thus, City would prevail in this instance, too.

In summary, it appears that the picketing statute is constitutional.

Answer to Question 11

1. Is the statute valid?

There are several ways in which Price (P) could attack the state A statute.

Due process:

P could initially contend that the state A statute violates his substantive due-process rights (contained in the Fourteenth Amendment) by purporting to tax the publisher of prohibited material, whether or not (1) he has any physical presence in state A or (2) the literature is ever distributed in state A (i.e., read literally, anyone publishing such materials, anywhere, is liable for the tax, whether or not (a) the written matter is ever distributed within state A or (b) the publisher knew, or had reason to believe, that the written matter would ever be distributed in state A). Thus, there is no sufficient nexus between the levying authority and the activity sought to be taxed. *Complete Auto Transit, Inc. v. Brady.* Although state A could assert in rebuttal that a reasonable construction of the legislation would be that it applied only to materials that were actually delivered to buyers within state A, P would still have insufficient contacts (merely responding to telephone orders initiated through literature mailed to potential buyers) with state A to satisfy due process.

Vagueness:

P could alternatively assert that the Due Process Clause of the Fourteenth Amendment is violated because the statute is unconstitutionally vague (i.e., a person of ordinary intelligence and aware of the statute would be uncertain as to whether her conduct is proscribed by the legislation). This contention would be predicated upon the assertion that whether material is "lewd" or "lascivious" is highly subjective. Because an unconstitutionally vague statute cannot serve as the basis of governmental action, the legislation is invalid. State A could respond in rebuttal that (1) the words in question are adequately defined in most dictionaries and are therefore sufficiently certain; and (2) *if the material in this instance was obscene* (the facts are silent as to this aspect), the words in question should be read as being equivalent to "obscene" (a term that has been defined by the U.S. Supreme Court). Nevertheless, the terminology in question would probably be deemed unconstitutionally vague, and therefore the statute would be invalid.

First Amendment:

P could alternatively assert that although printing entities are not immune from taxes of general application, the statute in question is a disguised regulatory measure that unconstitutionally infringes upon P's First Amendment rights (applicable to the states via the Fourteenth Amendment). This is arguably demonstrated by the facts that (1) the statute is directly related to the content of the printed matter in question (i.e., it applies to only lewd, lascivious, or obscene literature); and (2) the $1 fee applies to each publication, regardless of the number of pages or the price charged for the material. Although obscene matter may be constitutionally regulated—and even criminally proscribed—merely "lewd" and "lascivious" materials may not be. Although state A could contend in rebuttal that the levy is a mere "privilege" tax upon the right to undertake a specific activity (the sale of "lewd," "lascivious," or "obscene" matter within that jurisdiction), the content-related nature of the legislation would probably result in a finding in favor of P on this issue also.

2. May state A revenue agents seize and destroy copies of P's books?
Procedural due process:
Under the Due Process Clause of the Fourteenth Amendment, a state may not significantly affect property rights of an individual without a prior adequately noticed hearing. Because the destruction of the items would constitute an irreparable deprivation of property, P and the vendors of the books would contend that their procedural due-process rights were violated by the lack of any provision in the state A law for a hearing as to whether the materials were within the statute's purview. Unless state A could persuade the court that an intervening (i.e., between seizure and actual destruction of the books) hearing was implicit in the legislation, P and the vendors would probably be successful in their assertion of this theory.

Prior restraint:
P and the vendors of the books could alternatively contend that the statute constitutes an invalid prior restraint because it authorizes "large scale" seizures of materials without prior judicial determination that the items fall within the scope of the statute. *A Quantity of Books v. Kansas.* As a consequence, publishers would be reluctant to print questionable materials (i.e., if the items could be seized and destroyed, potential vendees might be hesitant to purchase them). Although state A could contend that, unless the seizure of the materials was immediate, it would be impossible to determine the appropriate amount of tax to be levied, this argument would probably fail. On the facts presented, (1) the evidence could be preserved by purchase of a single copy of the material by the governmental

authority, and (2) the precise number of books printed could probably be determined from invoices and order forms transferred among P and the book purchasers.

Thus, state A revenue agents may *not* lawfully seize and destroy copies of the books in state A.

Answer to Question 12

1. Is the federal statute constitutional?

Under Article I, §8, clause 3, of the U.S. Constitution, Congress has the right to legislate with respect to any commercial or economic activity that, aggregated across the national economy, substantially affects interstate or international commerce. *Wickard v. Filburn.* Federal courts ordinarily give great deference to congressional findings as to the impact of an activity on interstate commerce. Because people with reading difficulties would (1) be limited in the types of economic activities in which they could participate (i.e., participation in occupations that required significant reading skills or use of equipment would be precluded), (2) purchase fewer types of items (i.e., computers, sophisticated equipment, and machinery), and (3) travel less (i.e., such persons might be unable to read signs or menus), a plausible argument exists that the legislation is within Congress's power (i.e., the Interstate Commerce provision and the "Necessary and Proper" Clause attendant thereto).

On the other hand, the legislation does not directly relate to an economic activity; reading or learning to read does not involve commercial transactions (unlike engaging in loan sharking or buying or selling marijuana for medical use). The Supreme Court has invalidated laws that lack a sufficient and direct nexus to economic activities that affect commerce. *United States v. Morrison*; *Gonzales v. Raich.*

On balance, because the law does not directly regulate economic activity, it probably exceeds the scope of Congress's *commerce* power. On the other hand, if Congress wished to establish such a requirement, it could do so constitutionally through a conditional spending program. For example, it could link the receipt of federal funds for primary and secondary education to state-enacted mandates to meet the educational needs of children with learning disabilities. *South Dakota v. Dole.* Even so, it has not done so here.

2a. Assuming the federal statute is unconstitutional, what issues should the AB group raise against Board?

The AB group would raise equal-protection and due-process objections to Board's action.

In determining whether a law that is neutral on its face (as the present legislation, which discontinues *all* remedial reading programs) has a discriminatory purpose, a court may consider any pertinent data (including the statements made by Board's director). If intentional race-based discrimination could be shown, County's actions would have to satisfy the strict-scrutiny standard (i.e., a compelling state interest is furthered by the governmental conduct, and there is no less burdensome means of satisfying that objective). The director's statement that increased funds might lead to restoration of programs for children with disabilities but "not children of racial minorities who just need to improve their English language skills" is susceptible to multiple interpretations, including the notion that he harbors animus toward minority children (i.e., money so used is money wasted). On the other hand, the statement could reflect the difference in relative need—and nothing more. It is ambiguous, but could help to support a finding of intentional discrimination. Coupled with the extreme racially disparate *impact* of the decision, however, it helps to support an inference of discriminatory motive. Because the termination of the program has a disproportionately adverse racial impact (although racial minorities comprise 10 percent of County's population, they constitute 50 percent of the students enrolled in the program), in conjunction with the director's very strange public comments, Board would have the burden of proving that its actions were *not* racially motivated.

Board could argue that (1) its action was dictated by financial necessity, and (2) the effect of the program's termination also impacts upon nonminority students. In rebuttal, the AB group could contend that Board's purposeful discrimination is proven by the facts that (1) there were *increased* monies available for the dramatic-arts workshops (however, the total of this amount was only 15 percent of the funds that had been available for the remedial reading program), and (2) the director indicated disabled students would receive preference over minority students if adequate funding subsequently became available (although this could be defended by the fact that the latter group would completely fail to learn to read if their regular studies were not supplemented by the remedial program). Although statistics can be used to support an inference of intentional discrimination, the data here is far from conclusive and falls well short of constituting a "smoking gun." *Castenada v. Partida.* Assuming that the court found that the decision was *not* racially motivated, then County would only have to show that the program's termination bore a theoretical rational relationship to a legitimate state interest in order to sustain the decision. *Washington v. Davis.* County's showing that monetary pressures compelled cessation of the remedial reading program probably establishes this relationship, although the matter is not free from doubt.

The AB group could alternatively contend that the program's termination violated their substantive due-process rights. Under the Fourteenth Amendment, one cannot be deprived of fundamental "liberties" (i.e., rights recognized as essential to the orderly pursuit of happiness). The right to possess reasonably adequate reading skills is arguably "fundamental" because a failure to read proficiently inevitably results in lower-paying jobs and an overall diminished ability to enjoy life. The Supreme Court has held that there is no fundamental right to an equally financed education (i.e., all school districts within a particular county do not have to expend an equal dollar amount per child; *San Antonio School District v. Rodriguez*). Moreover, the Supreme Court has sustained a state law that would deny poor children free transportation to the local public schools, conceivably precluding their regular attendance. *Kadrmas v. Dickinson Public Schools.*

The only case to find a due-process violation for failing to provide an adequate public education was *Plyler v. Doe*, which involved a **complete** denial of all public educational services to the children of illegal immigrants in Texas. Here, the denial of services is limited, and the case would probably be controlled by *Kadrmas* rather than *Plyler*.

Some state supreme courts have enforced the state constitution's "right to a public education" guarantee very aggressively. In light of this development, AB might be more successful bringing a state constitutional claim in state court.

2b. Assuming the federal statute is unconstitutional, what issues would the CD group raise against Board?

The CD group could also raise the substantive due-process argument that reading skills are a "fundamental right" and therefore that the Board's abolition of the program should be subjected to strict scrutiny. The CD group would argue that cessation of the remedial program is tantamount to a complete denial of a public education, bringing its case within the scope of *Plyler*. The Board would respond that it has not closed the schools to the special-needs students, but rather has failed to provide the most appropriate program. The question would turn on whether *Plyler* and *Rodriguez* require state governments to provide an appropriate education for all students. Given the current Supreme Court's reluctance to expand the scope of substantive due-process rights, this claim would probably fail.

Alternatively, the CD group would contend that their equal-protection rights were violated. Although there is no case law supporting the proposition that educationally disabled students are a "suspect" or "quasi-suspect"

group, the Supreme Court has closely scrutinized local government decisions that appear to be motivated by animus toward those with mental
disabilities. *City of Cleburne v. Cleburne Living Center, Inc.* Abolishing
the program has an obvious and devastating effect on the special-needs
students; moreover, Board's director acknowledges this fact in his press
release. The plaintiffs have a reasonable chance of showing intentional discrimination that would trigger "rationality with bite" review.

In fact, the CD group's claims look very similar to the *Plyler* claims: An
unpopular group faced a complete loss of educational access. Although
disabled students are not a suspect class, neither were the children of illegal aliens. And, unlike *Rodriguez,* this case does not involve a quality-of-
education claim—instead, it presents a question of access.

Although it is a close issue, the CD group might prevail on an equal-
protection claim.

Answer to Question 13

Jurisdiction of the U.S. Supreme Court:

Review of state court decisions by the Supreme Court is limited to federal questions (i.e., those arising under the Constitution, a federal statute, or a U.S. treaty). Assuming Groups A, B, and C have each contended that the statutes in question were violative of their First Amendment rights (applicable to the states via the Fourteenth Amendment), this requirement is fulfilled. Review by appeal is permitted when a state statute is upheld against an assertion of invalidity under the Constitution. Thus, the Supreme Court may properly review these decisions.

Convictions of Group A:

Where a public figure is the subject of an allegedly defamatory statement, prosecution cannot successfully occur unless the defendant acted with actual malice (i.e., actual knowledge that the statement was false or reckless indifference to the truth or falsity of the statement). *New York Times Co. v. Sullivan.* Group A might initially contend that the statute is overly broad on its face (and therefore cannot constitute a basis for valid governmental action) because it purports to punish conduct that is constitutionally permissible (i.e., actual malice is not required by the statute). State X, however, will argue in rebuttal that, unless a statute gives the enforcing entity virtually unlimited discretion in deciding whether the law is applicable (i.e., the law is not substantially overbroad), it may serve as the basis of governmental action if it is constitutionally ***applied***. Given the relatively precise standard of "hatred, contempt, and ridicule," the statute is probably ***not*** substantially overbroad. Thus, Group A could be prosecuted under the statute (if it is constitutionally applied).

Actual malice is present where the defendant (1) knew her statements were false or (2) published with reckless indifference to their accuracy. Group A would have contended that (1) Senator X, being a state legislator, qualifies as a public official; and (2) because Senator X had "secretly" sold the apartments, the statements involved cannot be said to have been made with actual malice, that is, A neither had actual knowledge that Senator X's conflict of interest had been resolved through the sale nor acted recklessly in publishing the accusation. However, state X could argue in rebuttal that (1) the defamatory portion of the advertisement was the assertion that he had unduly influenced University officials in their decision to cease dormitory construction (rather than the statement that he owned private apartment houses that competed with the dormitories), and (2) it is unclear as to how Group A determined that Senator X had pressured X State University officials. If Group A premised its advertisements upon mere rumor or sheer conjecture, their statements could be deemed to have been made recklessly (and therefore the actual-malice standard would be satisfied).

The prosecution could have alternatively contended that *Dun & Bradstreet v. Greenmoss Builders, Inc.*, overruled earlier decisions and held that where a defamation pertains to matters of "private" (as opposed to "public") concern, state libel law applies (which often requires only that the statements in question have been false). Because the matter involved was private in nature (i.e., the senator had influenced University officials to cease dormitory construction for his personal financial gain), prosecution under the state law was appropriate. However, a decision about whether to undertake dormitory construction would very likely be viewed as relating to a matter of "public" concern. Moreover, abusing a government office to secure private financial gain undoubtedly constitutes a "matter of public concern." *Gertz v. Robert Welch, Inc.* Thus, even if the constitutional protection of an "actual malice" standard extends only to speech pertaining to matters of "public" concern, state X would still be obliged to show that Group A's communications did not satify this standard. On the facts presented, it appears that Group A's comments enjoy constitutional protection under the *Sullivan* standard, and therefore their convictions should be reversed.

Convictions of Group B:

Vagueness:

A statute is unconstitutionally vague where persons of ordinary and reasonable intelligence could not determine if contemplated conduct was prohibited. *Coates v. Cincinnati.* Group B could have contended that the phrase "circumstances tending to disrupt public order or tranquility" is too vague because it is unclear as to whether (1) the physical act of "congregating" must be the source of the public disruption, or (2) the message disseminated by those congregating may be the basis of prosecution. Additionally, the determination of what constitutes a "disruption" of the "public order or tranquility" is highly subjective in nature (i.e., would the stopping of vehicle drivers to shout their approval or disapproval of the message being publicized fall within this standard?). If a statute fails for vagueness, it cannot serve as the basis for governmental action. Although state X would probably argue in rebuttal that the "disruption" of "public order or tranquility" is sufficiently definite (i.e., where, as a consequence of a defendant's conduct, a possibility of violence or physical injury existed), Group B would probably prevail upon this contention.

Overbreadth:

Group B could have alternatively contended that the statute was overly broad on its face (i.e., the entity charged with enforcing the law had virtually complete discretion in determining whether it should be applied to a particular situation). The determination of when the "public order or tranquility" has been "disrupted" is highly subjective in nature. Therefore, the enactment cannot serve as the basis for governmental action. *Lovell v. Griffin.* State X could have argued in rebuttal, however, that the determination of what constitutes "disruption" of the "public order or tranquility" constitutes an adequate limitation upon its conduct to avoid application of the facially overly broad doctrine. Although a close question, state X properly prevailed on this issue.

Group B could next have argued that the statute is unconstitutional as applied. Although "fighting words" (communicative words or types of conduct that, by their very utterance or occurrence, have a tendency to incite an immediate breach of the peace) may be the subject of a criminal prosecution, there is no indication that violence was threatened in any manner (the facts state only that traffic was delayed by curious drivers who slowed down to view the picketing).

Thus, even if the state X statute survives attacks for vagueness and facial overbreadth, it would probably still be deemed unconstitutional as applied. Therefore, the Group B convictions should be reversed.

Public forum:

State X could have also contended that the area within one block of the administration building (although generally open to the public) is not a public forum. *Adderly v. Florida.* Therefore, speech may be completely prohibited in that area provided the regulation is viewpoint neutral (i.e., the area is closed to *all* speech activity) and otherwise "reasonable." *Cornelius v. NAACP LDF, Inc.* However, because the statute does not purport to preclude all demonstrations (but merely disruptive ones) from the locale in question, Group B's conduct probably could *not* be criminally sanctioned.

Moreover, a sidewalk on a public street is a quintessential public forum and presumptively should be available for speech activity. If the sidewalk outside the U.S. Supreme Court building cannot be closed to public protest, it would be difficult to argue persuasively that a university administration has a stronger case for peace and quiet. *United States v. Grace.*

Convictions of Group C:

Due process:

Group C probably contended that its due-process rights were violated because the statute failed to adequately advise them that their conduct was prohibited (i.e., the legislation punishes encroachment upon the lands of another only *after receiving notice prohibiting such entry*). The law does not purport to cover a refusal to leave land upon which the defendant had previously been invited. Although state X could have argued in rebuttal that a reasonable interpretation of the trespass statute would be that deliberately refusing to egress from land after receiving notice to leave was within the scope of the statute, Group C should have prevailed on this issue. Thus, the convictions of Group C should also be reversed.

Answer to Question 14

D's conviction for violating the Lakeport Smoke Abatement Code (LSAC):

Dormant Commerce Clause:

Pursuant to the Tenth Amendment, a state (and its subdivisions) is empowered to enact legislation for the health, safety, and general welfare of its populace. However, where local legislation places an undue burden on interstate commerce (i.e., the burden imposed outweighs the merits and purposes of the law), the local regulation will be invalidated. *Southern Pacific Co. v. Arizona.* D might contend that the LSAC would require expensive alterations (the facts are silent as to this point), with the consequence that compliance with the law would make it impossible for D to maintain its business of transporting cargo among several states. However, because (1) the LSAC does not appear to be in conflict with the laws of any other state to which D's vessel travels, and (2) the facts fail to indicate that a significant number of other ships are not in compliance with the LSAC, it is unlikely that mere enhanced expense would result in a finding that an undue burden on interstate commerce had occurred.

Preemption:

There would appear to be little doubt that the congressional act is valid because there is a constitutional basis for the law (seagoing safety) pursuant to both (1) the Commerce Clause and (2) Congress's right to legislate with respect to navigable waterways. *United States v. Appalachian Electric Power Co.*

There are three kinds of preemption under the Supremacy Clause of Article VI: express preemption, implied conflict preemption, and implied field preemption. Express preemption involves a congressional declaration of preemptive intent in the text of a statute; the facts do not mention the existence of such a statement. Accordingly, express preemption is not an issue.

Conflict preemption exists when a state law impedes either the ends or specific means that Congress (or a federal agency) adopts to advance a particular regulatory goal. The test for implied conflict preemption is *not* impossibility of compliance with both federal and state law, but rather whether the state law impedes or impairs the efficacy of the federal enactment (with respect to *both* ends and means). *Geier v. American Honda Motor Co.* Here, the facts do not suggest that state X's law overlaps with any specific federal law or regulation; absent some sort of significant overlap, implied conflict preemption does not exist.

Finally, D could argue that implied field preemption invalidates the LSAC. When Congress has enacted legislation with the intent that it occupy that field completely, local regulations pertaining to that area (even though not actually in conflict with the federal law) are deemed to be superseded. In the absence of a clear declaration of congressional intent, the Supreme Court may consider the following factors in deciding if the federal law was intended as exclusive legislation in that area: (1) whether the subject matter of the local enactment has traditionally been considered within a state's police power; (2) the completeness of the federal regulatory scheme; (3) whether the area covered by the federal law is one for which national, rather than local, regulation is more appropriate; and (4) the similarity between the federal and local enactments. Because there apparently is no legislative history that specifically indicates that the federal legislation was intended to be the exclusive body of law pertaining to vessel construction and operation, the intent of Congress must be determined from the other factors cited above. D could contend that the LSAC should be deemed to be superseded because of the "comprehensiveness" of the federal statute and the need to have legislative consistency where instrumentalities of interstate commerce are involved.

However, Lakeport officials could contend in rebuttal that (1) a similar municipal smoke abatement ordinance was sustained against a supersession attack in *Huron Portland Cement Co. v. City of Detroit*, (2) matters involving the public health or safety of citizens have traditionally been left to local government, and (3) the subject matter of the federal law was vessel safety (not emissions). This case, however, seems less directly on point than *United States v. Locke*, which held preempted state safety regulations for tanker ships operating on Puget Sound. In an area "where there has been a history of significant federal presence," such as shipping and navigation, the presumption should be in favor of implied field preemption. This rule would likely apply in this case.

In light of *Locke*, the LSAC probably would be deemed to be superseded by the federal legislation governing shipping and navigation.

Validity of the state X personal tax:
Consistent with due process, a taxpayer's domiciliary state may ordinarily tax the full value of an instrumentality of interstate commerce. Nevertheless, where the property involved has been "habitually employed" in another jurisdiction, the Commerce Clause requires apportionment of the value of such property to the extent that it has acquired a taxable situs

in another state (whether or not other states are actually taxing the item). *Central Railroad v. Pennsylvania.*

Because (1) the vessel in question only "enters state X's ports for occasional refueling and repairs," and (2) loading and unloading of transport is done at terminals in other states, D can probably prove that its vessel has acquired a taxable situs in several other jurisdictions. Thus, as a consequence of the Commerce Clause, D should not be liable for an amount of tax that exceeds the proportion of time that the vessel is located within state X relative to all time spent in other ports.

Note that application of a general property tax to vessels operating in interstate or international commerce would not violate the Tonnage Clause of Article I, §10. States may not impose tariffs on interstate shipping, either directly or indirectly. *Polar Tankers, Inc. v. City of Valdez.* Here, however, state X has applied a generic personal property tax to ships plying the state's waters, an exercise of taxing power that the Supreme Court specifically approved in *Polar Tankers.* Thus, if the tax were properly apportioned based on use, it would be constitutional as against a Tonnage Clause objection.

Answer to Question 15

1. Lease nonrenewal:
State X might initially assert that review by the U.S. Supreme Court is inappropriate because there is an adequate, independent state ground for the decision (i.e., under state X law, a tenant has no right to obtain an extension of her lease, even though the landlord's refusal to renew the agreement is based on the fact that the tenant has engaged in lawful activities). However, D could probably successfully argue in rebuttal that the essence of her case is that her First Amendment and due-process rights have been violated by the director's decision. *New York Times Co. v. Sullivan.* Therefore, a right of action exists under federal law, and so review by the U.S. Supreme Court is appropriate.

Substantive issues:
State action: Because the housing project was owned and operated by state X, there would be little question that official actions by the director with respect to operation of the facility would be attributed to state X. On the facts, the defendant *is* the state. *Lebron v. National R.R. Passenger Corp.*

Procedural due process: Although there is no case that stands squarely for the proposition that there is a Fourteenth Amendment property right to public housing, D's situation could be analogized to public employment. A "property" right to continued public employment may be found where there is some clear practice or understanding that the employee (in this instance, the lessee) will be terminated only for cause, such that an employee has a "legitimate claim of entitlement" to continued employment incident to a formal or even informal government policy. *Board of Regents v. Roth; Arnett v. Kennedy.* If leases at the housing project are ordinarily renewed automatically, D could contend that she had a justifiable expectation of continued occupancy at the project. *Perry v. Sindermann.* Therefore, she was constitutionally entitled to some type of adversarial hearing prior to the director's refusal to extend her leasehold interest. Although state X could argue in rebuttal that the renewal of outstanding leases is merely done as a matter of convenience (and therefore should not have created an expectation of automatic continuation of one's lease), D should prevail on this issue. Therefore, D would have a constitutional right to reinstatement of her leasehold interest.

First Amendment: D could alternatively contend that the director's action violated her First Amendment rights of free speech and association (applicable to the states via the Fourteenth Amendment) because one may not be deprived of public employment for speaking out on issues of public concern. *Pickering v. Board of Education.* Similarly, speech about a subject of great interest to lessees at a housing project (i.e., "poor judgment" on the part of the director) cannot be the basis for terminating a tenant's occupancy. State X would argue in rebuttal that a public employee's (in this instance, a public lessee's) First Amendment rights must balance against efficient performance of the governmental function being performed. *Connick v. Myers.* Because D's statements constitute nothing more than a personal attack against the director for his recommendations pertaining to operation of the housing project, D's First Amendment rights were outweighed by the harmful effects of her criticism. Alternatively, if D's statements related solely to a matter of private concern (rental rates), state X could argue that they do not implicate the Free Speech Clause of the First Amendment at all. *City of Borough of Duryea v. Guarnieri.*

Even if D's statements were incorrect (i.e., the director had not exercised "poor judgment" in recommending increased rents), her statement was more in the nature of an opinion about a matter of legitimate concern to residents of the housing project than factual criticism about the director. The statement also seems to relate to a matter of public concern (i.e., the management of the complex). Thus, D should prevail on this question, too.

Equal protection: Finally, D could assert that her equal-protection rights (embodied in the Fourteenth Amendment) were violated because, as a consequence of the refusal to renew her lease, D has been singled out for different, adverse treatment than that imposed on other residents of the housing project. The Supreme Court has held that a person subjected to irrational adverse treatment by a government officer has suffered an Equal Protection Clause violation, even if she constitutes a "class of one." *Village of Willowbrook v. Olech.* Accordingly, this contention should also prevail.

2. Contempt-of-court conviction:

Exhaustion of state X remedies:
State X would initially contend that review by the U.S. Supreme Court is inappropriate because D apparently failed to appeal her case to the highest court in state X in which a decision on her matter could be rendered. Assuming D was aware of the injunction and the order was appealable to an appellate court, this assertion by state X should be successful. For purposes of analysis, however, it will be assumed that the contempt conviction was not subject to review by a higher state X court.

A court order, even one that has been incorrectly issued, must be obeyed unless (1) judicial review of the injunction was deliberately made impracticable by the prosecuting entity, or (2) it is patently invalid on its face. *Walker v. Birmingham.* Because the injunction was issued on May 5 and presumably served upon D soon afterwards, D could *not* successfully contend that judicial appeal was impracticable. However, if there is no state X statute pertaining to public demonstrations, D could argue that the injunction was "patently invalid" because (1) it is well established that a public forum (such as a park) cannot be completely foreclosed to speech-related activity; and (2) although public forums are subject to reasonable regulations pertaining to time, place, and manner, the injunction in question completely precluded D's rally in the park (rather than simply limiting it to the appropriate number of persons). Nevertheless, given the strong presumption of validity with respect to court orders, state X should prevail on this question. Therefore, the contempt-of-court conviction would probably be upheld, assuming D's incarceration did not exceed six months. *Baldwin v. New York* (where a prison term of more than six months is imposed, a defendant is entitled to a jury trial).

If, however, the injunction was patently invalid on its face, D could probably successfully contend that the director's *ex parte* order constituted a deprivation of her Fourteenth Amendment due-process rights. Because the injunction affects a significant right (D's First Amendment right of speech and association), she was entitled to notice and an opportunity to be heard prior to issuance of the court order. Because the injunction was obtained almost one full month prior to the predetermined speaking date, the "emergency" situation that must exist to justify an *ex parte* order was not present in this instance.

Additionally, the injunction is probably invalid on due-process (i.e., vagueness) and First Amendment grounds, respectively, because (1) a reasonably intelligent person might have difficulty understanding what constitutes a "mass rally" (20, 50, 100, or 200 persons?), and (2) the order sought to preclude the rally entirely rather than place a reasonable limitation (i.e., 100 persons) on the number of individuals who could attend (without causing any interference with the normal traffic flow).

Answer to Question 16

The motion for dismissal:

Abstention:

A U.S. district court may abstain from hearing a case that challenges the constitutionality of an ambiguous nonfederal statute if the alleged defect might be cured by a narrowing interpretation by a state court. Although state A might contend that abstention is appropriate in this instance because no state court has yet construed the statute in question, Ajax and Ned (Plaintiffs) could probably successfully argue in rebuttal that a curative construction is unlikely because both the 30- and 60-year parameters and the specific testing requirements leave virtually no room for a saving construction if the age limits otherwise violate the Constitution.

Standing:

Article III of the Constitution requires that to have standing in federal court, a plaintiff must show a direct and immediate personal injury that is traceable to the challenged action. *Simon v. Eastern Kentucky Welfare Rights Organization.* State X might contend that Ned has suffered no injury because he has not been terminated from his employment, nor is there any indication that he is receiving less compensation than he received prior to the state A enactment. Ajax arguably lacks standing because it apparently has other drivers who are capable of obtaining the special driving permits (SDPs). Assuming, however, that (1) Ned's reassignment to other routes (a) ultimately results in lessened compensation (of any amount) for him or (b) is disadvantageous for any other reason (i.e., the substituted routes are more physically demanding because they are longer and/or more dangerous); and (2) altering driving assignments to comply with state A law could result in some drivers deciding to leave Ajax's employ, Plaintiffs probably have standing. On these facts, the plaintiffs can claim a concrete and particularized injury sufficient to establish a "case or controversy." *Lujan v. Defenders of Wildlife.*

The state A statute:

Pursuant to the Tenth Amendment, a state may ordinarily enact legislation that is aimed at promoting the health, safety, or welfare of its citizenry. Because the legislation in question is obviously aimed at decreasing the possibility of accidents involving explosives-carrying trucks, it would be constitutionally valid (unless it contravenes some federal interest).

Supremacy Clause:

Where a state statute conflicts with the language of, or purposes sought to be achieved by, a federal statute, the former enactment will be invalid under the Supremacy Clause. Plaintiffs will contend that the state A statute is inconsistent with the purposes sought to be achieved by the federal law because it would induce age discrimination (i.e., to avoid being obliged to juggle schedules to circumvent state A, employers would (1) hire drivers within state A's age parameters and (2) be more likely to terminate employees who could not travel within state A). However, state A could argue in rebuttal that (1) Plaintiffs' argument is premised on speculative secondary effects of its law, and (2) it is unlikely that Congress intended to preempt state legislation that was based on *bona fide* occupational qualifications (statistical studies support state A's age restrictions). Unless there is clear legislative history that Congress intended to totally preclude age as a consideration for employment, Plaintiffs probably would ***not*** succeed on this argument.

Equal Protection Clause:

Because the elderly have not historically been subjected to purposeful unequal treatment or relegated to a position of political powerlessness, neither the strict-scrutiny standard nor the intermediate-scrutiny standard would apply. *Massachusetts Board of Retirement v. Murgia.*

Plaintiffs might nevertheless contend that the state A statute does not satisfy the rational-relationship test (i.e., there must be a rational relationship between the classification drawn by the statute and the governmental object sought). This is because (1) the physical examination and driving test measure more accurately one's ability to drive safely than strict biological age; and (2) persons with perfect driving records could be excluded as a consequence of the statute, although others with negative driving histories might nevertheless qualify for an SDP. However, because the classification (1) need only be theoretically rational (i.e., maybe drivers over 60 are more prone to heart attacks) and (2) on the facts presented, is actually supported by empirical data, state A would probably prevail on this issue as well. *FCC v. Beach Communications, Inc.*

Dormant Interstate Commerce Clause:

State legislation that unduly burdens interstate commerce (i.e., the interference with interstate commerce outweighs the interest sought to be protected by the law) is invalid. *Bibb v. Navajo Freight Lines, Inc.* Plaintiffs could contend that the state A statute imposes a substantial burden on interstate commerce because interstate trucking companies will now be obliged (probably at substantial inconvenience and expense) to avoid state A or be compelled to hire additional employees who can acquire an SDP. State A, however, could argue in rebuttal that it has a strong interest in the legislation (i.e., the desire to avoid catastrophic explosions that have a potential for causing great loss of life and property). Moreover, the Supreme Court has sustained special permitting schemes applicable to trucking companies against both Dormant Commerce Clause and preemption challenges. *American Trucking Assns., Inc. v. Michigan Public Service Comm'n.* (Dormant Commerce Clause); *Mid-Con Freight Systems Inc. v. Michigan Public Service Comm'n.* (implied preemption doctrine). In light of these considerations, assuming that state A could show that most truck companies have drivers within their employ who qualify for an SDP (and therefore the statute merely results in the inconvenience of having to alter job assignments), it would again prevail.

Due-process rights:

Where a state statute conclusively presumes that certain facts exist that result in an adverse classification, the Supreme Court held at one time that the denial of an opportunity to challenge that presumption could violate an individual's Fourteenth Amendment's due-process right to demonstrate that the fact presumed is not true in his case. *Vlandis v. Kline.* Thus, under *Vlandis,* Plaintiffs could have argued that the presumption that persons over 60 were more prone to accidents than others was invalid (especially because Ned was capable of satisfying the physical examination and driving test requirements of state A). However, today the *Vlandis* rule allowing due-process scrutiny of irrebuttable presumptions applies only where, even apart from the existence of the presumption, there is reason to give heightened scrutiny to the classification. *Weinberger v. Salfi.* Because, as discussed above, age-based classifications don't get heightened equal-protection scrutiny, probably heightened due-process scrutiny of the irrebuttable presumption won't be applied either.

Even if the court were to scrutinize the irrebuttable presumption, state A could probably successfully contend that (1) there is no "property" interest in private employment, and (2) statistical studies (which were presumably methodologically sound) have established that drivers over 60 have a higher incidence of accidents than those under 60.

In summary, it is unlikely that Plaintiffs would be able to invalidate the state A statute.

Answer to Question 17

There are several contentions that Micro (M) could assert to invalidate the act.

There is little question that the act represents a valid exercise of Pacific's Tenth Amendment right to enact laws for the general welfare of its citizenry. The act arguably promotes and protects the morality of Pacific's citizens.

Impairment of contracts:

Pursuant to Article I, §10, of the U.S. Constitution, a state may not enact a law that substantially changes outstanding contract rights. The facts fail to indicate whether M's outstanding contracts with its subscribers stated that R-rated pictures would begin at 8:00 P.M. and NC-17-rated movies would commence at 10:00 P.M. If they did, M could contend that the act results in a substantial impairment of those agreements. The DJ could argue in rebuttal that merely changing the times (rather than completely precluding the showing of such pictures) does not result in a "substantial" impairment of the Micro-subscriber contracts. However, because most persons cannot practically watch movies through the latest hours of the night, M would probably prevail with respect to this contention.

Even a substantial impairment of a contract is permissible, provided that it is "reasonable and necessary to serve an important public purpose." *United States Trust Co. v. New Jersey.* This is called the "reserved-powers doctrine" and stands for the idea that the Contracts Clause does not strip states of the ability to exercise the police powers to advance the public good.

Here, Pacific seeks to protect minors from exposure to age-inappropriate adult-content programming. The Supreme Court has sustained similar restrictions applicable to broadcast television stations against a First Amendment challenge. *FCC v. Pacifica Foundation.* If protecting minors from broadcasts of such programming was sufficiently important to override First Amendment objections, it surely constitutes "an important public purpose" for purposes of Contracts Clause analysis. Although this issue is not free from doubt, M is unlikely to prevail on a Contracts Clause claim.

First Amendment:

M might next contend that its First Amendment rights were violated because the act, in effect, precludes speech that is constitutionally protected (i.e., there is no indication that the R or NC-17 movies are obscene). *Schad v. Mount Ephraim.*

The DJ could argue in rebuttal, however, that the act is a time and place regulation and therefore is valid if it (1) serves a substantial interest (i.e., protecting the morals of minors) and (2) does not unreasonably limit alternative avenues of communication (i.e., persons who want to view the films can simply stay up later). *Young v. American Mini Theatres.* The DJ could also cite *FCC v. Pacifica Foundation* for the proposition that the First Amendment affords less than complete protection with respect to speech that may be overheard by children and lacks "social value." Because the broadcasting in question involves violent and sex-oriented scenes, the act is arguably valid.

M would probably prevail upon this issue because the time parameters set forth in the act make it virtually impossible for most persons to practicably see R- or NC-17-rated movies. Although protecting children from exposure to sexually explicit or unduly violent programming is an important governmental objective, government cannot effectively preclude adult access to nonobscene materials in order to protect children. *Playboy Entertainment Group, Inc. v. United States.* Moreover the Supreme Court in *Playboy* expressly held that *Pacifica Foundation* does not apply to cablecasting because channel-blocking technologies present a less restrictive means of advancing the government's interest in protecting children. In addition, *Pacifica Foundation* involved the "uniquely pervasive" medium of free, over-the-air broadcast radio, rather than a subscriber-based cable television service. The government's rationale for comprehensive content-based regulation of *subscriber-based* services seems considerably weaker than that for free, over-the-air radio and television broadcasts because such services lack the "uniquely pervasive" nature of broadcast radio and television programming (i.e., if adult-oriented cable programming offends you, do not subscribe to it).

M should prevail on this claim.

Equal-protection rights:

M also might argue that its Fourteenth Amendment equal-protection rights were violated by the fact that, although private companies were regulated by the act, governmental subdivisions were not. However, it is well established that a legislature may "take one step at a time to remedy only part of a broader problem." *Williamson v. Lee Optical Co.* The legislature could have reasonably believed that governmental subdivisions, being more amenable to the will of their constituents, would be less likely to transmit questionable subject matter.

Thus, this contention by M would probably be unsuccessful.

Summary:
Because the act is probably unconstitutional on First Amendment grounds, it should be invalidated by a federal court.

Answer to Question 18

1. The Ut use tax:

It is assumed that Ut ordinarily charges a sales tax on toy purchases made in that state. If it did not, the use tax would probably constitute an impermissible discrimination against interstate commerce (i.e., local merchants would have a significant advantage over out-of-state vendors because sales by the latter group would be burdened with a tax that had not been imposed on the former group). It should also be mentioned that the Ut *use* tax could not exceed the difference between the Ut sales tax and the sales tax assessed by the state of Hio.

Arrow (A) could, however, contend that the Ut use tax violates its equal-protection rights because it applies only to mail-order sales (i.e., those persons who sell goods to Ut residents in a nonmail manner are exempted from the tax). A would assert that there is no rational basis for this distinction. However, Ut could probably successfully argue in rebuttal that (1) a state may deal with a problem (i.e., equalizing the taxation rate of in-state sales with those purchases made out of state, so that consumers are not encouraged to buy items in other jurisdictions) one step at a time; and (2) possibly, it is easier to identify mail-order sellers than other types of out-of-state vendors.

A might also assert that the tax violates the Privileges and Immunities Clause of Article IV of the U.S. Constitution. This clause prohibits discrimination against nonresidents with respect to "fundamental" rights (defined independently of "fundamental rights" protected under the Due Process and Equal Protection Clauses of the Fourteenth Amendment), unless the law in question is substantially related to an important governmental purpose. *United Building & Construction Trades Council v. Camden; Corfield v. Coryell.* However, use taxes are a recognized means of preventing in-state businesses (which are ordinarily required to assess a sales tax) from being disadvantaged by lower sales tax rates in other jurisdictions. Additionally, there is probably no "fundamental" right by an out-of-state seller to insist upon complete equality with respect to the imposition of a use tax.

Thus, the Ut use tax is probably valid.

2. Collection of the Ut use tax:

Under the Due Process Clause of the Fourteenth Amendment, a taxpayer must have sufficient contacts with the taxing state for the latter to be able to constitutionally require the former to pay taxes to it. It is well established that the solicitation of sales by mail does not satisfy the requirement of sufficient contacts enabling the imposition of a duty on an interstate seller to collect a use tax on sales to local residents. *National Bellas Hess, Inc. v. Illinois Department of Revenue*. Thus, A does ***not*** have to collect the Ut use tax.

3. The Penn highway use license fee:

A could assert that this tax is unconstitutional on due-process grounds because (1) it is too vague (i.e., a person of ordinary intelligence would be unable to determine if contemplated conduct was illegal) because the meaning of "regularly" is unclear, and (2) the tax (a flat amount) bears no relationship to the amount of actual highway use. The first argument is not a particularly strong one, although it is colorable.

As to the latter contention, Penn could probably successfully argue that the relatively nominal $20 fee is valid as long as the funds raised by the tax are used in a highway-related manner. *Capitol Greyhound Lines v. Brice*. Penn could have concluded that attempting to apportion the use tax among ***all*** actual users of its highways would simply be too cumbersome (and perhaps even impossible to do with sufficient certainty).

The Penn fee is probably not subject to attack on either Dormant Commerce Clause or federal preemption grounds. The Supreme Court has held that states may collect fees associated with the use of local roads, even from out-of-state transportation companies, provided that the companies make significant use of local roads on intrastate trips. Because A engages in substantial intrastate deliveries in Penn, Penn may assess the fee. *American Trucking Assns., Inc. v. Michigan Public Service Commn.* (Dormant Commerce Clause); *Mid-Con Freight Systems Inc. v. Michigan Public Service Commn.* (preemption).

As to A's vagueness argument, Penn could contend the validity of its fee would be determined by the particular circumstances to which it was applied (i.e., at a hearing, A could contend that (1) the number of times its trucks traveled on Penn highways and (2) the amount of mileage traveled by its vehicles in Penn did not constitute "regular" usage). Because it is unclear exactly how much A's trucks used Penn roads (i.e., the facts state only that "several large orders" were delivered to Penn each year in A's trucks), it is difficult to assess whether the tax could be validly applied against A's vehicles. However, assuming its trucks made at least limited use of Penn highways (i.e., four times per year, for an aggregate total of at least 100 miles), the Penn highway use tax would probably be sustained.

4. Ad valorem tax:

A state may ordinarily impose an *ad valorem* tax against personal property. Where instrumentalities of interstate commerce are concerned, the state in which the taxpayer is domiciled can ordinarily make this assessment against 100 percent of the taxpayer's property, unless the items have acquired a taxable situs elsewhere. In the latter event, due process requires that the assessment be reduced to the extent that the instrumentality was "habitually employed" in other jurisdictions. However, because A's trucks travel into Penn on an irregular basis (i.e., only whenever large orders must be delivered), A is probably *not* entitled to any type of apportionment.

Additionally, an equal-protection argument would probably not be successful (i.e., it is irrational to tax property owned by a taxpayer at one rate and that which is leased by her at a lower rate) because property that is merely being leased (and therefore must be returned to the owner at the end of the term) has less value to the taxpayer than that which the latter (as the owner) can sell at any time.

5. The leasehold tax:

The fact that A's use of federal property is being taxed does not necessarily lead to the conclusion that the tax is unconstitutional under the Supremacy Clause. *Detroit v. Murray Corp.* A could argue, however, that the 50 percent of leasehold value tax imposes an undue burden on the U.S. government's ability to lease surplus property and therefore violates the Supremacy Clause (especially in light of the fact that property leased from the state of Hio is not taxed at all, giving the state a significant advantage over the federal government). A should prevail on this contention, so the leasehold tax is probably unenforceable.

A could also contend that the tax violates its equal-protection rights because lessees of the state government have arbitrarily been exempted from the tax. Hio could argue in rebuttal that favoring itself is not irrational because (1) the state has numerous public functions to perform (all of which require money); and (2) without such an advantage, its used equipment (which presumably is often leased) might have to be sold for scrap at only a small fraction of its value. However, because Hio has numerous means at its disposal for raising the funds necessary to effectively perform its functions, this argument should fail. Thus, the leasehold tax is probably unconstitutional on equal-protection grounds also.

Answer to Question 19

1. The injunction against picketing:

The defendants in the state court action would probably contend that the injunction violated their First Amendment rights (applicable to the states via the Fourteenth Amendment). Regulations pertaining to traditional public forums (such as streets and parks) can ordinarily regulate only time, place, and manner. A university campus, at least in part, constitutes a traditional public forum. Because the injunction totally precludes picketing, it is arguably invalid. However, U could have argued in rebuttal that, even assuming streets within a college campus constitute a traditional public forum, activities that disrupt the educational functions of the college (i.e., the ability of students to traverse the campus to arrive at their next class in a timely manner) may be foreclosed entirely. *Grayned v. City of Rockford.* Nevertheless, the total ban on picketing by the NAACP is simply too broad to survive First Amendment review. The picketing can presumably be limited to a visible, yet noncritical area of the campus, where the message sought to be conveyed by the protestors can still be communicated. Thus, the injunction will probably be overturned, subject to a new order that permits the picketing to be carried out in a manner that does not interfere with U's ability to function.

Alternatively, U might argue that, given the antagonistic response of other students to the demonstrators, the ban was necessary to preclude a breach of the peace. *Feiner v. New York.* However, the speech in this instance was merely offensive to the listener's viewpoint. *Cox v. Louisiana.* Given the facts that (1) no physical violence appeared to be threatened as a consequence of the picketing (the opposing group of students merely heckled the protesters), and (2) potential violence could be suppressed by having an adequate number of police on hand, the injunction could *not* be validated on this basis without impermissibly validating a "heckler's veto," a course of action that the Supreme Court routinely has prohibited. *Forsyth County v. Nationalist Movement.*

2. The action for a declaratory judgment and injunction in federal court:

Abstention:

A U.S. district court may abstain from hearing a case that challenges the constitutionality of an ambiguous nonfederal statute or rule if the alleged defect might be cured by a narrowing state court interpretation. U might contend that abstention is appropriate because no state court has ruled on the validity of the U policy in question. However, the plaintiffs could probably assert in rebuttal that this doctrine is inapplicable because (1) no state court action is pending, and (2) the action of the U housing board is not susceptible to a curative interpretation (either it does or does not violate the Fourteenth Amendment's equal-protection rights of African American students). It is unlikely that the federal court will abstain.

Standing:

To have standing in federal court, an individual must show a direct and immediate personal injury that is traceable to the challenged action. *Simon v. Eastern Kentucky Welfare Rights Organization.* U could contend that (1) there is nothing to indicate that the three U students who joined the law-suit have ever attempted to procure housing through the bureau, or (2) they would have actually attempted to secure a room from one of the persons who had indicated that only Caucasians would be accepted. Without additional facts indicating that the three students had at least solicited the directory of available rentals from the housing bureau, it is unlikely they would have standing.

U could argue that the NAACP has no standing to assert the rights of students at U who had not been given the "whites only" list. However, a third party may assert another's rights where it would be highly burdensome for the latter to do so. The NAACP could respond that it would be difficult for African Americans at U to commence an action because they might fear reprisals from students, professors, or homeowners who were sympathetic with U's present housing policy. The antagonistic response to the picketing that occurred at U strengthens this argument. Given the strong national interest in eradicating racial discrimination, the NAACP would probably be deemed to have standing.

U might alternatively contend that, in any event, no injury was suffered by those African Americans who were not shown the "whites only" list. Because the homeowners on that directory would presumably have refused to rent to African Americans, African Americans have not been "injured" by being precluded from going through the futile action of being rejected by these lessors. This argument lacks merit. The plaintiffs could argue in rebuttal that, confronted with the unavoidable embarrassment of being compelled to reject an individual simply because of race, many "whites only" home-owners would overcome their prejudices and rent to African Americans. Local or state civil rights laws might also provide a civil cause of action, as would §1982 of Title 42. *Jones v. Alfred H. Mayer Co.* Section 1982, a statute that Congress enacted to enforce the Thirteenth Amendment, does not require that a defendant be a state actor, and refusals to rent or lease real property come within the scope of this law. Moreover, an actual injury occurs simply by the fact that facilities are foreclosed to African Americans solely because of their race. *Brown v. Board of Education.* Thus, the plaintiffs will prevail on this argument, too.

State action:
U could next contend that simply by honoring the wishes of local homeowners to be omitted from the list tendered to African Americans, the state is not discriminating against this group. U would argue that if it refused to comply with the wishes of the homeowners in question, the homeowners would disallow the listing of their names. However, the plaintiffs could probably respond that there is sufficient state involvement because (1) the housing bureau facilitates discrimination by allowing the "whites only" landlords to avoid the embarrassment of refusing to rent to African Americans; and (2) there is a symbiotic relationship in that (a) the homeowners involved are helping U make certain that there is adequate housing for its students, in return for which (b) the homeowners are permitted to avoid the distasteful experience of having to reject African American lessees. *Burton v. Wilmington Parking Auth.* Because it is at least possible that (1) a number of the "whites only" landlords would eventually agree to accept African Americans, and (2) some landlords would be financially obliged to accept African American lessees if a "whites only" list was ***not*** made available to students, state action probably exists. In any event, a state agency may not constitutionally encourage or facilitate private racial discrimination in real estate markets without violating the Equal Protection Clause. *Reitman v. Mulkey.*

Moreover, the Supreme Court has specifically found state action to exist when government acts to enforce racial discrimination in private housing markets. *Shelley v. Kraemer.* Although *Shelley* dealt specifically with the enforcement of racially restrictive covenants running with the land, and the Supreme Court generally has declined to extend this decision's precedential reach, the facts presented seem sufficiently analogous for *Shelley* to apply. *Reitman* also holds that states cannot encourage or facilitate private racial discrimination that the state itself could not engage in directly. By offering to maintain and distribute a "whites only" list of rental properties, the state has unconstitutionally encouraged private racial discrimination that would likely create equal-protection liability not only for the university but also for any private landlords on the exclusionary lists (under a "nexus" or "encouragement" theory of state action). *Reitman.*

Equal protection:

Classifications based on race must satisfy the strict-scrutiny standard (i.e., there must be a compelling state interest served by the legislation or policy involved, and there is no less restrictive means of accomplishing that objective). U could conceivably argue that (1) there is a compelling interest because campus housing is inadequate, and (2) there are no less restrictive means available (i.e., racially prejudiced landlords would otherwise refuse to make their homes available for additional housing). However, the plaintiffs could successfully contend in rebuttal that (1) it is unclear whether there would be insufficient housing accommodations if U refused to permit landlords to opt for a "whites only" directory, and (2) additional housing could be built by the state if the "whites only" landlords actually withdrew their names from the off-campus housing list. Under strict scrutiny, if any race-neutral means exist to achieve the government's compelling objective, the government must use them. *Adarand Constructors, Inc. v. Pena.* Here, obvious means of housing university students exist and must be used by U.

In summary, the U housing bureau can be enjoined from having a "whites only" listing of additional housing.

Answer to Question 20

Refusal to grant hearing:

Smith (S) might initially contend that, under the Due Process Clause of the Fourteenth Amendment, he was entitled to a hearing with respect to the rejection of his application. However, in the absence of circumstances that, under applicable state law, would create a legitimate claim of entitlement to continued public employment, a governmental worker has no right to a pretermination hearing. *Perry v. Sindermann; Bishop v. Wood.* Unless the Centerville School District (District) had an established policy of giving hiring priority to existing temporary teachers whenever a full-time position became vacant, S would have no reason to anticipate being rehired (and therefore would *not* be entitled to a hearing pertaining to rejection of his application because he lacks a cognizable property interest in continued public employment).

Refusal to hire:

Even if S was not entitled to a hearing on his application to become the full-time science teacher, the refusal of District to hire him could *not* be predicated on an unconstitutional basis. If it were, S would be entitled to an order requiring that his application be reconsidered. However, if any constitutionally valid basis for rejection of S's application exists and was the primary reason for the decision, the fact that it was partially premised upon unconstitutional grounds would be irrelevant. *Mt. Healthy City School District Board of Education v. Doyle.* Under such circumstances, the burden would be on the defendant to establish that the same decision would have been made in the absence of the unconstitutional consideration(s).

First Amendment:

S could contend that refusal to accept his application for the full-time position violated his First Amendment right of free speech (applicable to the states via the Fourteenth Amendment). One may not be deprived of public employment for speaking out on issues of general importance. *Pickering v. Board of Education.* S would argue that his contention that other teachers were incorrectly instructing their students with respect to evolution constituted a matter of public concern. District could respond, however, that (1) a public employee's First Amendment rights must always be balanced against efficient performance of the particular governmental function involved, and (2) constantly accusing other teachers of misinforming their students would lower morale and engender dissension among the staff at the high school. It is unclear from the facts whether S had, despite his personal beliefs, previously taught his science class in accordance with the board's viewpoint on the question of evolution. If he had, his "verbal attacks" would probably have to be highly offensive (rather than merely persistent and unpopular) to be the basis for not hiring him.

Free Exercise Clause:
A general law that incidentally burdens religious practices does not generally violate the Free Exercise Clause of the First Amendment (applicable to the states through the Due Process Clause of the Fourteenth Amendment). *Employment Division v. Smith.* To overcome this rule, S would have to show that the 9:00 A.M. to 3:30 P.M. school day was established with the specific intent of interfering with his religious practices or that it also violated some other constitutional right (such as the right of privacy). *Church of the Lukumi Babalu Aye v. City of Hialeah.*

Absent extraordinary facts not provided, the board will prevail on the Free Exercise Clause claim.

Equal Protection Clause:
Although legislation pertaining to legal aliens is usually analyzed under some form of heightened scrutiny, mere "rationality" is required where public school teachers are involved. *Ambach v. Norwick.* In *Ambach*, legal aliens who had shown an unwillingness to acquire U.S. citizenship were barred from becoming teachers in public schools. This classification was deemed rational in accomplishing the state's goal of fostering in its students (1) respect for governmental processes and (2) a sense of social responsibility. However, the board's concern in this instance seems to be with the quality of S's previous training, rather than with his status as a legal alien.

Although the board's precise reasons do not square with those set forth in *Ambach*, the board's concern for local unemployment among citizens is certainly "rational." Moreover, if the board's concern with local training relates to the values identified in *Ambach*, the board's policy could fall squarely under this precedent. Without additional facts, it is difficult to determine the outcome of this claim. Assuming that *Ambach* applies, the board should prevail.

Summary:
The board will likely prevail on the procedural due process, Free Exercise Clause, and Equal Protection Clause claims. It is possible, though not likely, that S will prevail on the free-speech claim. However, even if S should prevail on the First Amendment claim, the board will not face liability if it can show that the decision would have been the same even absent the impermissible considerations.

Answer to Question 21

Federal authority:

Orange (O) might initially argue that the federal statute was unconstitutional because Powerco's business operations occurred solely within O. Therefore, the Interstate Commerce Clause was not a proper basis for the law. However, Powerco (P) could contend in rebuttal that the act was constitutional under **both** (1) the Interstate Commerce Clause, because the activity itself (the regulation of nuclear reactors) constitutes economic activity (the generation and sale of electrical power for sale to others) that has, in the aggregate, an appreciable effect on interstate commerce; and (2) the War Power Clauses (U.S. Const. art. I, §8, cl. 11, 12, 13, and 14), because atomic reactors under appropriate supervision can be used for military and national defense purposes. Thus, the federal legislation is valid.

It is well established that, pursuant to valid legislation, Congress may delegate its authority to a commission. Although the guidelines conferred on the AEC in this instance are somewhat broad (i.e., the AEC is authorized to "license" the commercial uses of nuclear reactors and "regulate the emission of radioactive waste"), Congress's grant of power to the AEC would be sustained. *American Trucking Assns. v. Whitman.*

Preemption:

O could contend that there was no "conflict" with the AEC's emission levels because its standards were more stringent than those promulgated by the federal entity (i.e., the Pollution Law encompassed the federal emission standard within it). Thus, the Pollution Law is **not** invalid under the Supremacy Clause. However, P could make two arguments in rebuttal.

First, P would assert that the act was intended to preempt the entire field of atomic energy, and therefore **any** state legislation within its sphere was unconstitutional under the Supremacy Clause. In determining if this was Congress's intent, several factors would be considered: (1) any language in the federal enactment that indicates such a purpose; (2) whether the subject matter of the local enactment has traditionally been dealt with under the states' police powers; (3) the completeness of the federal regulatory scheme; and (4) whether the area is one for which national, rather than local, regulation is more appropriate. P would argue that, given (1) the broad policy language in the first clause of the act (referring to (a) the general welfare and (b) the common defense and security), (2) the broad grant of legislative authority to the AEC (presumably so that additional ordinances could be promulgated expeditiously and on a continuing basis), and (3) the importance of developing a coherent nuclear energy policy, the act was intended to preempt the entire field of atomic energy. Although O could respond that (1) Congress could have, if it had desired to do so, easily exempted the area of nuclear power from state regulation by the simple expedient of clear language to that effect; and (2) the states have traditionally legislated in the area of environmental pollution, P would probably prevail on this issue. Thus, the portion of the Pollution Law pertaining to emission standards is probably invalid. *United States v. Locke.*

Alternatively, P could contend that, even if Congress did not intend to preempt the entire field, the emission provisions of the Pollution Law would frustrate the particular purposes and the specific means sought to be achieved by the act (i.e., the development of energy resources). *Geier v. American Honda Motor Co.* P can apparently show that it would **not** be economically feasible to comply with O's emission standards. Again, P's argument would probably be successful.

Thus, the emission standards contained in the Pollution Law are probably unconstitutional under the Supremacy Clause.

The O license tax:
P could attack the license tax on both Supremacy Clause and due-process grounds.

Because the AEC has been specifically authorized to "license" the commercial use of atomic reactors, O would probably be preempted from introducing new requirements into this area.

Licensing fees must be proportional to the services that are provided by the taxing authority. *Complete Auto Transit, Inc. v. Brady.* Here, P owns and operates the plant entirely within O; accordingly, O may tax the physical plant and the goods that it produces.

A state is free to use taxation as an instrument of public policy and to raise general revenues. A tax of $500,000 per year on a multibillion-dollar facility seems entirely reasonable—certainly no serious due-process or equal-protection issues exist. The harder question relates back to the preemption issue; the tax plainly exists to discourage the construction and operation of nuclear power plants in O. This constitutes an effort to frustrate the achievement of a federal policy of encouraging the use of nuclear power. Although this issue is a close one, the tax arguably should be held preempted on the authority of *American Honda.*

The gross-receipts tax:

Gross-receipts taxes are ordinarily upheld, provided that (1) they bear some relationship to the services provided by the state, and (2) the taxpayer is not obliged to pay for the same services received from the state more than once (these are both due-process considerations). In the absence of facts not provided, the tax is probably valid. Because a number of governmental instrumentalities are available to P (i.e., police protection, fire department, etc.), O would be entitled to assess a tax that is fairly related to these services. Moreover, the facts do not suggest that an issue of double taxation exists.

Answer to Question 22

Agency would probably raise the following issues before the U.S. Supreme Court.

State action:

Agency would initially argue that no governmental action is involved because it is a private corporation. The fact that it is licensed and extensively regulated by state X does not transform Agency's decision into state action. *Jackson v. Metropolitan Edison Co.* H and W could argue in rebuttal, however, that adoption should be viewed as an "exclusive governmental" function, and therefore the conduct of the entity undertaking that function is properly viewed as state action. *Rendell-Baker v. Kohn.* They could argue alternatively that there is significant state "entwinement" because state X has legislatively mandated most of the standards that Agency must apply in deciding if potential parents should be permitted to adopt children, licenses the entities applying the standards, and retains some level of overall responsibility for children taken from the custody of their biological parents. *Brentwood Academy v. TSSAA.* Although the argument that adoption has been the exclusive province of the state should be persuasive, their second argument based on entwinement is compelling. Thus, the state action requisite is probably satisfied.

H and W's agnosticism:

H and W could assert that their lack of religious affiliation cannot constitutionally be considered in determining if they should be permitted to adopt. A state regulation violates the Establishment Clause of the First Amendment (applicable to the states via the Fourteenth Amendment), unless (1) it has a secular purpose, (2) its primary effect doesn't advance or inhibit religion, **and** (3) it produces no excessive entanglement between religion and the state. H and W could assert that there can be little question that the effect of the law would be to generally promote religion because nonreligious persons in state X would be precluded from adopting children. Because state X appears to have no satisfactory response to this assertion, H and W probably have a constitutional right to have their lack of religious affiliation excluded from the determination of whether they should be permitted to adopt.

The difference in H and W's ethnic (i.e., racial) backgrounds:

H and W could contend that rejection of their application as a consequence of their different ethnic backgrounds violates their (1) due-process **and** (2) equal-protection rights.

Due process:

As to the due-process assertion, H and W would argue that the right to adopt children, like the right to procreate (*Skinner v. Oklahoma*) and the right to marry (*Loving v. Virginia*), is fundamental. Therefore, state X may burden this interest only if the regulation meets the strict-scrutiny standard (i.e., there is a compelling reason for the classification, and there is no less burdensome means of accomplishing the governmental objective). Although state X certainly has an interest in attempting to ensure the well-being of a prospective adoptee, completely excluding an interracial couple from adoption fails to advance a compelling governmental interest and lacks narrow tailoring. *City of Richmond v. J. A. Croson Co.* Assuming applicants were otherwise qualified, the state cannot absolutely condition adoption rights on the race of the prospective adopters.

Procedural due process:

When the government impinges on important liberty interests by adopting classifications that are arguably overinclusive, a person's procedural due-process rights are violated in the absence of some reasonable opportunity to rebut the presumption implicit in the classification. In *Stanley v. Illinois,* a state law provided that the natural father of a child born to unmarried parents automatically lost custody of the child upon the death of the child's natural mother. The Supreme Court held that the father had a right to a hearing on the question of whether he was a suitable parent. A law or policy that absolutely (1) requires an adoptee's new parents to be of the same racial affiliation as her natural mother or (2) precludes parents from adopting solely because of their diverse racial backgrounds is arguably defective because the parents desiring to adopt have no opportunity to rebut the implicit presumption that they are not qualified. Because Agency has already declared that H and W would (except for their differing ethnic backgrounds) be qualified to adopt a child, a hearing on their fitness is unnecessary. Thus, Agency should be ordered to permit H and W to adopt.

Equal protection:

H and W's equal-protection argument would be predicated on the assertion that where a classification involving a married couple is made on the basis of their different ethnic backgrounds, it is subject to strict scrutiny. *Palmore v. Sidoti.* In *Palmore,* the Supreme Court invalidated the transfer of custody of a child back to her biological father solely because her mother had, following her divorce from the biological father, wed an African American man. The Court acknowledged that the child would probably

suffer some "social stigmatization" from her peers, but held that the state
of Florida could not itself endorse these prejudices by using them as a basis
for terminating an otherwise fit custodial parent's right to continued custody of her daughter. The *Palmore* Court reasoned that for the state to act
on the social fact of widespread racial prejudices would have the effect of
validating them and also would perversely help to sustain racial prejudices
in society over time. Because custody of a child cannot be altered merely
because her parents are racially diverse, similar reasoning would dictate
that adoption procedures also ***cannot*** be predicated exclusively on this
factor.

Requirement that the race and religious affiliation of the adopting parents be the same as the natural mother's:

Although Agency did not state that its rejection of H and W was premised
on the state X requirement that adoptive parents be of the same racial background and religious faith as the adoptive child's mother (Agency asserted
that the racial diversity of the parents was a sufficient reason for denying
their application), H and W would probably seek to have this requirement
declared unconstitutional so that it not be used against them when Agency
reconsiders their application.

Government cannot condition the imposition of burdens or the conveyance of benefits on the religious beliefs (or lack thereof) held by citizens.
McDaniel v. Paty; Torcaso v. Watkins. Although the state could take the religious upbringing of a child into account when placing a child with either
foster or adoptive parents, an absolute requirement of correspondence of
religious beliefs goes too far in making religious belief a precondition for
serving as an adoptive or foster parent. Certainly, less restrictive means of
respecting a child's religious heritage and, in the case of older children,
religious upbringing, plainly exist.

Answer to Question 23

Standing:

The president (P) could initially contest Jones's standing.

Jones (J) would argue that Congress has specifically permitted taxpayers to contest the validity of P's executive order permitting warrantless wiretaps. Pursuant to Article III of the U.S. Constitution, the existence of federal courts (other than the U.S. Supreme Court) is left to the discretion of Congress. Because Congress has the power to create federal courts, this authority would presumably embody the right to determine what groups of persons can assert a particular cause of action within the federal judicial system.

However, P could contend in rebuttal that the Constitution provides that federal courts are competent to hear only "cases and controversies." U.S. Const. art. III, §2. Congressional acts cannot, of course, override the Constitution. *Lujan v. Defenders of Wildlife.* Thus, persons contesting executive orders must still show that an actual or imminent injury, which is also concrete and particularized, has occurred or is highly likely to occur as a consequence of the challenged activity. *Summers v. Earth Island Institute.* P would therefore assert that J lacks standing because (1) J is not an alien and so would *not* be covered by the executive order in question; and (2) even if J occasionally had telephone discussions with aliens (and therefore might coincidentally be overheard during an allegedly illegal wiretap), he would still be obliged to show that the telephones of the particular aliens with whom he spoke had been tapped (i.e., those aliens were perceived by the FBI as being persons suspected of espionage or subversion).

A taxpayer (who has suffered no direct harm) ordinarily has no right to challenge governmental actions of federal officials, even if no one would otherwise have standing. *Schlesinger v. Reservists Committee.* (Our situation does not deal with a congressional appropriation to a church or religious organization that allegedly infringes the Establishment Clause. *Hein v. Freedom from Religion Foundation, Inc.*; *Flast v. Cohen.*)

Because J has not established a concrete and particularized injury in fact, it therefore appears that J lacks standing to contest the executive order in question, notwithstanding Congress's desire to convey standing by statute. However, additional issues will be discussed in the event that this conclusion is erroneous.

Presidential authority:

J could contend that the Fourth Amendment protects persons from unreasonable searches and seizures. As a consequence, wiretaps (which constitute a search) are invalid unless issued by a *judicial* officer upon probable cause. Because the executive order permits a wiretap to be installed (1) in the case of "suspected" espionage or subversion and (2) without the authorization of a judicial order, it is unconstitutional.

P could argue in rebuttal that his action was proper because implicit in the power of the presidency is the right to undertake emergency measures that are necessary to protect the country from hostile forces. Because the aliens in question are allegedly contemplating acts of espionage and subversion (activities that could presumably result in loss of life), the executive order should be sustained. However, because (1) the facts fail to indicate that any violent acts (i.e., explosions, fires, etc.) are imminent, and (2) P is not responding to a current "crisis" situation precipitated by a foreign government (*Dames & Moore v. Regan*), it is unlikely that P would be successful. Presidential authority, even in times of crisis, remains subject to constitutional constraints. *Hamdi v. Rumsfeld.* Thus, the executive order is probably invalid.

Due process:

Even assuming a national emergency did exist, the Fifth Amendment due-process rights of aliens have arguably been violated by P's action because the executive order extends to the entire class of aliens (without any type of judicial finding that the persons whose phones have been tapped intended to engage in espionage). Although P might contend that the FBI's determination as to those persons who represented a threat to the national security was an adequate limiting standard, this contention would probably fail. Thus, the directive's overbreadth and lack of any independent review of the actions undertaken by the executive branch would probably cause the executive order to be deemed unconstitutional. *Hamdi v. Rumsfeld.*

Additionally, the term "subversive" is arguably too vague (i.e., a person of ordinary intelligence and who had knowledge of the executive order could not determine if contemplated conduct was proscribed) to serve as the basis for governmental action. This term has been deemed to be unconstitutionally vague in the context of a loyalty-oath requirement. *Baggett v. Bullitt.* Although P could argue in rebuttal that "subversive" should be interpreted as being equivalent to "illegal activities that threaten the national government," J would probably prevail on this issue. Thus, the executive order is probably illegal on due-process grounds also.

Executive privilege:

The Supreme Court has recognized a limited executive privilege protecting the disclosure of presidential communication. *United States v. Nixon.* However, in the context of criminal cases, these communications are only presumptively privileged. Thus, J would contend that P's communications are subject to an ***in camera*** review by the trial judge for the purpose of determining whether they were sufficiently related to the performance of executive activities (i.e., to protect the country from illegal conduct by foreign agents). P could argue in rebuttal, however, that *United States v. Nixon* dealt with a criminal proceeding. The Supreme Court has declined to extend executive privilege to convey an absolute immunity even in civil cases involving the president. *Clinton v. Jones.* Given the gravity of the interest at stake—a fundamental right secured by the Fourth Amendment—J would probably prevail on this issue. Thus, the judge would be permitted to make an ***in camera*** review of the materials in question. If the materials do ***not*** relate to matters of national security, J would be permitted to obtain them. *Hamdi v. Rumsfeld.*

Answer to Question 24

1. M's lawsuit:

State action:

The PTA could initially contend that no state action is involved because it is a private organization, consisting of nonschool officials or employees. Thus, its activities are not subject to constitutional limitations. However, M could argue in rebuttal that where a governmental entity is significantly involved with the allegedly unconstitutional activity, the state action requirement is satisfied. *Brentwood Academy v. TSSAA.*

State action would probably **not** exist here because the PTA is a private group and does not have any formal links to the school; the school does not control membership, establish organizational rules, or act in concert with the PTA. In fact, one would expect that the PTA would often find itself in an adversarial relationship with the public school (over program cuts, teacher assignments, etc.).

Many organizations use school facilities before and after regular school hours—federal law mandates such access. The Supreme Court has held that schools cannot ban pervasively sectarian entities from access to school facilities. *Good News Club v. Milford Central School.* If mere use of school facilities after hours transformed organizations into state actors, *Good News Club* was wrongly decided. On the other hand, the school distributes PTA materials during school hours and facilitates transportation home after the PTA-sponsored classes. It seems likely that the other private organizations, such as the Boy Scouts and Girl Scouts, enjoy similar support—and are not state actors as a result of it. Although it is a close question, the PTA is probably **not** a state actor on these facts.

Standing:

The PTA could next assert that M lacks standing (i.e., she has suffered no direct, immediate, and concrete injury because it is her daughter, not M, who has been denied admission to the Baseball Practice class). However, M could probably contend in rebuttal that (1) she is "injured" in the sense that M will be precluded from the enjoyment of watching her child engage in this activity, and (2) standing is often found to exist when there is a special relationship between the claimant and the party who has directly suffered the alleged harm. Moreover, the Supreme Court did not suggest that standing problems existed for the plaintiffs in the *VMI* case, which involved gender-based denials of admission to a state-sponsored institution of higher learning. *United States v. Virginia (VMI).* The Supreme Court also has held that voters possess standing to challenge voting districts drawn using a suspect classification (race), because invidious governmental classifications presumptively cause a constitutionally cognizable injury. *Shaw v. Reno.* Because matters affecting a child's development invariably affect her mother (at least to some degree), a reviewing court is very likely to find that standing exists.

Equal protection:

Although state action arguably does not exist, I will nevertheless consider possible constitutional claims that would exist if the PTA were a state actor. M could contend that A's Fourteenth Amendment equal-protection rights were violated by the PTA's exclusion of girls from the Baseball Practice course. When government uses a gender-based classification, an intermediate level of scrutiny is ordinarily applied (i.e., an "important" or "significant" governmental interest must be involved, and the legislation must be substantially related to the achievement of that objective). *Mississippi University for Women v. Hogan.* M could argue that the PTA's claim that there might be possible "behavior problems" if Baseball Practice were coeducational is too inadequate to constitute a "substantial state" interest. *VMI.* Because boys and girls interact in regular classes, there is no reason to believe that they couldn't coexist during Baseball Practice. Moreover, there is no reason to believe that some girls can't play baseball as well as or better than some boys; equal protection mandates that they be given the chance. *VMI.* M would probably prevail. Finally, excluding girls from the baseball practice offering seems to rely on and to ratify longstanding gender-based stereotypes—discriminatory behavior that the Supreme Court has repeatedly and expressly *rejected* as a substantial or important government interest.

Procedural due process:

It will be assumed that M can show that, if her car had not gotten a flat tire, she would have arrived at the school in sufficient time to register H for Creative Crafts (i.e., the other parents were not queued up to register their children in advance of the time that M would have arrived, even had the flat tire been avoided). Without such a showing, M would be unable to prove a causal relationship between the alleged constitutional infringement and the "harm" that she suffered, and she would therefore lack standing.

M could contend that the exclusion of H from Creative Crafts violated her procedural due-process rights because participation in that activity should not be dependent on so fortuitous an event as arrival at the school at a particular time. However, enrolling in a Creative Crafts class is probably *not* a sufficiently important interest for procedural due-process rights to attach (i.e., elementary school students could presumably become productive, successful adults without special training in this activity). Indeed, because the right to enroll was not guaranteed, the PTA could argue that H lacked a legitimate claim of entitlement to enrollment and thus did not possess a liberty or property interest sufficient even to trigger procedural due-process protections. *Board of Regents v. Roth*; *Perry v. Sindermann*. Additionally, assuming the existence of a cognizable liberty or property interest (a doubtful assumption), even if there was a "right" to notification prior to exclusion from the class, enrolling applicants on a "first come, first served" basis would probably constitute a fair methodology for selecting a limited number of potential enrollees. Thus, any applicable procedural due-process concerns are satisfied.

2. Claims of the other two parents (Ps):

Standing:

The facts fail to indicate that the children of Ps were (1) interested in joining any of the PTA's classes or (2) in any manner excluded from doing so. Unless a taxpayer is personally injured, he ordinarily has no standing to contest particular governmental conduct, except where it can be shown that a spending measure violates the Establishment Clause by directly appropriating public money to a church or other religious organization. Because the public school district does not provide any direct financial subsidy to the Bible Studies class, Ps cannot meet this standard. Thus, Ps would *not* have standing to raise their claims in federal court.

Equal protection:

Assuming, however, that Ps were deemed to have standing (i.e., their children were denied admission to one or more of the PTA activities because of gender), they could assert basically the same arguments made by M with respect to the Baseball Practice class. Given the Supreme Court's strong presumption against gender-based stereotypes in affording educational opportunities (*VMI*), these claims would have merit.

Establishment Clause:

Ps could also assert that the existence of the Bible Studies class violates the Establishment Clause of the First Amendment (applicable to the states via the Fourteenth Amendment) because (1) it does not have a secular purpose (i.e., the Bible is the major sourcebook of many religions), (2) its primary effect is to further religion (i.e., persons who read the Bible would arguably acquire a greater religious orientation), and (3) it would result in excessive entanglement between church and state (i.e., classes are held on school grounds, and teachers might encourage their pupils to adopt a particular religious view). However, the PTA could argue in rebuttal that academic study of the Bible merely acquaints students with a renowned piece of literature; it does not indoctrinate them with a particular religious belief. *Abington School District v. Schempp*. Additionally, because school facilities are being made available for other types of PTA activities, precluding the Bible Studies class would arguably violate the Establishment Clause by deliberately impeding religion. *Widmar v. Vincent*. Because the PTA programs (1) are voluntary, (2) are taught by nonschool personnel, and (3) occur after school, there is no indirect coercion of nonobserving individuals. *Engel v. Vitale*.

Finally, the Supreme Court specifically has held that "release time" programs for religious instruction do not violate the Establishment Clause. *Zorach v. Clauson*. If a release-time program that disrupts the regular instructional program passes Establishment Clause review, an entirely voluntary after-school program undoubtedly does, too.

In summary, it is unlikely that a reviewing court would find a violation of the Establishment Clause on the facts presented.

Answer to Question 25

1. Does Guy (G) have standing with respect to §§1 and 2 of the act?

To have standing in federal court, a plaintiff must ordinarily show that he has been injured (or is threatened with injury) as a consequence of the allegedly unconstitutional conduct. The facts do not state whether G (1) ever fished for river salmon himself or (2) merely guided others. If G actually fished in the lake and carried his catch out of state X, he would probably have standing to challenge §§1 and 2 of the act. Even if he did not, G could assert that, as a guide, he has a close financial association with nonresidents who would be affected by §§1 and 2 of the act. *Craig v. Boren.* The standing requirement is probably satisfied.

2. Are the various provisions of act unconstitutional?

Invalid delegation of congressional power:

G might initially argue as follows: (1) the lake in question is a navigable waterway; (2) navigable bodies of water are within the admiralty and maritime power of Congress (*Oklahoma v. Guy F. Atkinson Co.*); (3) Congress may not delegate this authority to the states; and (4) therefore, any state X regulations pertaining to the lake are unconstitutional. However, state X could contend in rebuttal that its authority to pass the act was not dependent on federal legislation. Under the Tenth Amendment, state X retained the right to enact legislation pertaining to the lake (provided no conflict existed between the act and federal statutes). Thus, the act probably could *not* be invalidated on the ground that it was passed pursuant to an unconstitutional delegation of congressional authority.

Privileges and Immunities Clause of Article IV:

Under the Privileges and Immunities Clause of Article IV, §2, states may not discriminate against citizens of other jurisdictions with respect to "fundamental" interests, unless the classification is substantially related to an important state interest. *Hicklin v. Orbeck.* G could assert that the act discriminates against U.S. citizens who are not residents of state X because they (1) must pay a higher license fee, (2) cannot carry river salmon back to their own states, (3) must be accompanied by a licensed state X guide, and (4) cannot obtain licenses to become guides. State X could argue in rebuttal, however, that (1) recreational fishing, as opposed to commercial fishing, does not implicate a "fundamental interest" for purposes of the Article IV, §2, Privileges and Immunities Clause (*Toomer v. Witsell*); and, in any event, (2) substantial state interests are involved: (a) (presumably) §1 merely equalizes the overall and long-term expense to state X of maintaining the lake (which was previously paid for via taxation of state X citizens), (b) §2 preserves state resources, and (c) §3 was dictated by the desire for water safety (i.e., state X residents would ordinarily be more familiar with the lake and local customs pertaining to boating safety than individuals from outside of the jurisdiction). *Baldwin v. Fish & Game Commission.*

It is unclear from the facts whether G derived his primary income as a fishing guide at the lake. If relatively significant income was earned by G as a guide, §3 of the act would probably violate the Privileges and Immunities Clause of Article IV because an essential activity (i.e., earning a living) would be involved. *United Building & Construction Trades Council v. Camden.* Section 1, however, would probably not be invalid because the licensing fee provision does not affect out-of-state residents with respect to an interest of a fundamental nature that implicates sufficiently the promotion of interstate harmony among and between the states. *United Building & Construction Trades Council.*

The state's interest in control and management of its natural resources ends when a fish is lawfully caught or taken. State X cannot attempt to prevent the exportation of fish out of state once the fish have been caught. *Hughes v. Oklahoma.* This rule applies regardless of whether a citizen or noncitizen of X attempts to export the fish. Accordingly, §2 of the act is invalid on Dormant Commerce Clause grounds.

Commerce Clause:

State laws that facially discriminate against commerce with another state are invalid, unless the first state can demonstrate that (1) an overriding local interest is achieved by the legislation, and (2) there is no nondiscriminatory means of accomplishing that objective. *Maine v. Taylor.* Because there is a better means of impeding the depletion of river salmon (i.e., limiting both the net total catch per year and also the amount of fish that a person may extract from the lake over a specified period of time), §2 of the act is probably invalid under the Commerce Clause. *Sporhase v. Nebraska.*

Equal Protection Clause:

The Equal Protection Clause of the Fourteenth Amendment requires that classifications be reasonably related to a legitimate state purpose. *Williamson v. Lee Optical Co.* As described above (under the discussion with respect to the Privileges and Immunities Clause of Article IV, §2), state X could advance justifications for each provision of the act. However, limiting lake guides to citizens of state X is arguably irrational because out-of-state residents (such as G) could be or become equally familiar with the lake and the necessary safety procedures. Also, the Supreme Court has applied the rationality test with greater vigor in the context of discrimination against out-of-state business interests. Thus, limiting lake guides to state X citizens is probably invalid. *Metropolitan Life Insurance Co. v. Ward.*

Summary:
Based on the discussion above, only §1 of the act appears to be valid.

Answer to Question 26

Abstention:

A U.S. district court may abstain from hearing a case where the plaintiff is challenging the constitutionality of an ambiguous nonfederal statute, if the alleged defect might be cured by a narrowing interpretation by a state court. State X might contend that abstention is appropriate in this instance (i.e., any attacks that Doe (D) could make against the law might be cured by a state court's interpretation of the legislation). However, because (1) D is presently being prejudiced by his inability to obtain a teaching certification, and (2) a First Amendment right (applicable to the states via the Fourteenth Amendment) is allegedly at issue, it is unlikely that a federal court would abstain in this instance.

1. Section 1:

Bill of attainder:

A bill of attainder (a legislative act that punishes named individuals or an ascertainable group without trial) is unconstitutional. D could assert that the state X certification law is essentially a bill of attainder because it non-judicially punishes members of the Nazi Party by precluding them from becoming teachers. *United States v. Brown.* However, state X would contend in rebuttal that the prejudice suffered by the complainant must have been intended as a punishment by the legislature. *Nixon v. Administrator of General Services.* Because the statute in question was arguably only a means of assuring that impressionable young students would not be influenced to break the law (rather than a means of penalizing members of an organization), the initial clause is *not* a bill of attainder. Because state X has a legitimate interest in assuring that teachers advocate respect for the law, it should prevail on this issue.

Overbreadth:

D could next contend that §1 of the statute is facially overbroad and therefore cannot serve as the basis for governmental action. This contention would be premised on the facts that (1) the statute precludes persons from being teachers even though they may not presently be members of a prohibited organization (*Schware v. Board of Examiners of New Mexico*), and (2) there is no requirement that refusal of certification be based on the applicant's specific intention of furthering the illegal goals of the organization (*Elfbrandt v. Russell*).

State X could contend in rebuttal, however, that a statute is not facially invalid unless its overbreadth is substantial. *Broadrick v. Oklahoma.*

Because the determination of the standards to be applied in deciding who may become a teacher is not totally discretionary with the licensing body, it is unlikely that the statute would be deemed to be facially overbroad. *Arnett v. Kennedy*.

Overbreadth as applied:

Requiring disclosure that a person is a member of a particular group violates his First Amendment right of association, unless the information demanded serves a substantial governmental interest and is closely tailored to satisfy that concern. *Buckley v. Valeo*. D could contend that because the certifying committee did not inquire as to (1) whether he was presently a member of the Nazi Party and, if so, (2) whether he had the specific intent to further the illegal aims of that organization, the certification process as applied to him was unconstitutional. *Law Students Civil Rights Research Council v. Wadmond*. However, the committee could contend in rebuttal that they were not obliged to undertake an obviously futile act. Because D had announced that he would not answer any questions pertaining to his membership in the Nazi Party, the committee probably was not compelled to proceed further.

Fifth Amendment:

As a technical matter, any right against self-incrimination in this case would arise under the Fourteenth Amendment, which is applicable to the states, rather than the Fifth Amendment itself, which only applies directly against the federal government. *Barron v. Baltimore*. The right against self-incrimination is sufficiently fundamental to ordered liberty to justify incorporation against the states through the doctrine of substantive due process. *Malloy v. Hogan*. A potential employee cannot be obliged to forgo the privilege against self-incrimination as a precondition to public employment. *Spivack v. Klein*. Thus, D could contend that his refusal to answer questions about his membership in the Nazi Party could not be a basis for denying him certification. However, state X could argue in rebuttal that (1) D never claimed that he was asserting the Fifth Amendment to avoid self-incrimination (rather, he alluded to a "right of privacy"); (2) merely being a member of the Nazi Party would probably not constitute a crime because advocating the propriety of overthrowing the government by force or violence is not criminal, but rather is constitutionally protected speech, unless a speaker advocates *immediate,* lawless action under circumstances where members of the audience seem likely to act on the suggestion (*Brandenburg v. Ohio*); accordingly, the Fifth Amendment right against self-incrimination is *not* applicable; and (3) the Fifth Amendment privilege could not properly be asserted by D until a question that might expose him to criminal culpability was actually asked (i.e., D announced his refusal to answer any questions at the commencement of the hearing). Because D probably lacked both an actual and an objective good-faith basis for asserting the Fifth Amendment, his refusal to answer any questions pertaining to his membership in the Nazi Party was incorrect. As described above, questions pertaining to membership in an organization that advocates the violent overthrow of the government are considered appropriate in determining fitness for employment in significant governmental positions. *Konigsberg v. State Bar of California, II.*

2. Section 2:

Overbreadth:

D could also contend that §2 of the statute is overly broad in that it permits denial of certification, even though the applicant may have been privileged to refuse to respond to the inquiry. However, a court would probably rule that the right to assert constitutional privileges (without prejudice) is implicit in the statute.

Additionally, D could assert that the term "relevant" is vague (and therefore violates his due-process rights) because the party making the inquiry has no guidelines to determine how the term should be applied. However, state X could again probably successfully contend in rebuttal that "relevant" would be construed as meaning information that was directly related to the applicant's fitness to teach in public or private schools.

Summary:

A federal court would probably direct that a rehearing be held on D's teaching certification, with the further directions that (1) §1 be construed and applied in accordance with the *Schware* and *Law Students Civil Rights Research Council* cases; (2) present, knowing membership in the Nazi Party with the specific intention to further its illegal goals is a legitimate subject of inquiry (and would be a valid basis for denying certification to D); ***and*** (3) D's assertion of the Fifth Amendment may be based only on a good-faith belief that his response would subject him to criminal culpability.

Answer to Question 27

1. Val's (V's) request:

V could contend that scheduling the graduation ceremonies on a Saturday morning violates the Establishment and Free Exercise Clauses of the First Amendment (applicable to the states via the Fourteenth Amendment).

A three-part test is employed to determine if a law that allegedly impacts on religion is constitutional (i.e., does it have a secular purpose, was its primary effect to benefit or diminish religion, and would it result in excessive entanglement between religion and a governmental entity?). *Lemon v. Kurtzman.* District's selection of Saturday would seem to satisfy this test: There is a secular purpose (to choose a time and day when many parents and students probably would *not* be at work), its primary effect does not benefit or diminish religion (any persons who observe Saturday as their Sabbath would merely have to bypass a particular, nonessential ceremony), and it would not produce entanglement between religion and government. Thus, V's Establishment Clause argument should fail.

V could alternatively contend that District's rule violates the Free Exercise Clause of the First Amendment. A law of general applicability is subject to invalidation on Free Exercise Clause grounds only if it was the product of religiously motivated animus or if the plaintiff can show that the general law burdens free exercise and some other constitutionally protected interest. *Employment Division v. Smith.* On the facts presented, no evidence exists suggesting that District selected a Saturday graduation date as a result of purposeful religiously based discrimination against V. Moreover, no other constitutional right supports V's preference for commencement exercises on a day other than a Saturday. District will prevail on this claim.

2. NFO's application:

Board could initially contend that high school auditoriums are *not* traditional public forums, and therefore NFO has no right to require Board to make these facilities available to it. However, NFO could argue in rebuttal that where a governmental agency has opened up a nontraditional forum to the public for a particular type of activity (i.e., meetings of community organizations), it creates either a designated or "limited purpose" public forum and must make that forum available to would-be users of the forum whose activities or speech falls within the scope of the government's designation. *Southeastern Productions, Ltd. v. Conrad.* Because Board has chosen to open the auditorium for rent to community groups in general, NFO *cannot* legally be refused access to that facility merely because Board disapproves of the viewpoints that the organization espouses.

Board might next contend that it could nevertheless refuse NFO's application because of the hard-intelligence information that the police have received (i.e., that a militant antifascist group plans to expel NFO members by force). Under the "fighting words" doctrine, where a speaker's words are likely to make the persons to whom they are addressed commit an act of immediate violence, they are **not** protected by the First Amendment. However, NFO could assert in rebuttal that although its message might be offensive to the racial and religious groups against which it advocates discrimination, advocacy cannot be proscribed simply because it stirs the listeners to anger. *Forsyth County v. Nationalist Movement.* The police can intervene to stop constitutionally protected speech only if they are, in fact, physically incapable of preventing imminent violence. Because the anti-NFO group might not actually materialize at the auditorium and the police are (presumably) capable of being present in sufficient force to dissuade those who desire to physically harm NFO members, Board cannot legally refuse the NFO's application on this ground.

Finally, if it were illegal for private parties to engage in religious or racial discrimination in this jurisdiction, Board might contend that it is entitled to prohibit speech aimed at inciting such conduct. However, under the *Brandenburg v. Ohio* test, the speech in question must be likely to incite "imminent" lawless conduct. There is no indication that those attending the NFO meeting for the purpose of joining that group would immediately engage in such illegal conduct. Rather, it is more probable that these persons would discriminate against others on the basis of religion and race at a subsequent time (in their business or social affairs). Additionally, the gathering in question is merely a recruitment meeting, and NFO's views might not even be aired at the meeting.

In summary, Board would probably be legally obliged to grant NFO's application.

Answer to Question 28

The district court should *not* dismiss Boole's libel suit against the *National Explorer* because, on the facts presented, plaintiff Boole might be able to meet the *Sullivan* "actual malice" standard.

Actual-malice standard:

Under the governing standard of *New York Times v. Sullivan*, a public figure suing a media defendant must establish that the defendant acted with "actual malice," meaning that the plaintiff must show that (1) the statements at issue were false, and (2) the publisher either knew them to be factually false or published them with reckless indifference to truth or falsity. The issue is one of constitutional fact, meaning that if a media defendant loses a libel judgment at trial, the appellate court must review the record *de novo* to ensure that the plaintiff met the actual-malice standard with "clear and convincing" evidence. *Philadelphia Newspapers v. Hepps.*

Application of the governing standard to the facts presented:

Given Susie Boole's exposure to the public on the television show, she probably constitutes a public figure and therefore must meet the *Sullivan* standard of fault in order to recover against the *National Explorer. Hustler Magazine, Inc. v. Falwell.* The use of heroin and sharing heroin with a cat, a form of animal cruelty, also likely constitute a matter of public concern. *Gertz v. Welch.* Indeed, even if Boole were not a public figure (which seems unlikely for the reasons stated earlier), a story about a matter of public concern would trigger the *Sullivan* standard regardless of whether the plaintiff is a public figure or a government official. Accordingly, to prevail on the merits, Boole must show by clear and convincing evidence that the newspaper published a false story with either actual knowledge of falsity or reckless indifference to truth or falsity. This will be a difficult, but not impossible, task for Boole.

Here, the *National Explorer* published a factual assertion that Boole uses heroin and also gives heroin to her pet cat, Miss Pickles. These both constitute assertions of fact that, if Boole proves to be false, would be libelous. The *National Explorer* will undoubtedly claim that it believed the story to be true based on Harry Gibbons's statement to the newspaper, asserting the heroin use and the sharing of heroin with Miss Pickles. However, the *Sullivan* standard does not immunize a publication from liability based on willful blindness to falsity; if a newspaper acted with *reckless indifference* to truth or falsity, liability could attach to the *National Explorer.* That said, it does seem unlikely, given the statement by Gibbons to the newspaper, that Boole could prove knowledge of falsity.

To prevail, Boole would have to show by clear and convincing evidence that the *National Explorer*'s reliance on Gibbons as a source constituted "reckless indifference" to whether the defamatory statements were factually true. It seems doubtful that a reasonable newspaper publisher would credit "a homeless man with a long criminal record" who presently "lives under an expressway overpass" as a reliable source; at a minimum, a nonreckless newspaper would probably seek a corroborating source who presented less risk of proving to be unreliable. That said, this is a mixed question of law and fact that would be determined at trial and again on appeal.

On a motion to dismiss, however, a reviewing court should review the facts in the light most favorable to the plaintiff. So viewing the facts, it seems entirely possible that Boole could establish that a nonreckless newspaper would not have relied on Gibbons as the sole source for a *per se* libelous accusation of this sort. It will be difficult, if not impossible, for Boole to show knowledge of falsity on the *National Explorer*'s part, given that the tabloid actually has a source for the libelous factual assertions. This means that Boole must rely on the "reckless indifference" prong of the actual-malice standard: Boole will have to establish that the source, Gibbons, is simply too unreliable for the newspaper to escape a finding of reckless indifference to truth, even under a "clear and convincing" standard of proof.

Conclusion:

In sum, the district court judge should **deny** the motion to dismiss because plaintiff Boole could show at trial, by clear and convincing evidence, that the newspaper published a false statement of fact with reckless indifference to the truth or falsity of the statement.

Answer to Question 29

Sections 9 and 10 of the Emergency Relief Act (ERA) are both subject to challenges under the Contracts Clause, the Takings Clause, the Equal Protection Clause, and the doctrine of substantive due process. The Contracts Clause and Takings Clause claims are undoubtedly the strongest potential claims for Magnolia Properties to assert in federal district court. Although there is some chance of prevailing on a Contracts Clause or Takings Clause claim, it seems more likely that Mississippi will be able to defend these provisions as a necessary, proportionate, and justifiable response to a public emergency. *Home Building & Loan Assn. v. Blaisdell*; *Penn Central Trans. Co. v. City of New York.* The strongest potential claim would assert that the ERA works a regulatory taking.

The Contracts Clause claim:

Section 9 of the ERA suspends mortgage foreclosures, regardless of payment history, for real property located in the Hurricane Blanche impact zone; §10 of the ERA suspends eviction proceedings for up to 12 months (or less if the lease expires in less than 12 months) for persons renting real property within the Hurricane Blanche impact zone. Neither provision has the effect of eradicating the mortgage payment or rent payment obligation; but both provisions impair the collection of mortgage payments and rent payments for a period of up to 12 months. Moreover, both provisions have the effect of invalidating private contracts that require regular and timely mortgage and rent payments.

The Contracts Clause, Article I, §10, clause 1, prohibits any state from enacting a law "impairing the obligation of contracts." Clearly, the ERA has this effect and is designed precisely to bring about an abrogation of contractual rights held by those holding a mortgage or lease agreement.

In *Blaisdell*, the Supreme Court sustained an emergency measure that Minnesota adopted to provide relief from foreclosures on mortgages. The Court explained that the Great Depression "furnished a proper occasion for the exercise of the reserved power of the State to protect the vital interests of the community," that "the relief afforded and justified by the emergency" was "appropriate to the emergency," and that the "conditions upon which the period of redemption is extended do not appear to be unreasonable." Justice Holmes also placed emphasis on the fact that "[t]he legislation is temporary in operation." The Minnesota law was enacted in 1933 and limited relief to May 1, 1935.

Here, the Mississippi ERA seems consistent with the holding in *Blaisdell*: It constitutes a limited response to an emergency (here a hurricane, rather than an economic crisis), it lasts for a limited period of time (not more than 12 months), and it does not permanently cancel either mortgage or rent debts. Magnolia Properties could attempt to distinguish *Blaisdell*, but it would be difficult to do so persuasively.

Modern Contracts Clause cases require a state law that abrogates or impairs a private contract to "be upon reasonable conditions and of a character appropriate to the public purpose justifying its adoption" (*United States Trust v. New Jersey*) or a two-step test asking whether a law "operates as a substantial impairment of a contractual relationship" and, if it does, then balances the severity of the impairment against the public interest at stake (*Allied Structural Steel Co. v. Spannaus*). Even if a court were to apply the more recent precedents, rather than *Blaisdell*, it seems unlikely that Magnolia Properties could prevail; a reviewing court is likely to view with sympathy a temporary measure aimed at providing short-term relief to the victims of a hurricane.

The Takings Clause claim:

The Fifth Amendment provides that "nor shall private property be taken for public use, without just compensation." The Takings Clause (applicable to the states through incorporation by the Fourteenth Amendment's Due Process Clause) prohibits not only direct expropriations of private property but also "regulatory takings" that adversely affect the fair market value of a property interest. *Pennsylvania Coal Co. v. Mahon.* The modern test for a regulatory taking inquires into (1) the effect of the regulation on the value of the property interest; (2) the reasonable, investment-backed expectations of the property's owner; and (3) the character of the government's action. *Penn Central Transportation Co.* One also should note that even the temporary deprivation of a property interest can constitute a taking. *First English Evangelical Lutheran Church of Glendale v. County of Los Angeles.*

Applying the relevant legal test, §§9 and 10 arguably constitute regulatory takings: The ERA destroys the current present value of mortgage and rent payments; it could not have been foreseen by Magnolia Properties at the time it entered into the mortgage and lease agreements; and the character of the government's action is, by historical standards, unusual. Many hurricanes have hit populated areas of the United States over the past 200 years, but the ERA constitutes a relatively novel response to a hurricane; this sort of law is certainly far from commonplace. A plausible claim for a regulatory taking could be pursued in federal district court. If Magnolia Properties were to prevail, the likely remedy would be the invalidation of the ERA. *Eastern Enterprises v. Apfel.* We would then be free to pursue both foreclosures and evictions in the Hurricane Blanche impact zone.

A cautionary note is in order, however. After Hurricane Katrina, a serious risk exists that a reviewing court might conclude that the ERA does not impose an unreasonable burden in light of the challenges facing an area recovering from a major hurricane. The *Penn Central* test considers the "character of the government's action," and it is possible that in the context of a recovery effort of this sort, a reviewing court would decline to find a regulatory taking. In any event, a Takings Clause claim appears to have a greater probability of success than a Contracts Clause claim.

Equal-protection and substantive due-process claims:

The Fourteenth Amendment requires state governments to provide "equal protection of the laws" to all persons, including corporations such as Magnolia Properties, and also secures "due process of law" to all persons. Economic and social legislation may be challenged on either equal-protection or substantive due-process grounds; a reviewing court will determine whether the statute at issue bears a rational relationship to a legitimate state interest. *FCC v. Beach Communications, Inc.* In such cases, the plaintiff bears the entire burden of showing that no rational relationship to a legitimate state interest exists (or even could *theoretically* exist); the government has no burden of proof in such challenges, and the federal courts will presume the validity of the law.

Sections 9 and 10 of the ERA could be challenged on either due-process or equal-protection grounds, but in either case the probability of success is very low. Since the 1930s, the Supreme Court has invalidated only one law as lacking the requisite rational relationship to a legitimate state interest (*Morey v. Dowd*), and the Supreme Court subsequently repudiated this decision in *New Orleans v. Dukes.* It seems highly unlikely that Magnolia Properties would prevail on such a claim. Indeed, even raising such a claim could undermine claims with greater promise, such as a possible Takings Clause claim.

Conclusion:

Magnolia Properties should consider challenging the ERA as a regulatory taking. We also should consider raising a Contracts Clause claim, although the prospects of success with such a claim seem limited in light of *Blaisdell.* We should not pursue an equal-protection or substantive due-process challenge because we are virtually certain to lose such a claim, and its inclusion could undermine the credibility of our other, more meritorious claims. In the end, it will likely be difficult to convince a federal judge to invalidate a targeted effort to provide temporary relief to the victims of Hurricane Blanche. That said, however, we could mount a strong case based on the Takings Clause.

Answer to Question 30

Short answer/overview:

Congress possesses multiple means of regulating or prohibiting the manufacture, transportation, sale, and possession of tobacco and tobacco products. The most obvious source of legislative authority is the Commerce Clause, Article I, §8, clause 3, which expressly grants Congress the power to "regulate Commerce with foreign Nations, and among the several States, and with the Indian Tribes." Under the post-1937 understanding of the federal commerce power, the manufacture, transportation, sale, and possession of tobacco would all fall within the federal commerce power. Additional potential constitutional sources of authority for Congress to regulate tobacco include the taxing power, the conditional spending power, and the Necessary and Proper Clause, a kind of catchall provision. This memorandum will consider each of these sources of authority over tobacco products in turn, starting with the power to regulate commerce. Even if the tobacco industry were to challenge such federal regulation, it is likely that the federal courts would find that all four congressional powers support comprehensive regulation of tobacco and tobacco products.

1. The commerce power:

The Commerce Clause encompasses the channels and instrumentalities of interstate commerce, goods and services moving in interstate commerce, and any economic activity that, aggregated across the national economy, substantially affects interstate commerce. *Gonzales v. Raich.* The production of tobacco constitutes economic activity that, aggregated across the national economy, substantially affects it. *Raich; Wickard v. Filburn.* Consequently, Congress could, if it wished to do so, criminalize the growing of tobacco plants incident to the power to regulate interstate commerce. Congress could also prohibit the interstate transportation or shipment of tobacco or tobacco products. *Champion v. Ames.* In fact, the commerce power alone would provide an adequate basis for comprehensive regulation of tobacco and tobacco products. Given that the Supreme Court recently held in *Raich* that the growing of marijuana plants, by itself, solely for personal use, and using only local materials came within the scope of Congress's power to regulate commerce, the question is not a particularly close one.

2. The taxing power:

If Congress would prefer not to invoke its power to regulate commerce, it could rely instead on its power to tax to regulate, or effectively ban, tobacco products. As Chief Justice Marshall said in *McCulloch v. Maryland*, "the power to tax involves the power to destroy." Congress could impose very high excise taxes on tobacco products, taxes sufficiently high that they would effectively close the lawful sale of tobacco products. Even the *Lochner*-era Supreme Court refused to determine whether a tax had a regulatory purpose; if Congress chooses to tax an item, the federal courts will generally defer to that decision. *United States v. Butler*. As the Supreme Court explained in *United States v. Kahriger*, "the constitutional restraints on the taxing power are few" and "it is hard to understand why the power to tax should raise more doubts because of indirect effects than other federal powers." The Supreme Court has sustained confiscatory taxes on certain firearms, narcotics, and unlawful gambling earnings under this theory. Accordingly, Congress could, if it wished, tax tobacco into oblivion.

3. Conditional spending to encourage state tobacco bans:

Given that Congress possesses effectively plenary power to regulate tobacco under either the Commerce Clause or incident to the taxing power, it probably would not need to rely on its power to offer conditional spending grants to the states. However, if Congress wished to enlist state law enforcement in aid of its effort to ban tobacco products, it could do so by conditioning aid to local and state law enforcement agencies on the enactment and enforcement of a state law banning tobacco products. Alternatively, the condition could be tied to federal subsidies of health care or health care providers, such as the Medicare or Medicaid programs.

Under the holding in *South Dakota v. Dole*, conditional spending is valid against a Tenth Amendment federalism objection if the spending promotes the general welfare, the condition is clear and unambiguous, the decision to accept or reject the federal funds is entirely voluntary, and a reasonable nexus exists between the condition and the purpose of the federal program. Here, either law enforcement subsidies or federal subsidies for medical care could be conditioned on state governments' adopting tobacco bans. Thus, even though Congress could not directly require states to adopt tobacco regulations (*New York v. United States*), and it could not directly order state law enforcement officers to enforce a federal program (*Printz v. United States*), it may require adoption of tobacco regulations, up to and including a ban on tobacco sales within the state, as a condition of receiving federal funds that relate in a plausible way to the social and legal effects of tobacco consumption.

4. The Necessary and Proper Clause:

In *McCulloch v. Maryland*, Chief Justice Marshall broadly construed the Necessary and Proper Clause, Article I, §8, clause 18, to enhance the other congressional powers enumerated in Article I of the Constitution. In doing so, he upheld the constitutionality of the Second Bank of the United States, finding that a bank was reasonably related to the execution of multiple delegated powers. Thus, if Congress seeks to advance a legitimate end, it may deploy any means reasonably calculated to achieve that end under the rubric of the Necessary and Proper Clause. Accordingly, if any residual doubts exist about whether Congress possesses the constitutional authority to prohibit tobacco products under the Commerce Clause, taxing power, or conditional spending power, the Necessary and Proper Clause would require a reviewing court to resolve those doubts *in favor* of the validity of the legislation banning tobacco. Although it is doubtful that Congress would need to invoke this clause in light of the strength of the other arguments, set forth above, it bears noting that the Necessary and Proper Clause provides a final "catchall" basis on which to sustain the proposed legislation.

5. Best arguments against the constitutionality of the ban:

Although there are many close questions in constitutional law, this is not one of them. Simply put, the tobacco industry lacks sound constitutional arguments against the constitutional validity of a federal statute that bans tobacco products. As the preceding discussion demonstrates, Congress has ample authority to regulate, or ban, tobacco products (either directly or indirectly via taxation or conditional spending). The best potential argument would invoke the Tenth Amendment's reservation of powers not assigned to the federal government to the states; this argument would rely on pre-1937 understandings of reserved state police powers over the health, safety, and morals of their citizens as a limit on the scope of the commerce, taxing, and spending powers. The argument would posit that in light of the long national tradition of permitting tobacco products to be sold, subject only to state and local regulation, a national ban exceeds the scope of federal regulatory authority. However, if Congress may apply the Controlled Substances Act to prohibit marijuana grown solely for personal use, using entirely local materials (*Gonzales v. Raich*), the argument against an identical power to ban tobacco appears unlikely to succeed. Thus, the Tenth Amendment's reservation of undelegated powers to the states presents the best potential argument for the tobacco industry to make, but it is not a very strong argument.

6. *Summary:*

Congress has clear constitutional authority to regulate, or even ban, tobacco products if it wishes to do so. A constitutional challenge to such legislation as beyond the scope of Congress's legislative powers would almost certainly fail, at least with respect to legislation adopted incident to the commerce power, the taxing power, or the spending power.

Answer to Question 31

The law governing the substantive due-process right to use (or refrain from using) contraceptives and the right to terminate a pregnancy currently use different standards of review. Cases arising in the *Griswold v. Connecticut* line of cases, such as *Eisenstadt* and *Carey*, apply strict judicial scrutiny to laws that prohibit the possession or use of birth control devices to prevent conception. This means that the government bears the burden of proving a compelling state interest in the regulation and that achievement of this compelling state interest cannot be secured with any more narrowly tailored means. By way of contrast, since the joint opinion in *Casey* and ratified in *Stenberg v. Carhart*, the federal courts review regulations of access to abortion under an "undue burden" standard and ask whether a particular regulation imposes an "undue burden" on a woman's right to determine whether or not to carry the fetus to term. The Supreme Court has not explained whether the undue-burden test has broader application in other areas of the substantive due-process right of privacy. Accordingly, the North Dakota law should probably be reviewed under both the strict-scrutiny and undue-burden tests. Under either test, however, this court should probably find the act unconstitutional.

1. A preliminary matter: standing:

To test the validity of the act, the plaintiffs must establish that they possess Article III standing: an injury in fact that is concrete and particularized, as opposed to a generalized grievance; an injury that is traceable to the subject matter of the suit; and an injury that a federal court could redress effectively. Here, Planned Parenthood of North Dakota (PP) has standing.

An organization has standing to assert the rights of its members; if any member of the organization has standing, the organization ordinarily may sue on behalf of that member. On the facts presented, it seems very likely that members of PP who use or wish to use contraceptives will be subject to the new taxes; this would be sufficient to convey standing. Also, as a direct seller of contraceptive devices, PP itself would be directly harmed by the new tax. *Craig v. Boren.* Under either theory of standing, PP has standing to prosecute a challenge to the act. In addition, PP's North Dakota clients, assuming that they currently use birth control devices subject to the new taxes, would also have standing to challenge the act (i.e., they have a concrete and particularized injury, it is traceable to the act, and a federal court could remediate the injury by invalidating the act).

2. Strict scrutiny:

Assuming for the moment that the undue-burden test applies only to abortion regulations, North Dakota would have the burden of establishing a compelling state interest and narrow tailoring in order to save the act from invalidation on substantive due-process grounds. One possible defense to the suit would be for North Dakota to argue that the law does not regulate birth control at all, but rather simply constitutes a revenue measure. This argument should not succeed.

As Chief Justice Marshall explained in *McCulloch*, "the power to tax involves the power to destroy." North Dakota has not imposed a general sales tax on contraceptives, but instead has adopted a targeted tax directed toward coercing unwanted pregnancies that will almost certainly result from unprotected sex. The title of the act—Re-Populate North Dakota Now!—clearly bespeaks the purpose of burdening access to birth control in order to coerce North Dakotan women into pregnancy and childbirth. Although the state can adopt incentives to encourage pregnancy and child rearing, and may also choose not to subsidize access to birth control or abortion (*Maher v. Roe*), it may not attempt to force its citizens to become pregnant. The purpose of the law is clear, and it will have the effect of burdening a fundamental liberty interest; this court should therefore apply strict judicial scrutiny under *Eisenstadt* and *Carey* to the act. Even if North Dakota has a compelling interest in increasing the state's population (a highly contestable proposition), far more narrowly tailored means of achieving this interest exist, and these alternative means could easily be used to achieve this purpose. The state could offer financial incentives for voluntary pregnancy and childbirth, for example, or it could create financial incentives for relocating to North Dakota from other states (e.g., low-interest mortgages or free educational benefits at the state's universities). Given the vast array of options available to the state, burdening access to birth control through a targeted tax on contraceptives plainly constitutes an impermissible means for the state to adopt.

3. The undue-burden test:

In *Casey* and *Stenberg*, the Supreme Court declined to apply strict judicial scrutiny to state laws burdening access to abortion services. Similarly, in *Troxel*, the Supreme Court plurality decision failed to apply the strict-scrutiny test when evaluating a Washington State law that burdened a biological custodial parent's ability to limit visitation by third parties. Accordingly, an argument exists that this court should apply the undue-burden test, rather than strict scrutiny, to the act. Moreover, because this is a less demanding standard of review, North Dakota will certainly argue that the court should use it, rather than strict scrutiny, in this case.

Whether a regulation constitutes an undue burden is difficult to determine, primarily because the test seems so open ended; reasonable people applying this test are likely to reach differing conclusions on the same facts. If one assumes, however, that condoms routinely cost a few dollars per box, a $5 per condom tax increases the expense of birth control by an astounding percentage, something like 600 percent; a half dozen condoms would cost $30 in tax alone, rather than something like $5 or $6. The tax has the same effect on the price of other forms of birth control, such as contraceptive sponges. Whether this poses an "undue" burden is not entirely clear; it certainly constitutes a cognizable burden. Although the matter is not free from doubt, the North Dakota law should probably also fall under the undue-burden test, given its extreme effect on the cost (e.g., a 600 percent increase in cost) and thereby access to traditional forms of birth control.

4. An as-applied exemption for indigent persons:
Even though a state government is not required to subsidize the exercise of fundamental rights (*Maher*), it may be required to remove obstacles to the exercise of a fundamental right that the state itself creates. *Boddie v. Connecticut.* If a state must waive the filing fees for a marriage license or a divorce and provide a free transcript for an appeal of an adverse family court decision that will permanently terminate parental rights, it seems likely that a state would be required to waive the birth control taxes for indigent persons.

Indeed, as applied to the indigent, the act plainly creates an "undue burden" on the right of privacy. Even if the act might be found constitutional on its face, North Dakota plainly must exempt indigent persons from the taxes in order to avoid running afoul of the equal-protection (and/or substantive due process) rule announced and applied in cases such as *Boddie* and *M.L.B.* Whether the court characterizes this result as a function of the undue-burden test or as an application of the rule that the state cannot preclude the indigent from exercising fundamental rights, the outcome of an "as applied challenge" by this group seems clear: The act is an unconstitutional infringement of a fundamental right.

5. Prenatal and postnatal medical care subsidies for indigent women:
The act provides targeted subsidies to indigent women for prenatal and postnatal care. As noted earlier, a state may constitutionally subsidize prenatal and postnatal care, but not abortion or contraceptives. *Maher.*

Although the funding mechanism for this program is probably unconstitutional (see above), North Dakota is free to establish and maintain such programs. A state constitutionally may subsidize a decision to give birth, but decline to subsidize access to contraceptive or abortion services.

Summary:

The act will not survive strict judicial scrutiny; if this is the controlling standard of review, this court should invalidate the act as failing the narrow-tailoring requirement. The act should probably be invalidated under the undue-burden standard as well; a 600 percent increase in the cost of commonly used contraceptive devices should be deemed to constitute an "undue burden" on access to them. An as-applied challenge for indigent persons plainly would have merit, but the law is likely unconstitutional on its face. Finally, North Dakota may provide targeted subsidies to encourage pregnancy, childbirth, and child rearing, but it may not adopt an unconstitutional tax to fund such a program.

Answer to Question 32

1. S. has a strong First Amendment claim

In general, the government may not regulate (or prohibit) speech because of either the content or viewpoint of the speech. *Ashcroft v. American Civil Liberties Union.* When government adopts content-based speech regulations, it bears a very high burden of justification—the regulations must be narrowly drawn to achieve a compelling state interest.

Exceptions to this rule exist for certain limited categories of speech, including libel, obscenity, fighting words, and graphic child pornography. *New York v. Ferber.* If violence were among these categories of proscribable speech, Congress would be free to regulate, and even ban, speech featuring violent content. The Supreme Court, however, has squarely held that speech featuring violent content *is not* a separate category of unprotected speech. *Brown v. Entertainment Merchants Ass'n.*

Moreover, the fact that the ban relates to minors does not affect the analysis. Persons under 18 enjoy First Amendment rights and, although doctrines involving unprotected forms of speech, like obscenity, may be tailored to fit this class, there is no general exception for government regulations that restrict minors' access to expressive materials. *Brown; Tinker v. Des Moines Indep. Community School District.*

Accordingly, because Congress has adopted a content-based restriction on protected speech, the government must show that the law survives strict judicial scrutiny in order to prevail. (S. clearly has standing—the company has suffered an injury in fact (lost sales), the injury can be traced to the Act, and invalidation of the Act would provide an effective remedy. No more needs be said about this aspect of the question.)

2. Can the government successfully defend the Act?

At first blush, protecting children from exposure to violent video games would seem to advance a compelling government interest—protecting kids from exposure to age-inappropriate content. The Supreme Court has sustained laws aimed at protecting children from exposure to sexually graphic materials, for example, that would not be obscene with respect to an adult audience. *Ginsberg v. New York.* However, *Ginsberg* involved adjusting the boundaries of a preexisting category of unprotected speech, not creating an entirely new category of unprotected speech. Whatever the merits of taking such a step, as noted above, the Supreme Court has flatly rejected the notion that speech featuring violent content, even graphic violence, constitutes a special unprotected category of speech. Because the government may not treat the speech as intrinsically harmful, it lacks a compelling interest in shielding children from it. *Brown*; *U.S. v. Stevens*.

In *Brown*, California was unable to convince the Supreme Court that it possessed a compelling interest in prohibiting the sale of violent video games to minors, and the facts in this case do not present any new evidence that might be offered to distinguish the Act from the state law invalidated on First Amendment grounds in *Brown*. Again, the key difficulty is that violent content does not, per se, affect the protected status of speech (or video games).

Even if the federal government could proffer a compelling interest, it also is far from clear that the Act is "narrowly tailored." More precisely, the Act bans all sales to minors, even if a minor's parents do not object to the sale. It also seems likely that the state might have a stronger interest in protecting very young children from certain content than it would with respect to a person one week shy of her eighteenth birthday. In other words, a more narrowly drawn statute that included a parental bypass and that targeted the most vulnerable child audience would stand a better chance of surviving constitutional review, particularly if the government could produce credible expert evidence showing that exposing young children to graphic depictions of violence is harmful to them (e.g., correlates with aggressive or anti-social behavior). Even a more narrowly drawn statute, however, would have to overcome the difficulty that the Supreme Court simply does not recognize that exposure to materials featuring graphic violence harms children. Thus, because graphic violence is immaterial to First Amendment analysis under *Brown*, even a more carefully crafted federal law might well be invalidated. The scope of this law, however, which seems largely identical to the law invalidated in *Brown*, makes it virtually certain that the government would be unable to meet the narrow tailoring requirement.

3. Conclusion
Because the Act is a content-based restriction on speech, the federal government must show that it advances a compelling interest in a narrowly tailored way. Absent facts not given, it will not be able to sustain this burden. Accordingly, the district court should rule in favor S. and invalidate the Act on First Amendment free speech grounds.

Multiple-Choice
Questions

1. Under a recent federal statute, the U.S. government was to clean up heavily used water areas (including the beach in Santa Monica, California). Kevin (who is a U.S. citizen living in Los Angeles) believes that the secretary of the interior is not performing his duties under this statute in an adequate manner. Kevin sues the secretary of the interior, alleging that he occasionally (six to eight times per year) swims at the Santa Monica beach, that he intends to continue to do so, and that his enjoyment of this activity is diminished by the secretary's failure to enforce the statute in an adequate manner.

   Based on the foregoing, if the secretary of the interior contends that Kevin lacks standing, it is most likely that

   A. Kevin will prevail because any U.S. citizen can sue federal government officials for a failure by the latter to perform their duties.

   B. Kevin will prevail because he has suffered a direct and immediate injury.

   C. Kevin will not prevail because U.S. citizenship is not, *per se*, a basis for standing against a federal government official.

   D. Kevin will not prevail because he has suffered no direct economic loss as a consequence of the secretary's failure to perform his duties.

2. The state of Utopia recently passed legislation stating that if administrative school personnel believe that a child may have psychological problems, that child is to be tested by a school psychologist who works at a public school and is licensed by Utopia. If those tests are positive, the child promptly receives remedial counseling by a licensed school psychologist located at one of the public schools.

   Where a psychological problem is detected at a religious school, a licensed school psychologist comes to the institution and tests the child there. If the results are positive, the child is obliged to come for counseling at a psychologist's office at the nearest public school. The statute also provides for reimbursement of any travel expenses incurred by the child in this situation.

   Believing that his tax dollars were being used to sustain religious institutions, Ralph, a Utopia citizen and taxpayer, brought an action in federal court. He contends that application of the statute to students at religious schools violates the Establishment Clause.

   Based on the foregoing, it is most likely that

   A. Ralph will prevail because services (the initial testing) are being provided by public employees at religious institutions.

B. Ralph will prevail because monies are being expended in assisting students at religious schools for travel to and from the counseling sites.

C. Ralph will not prevail because state services may be provided to students at a religiously affiliated school on a "neutral" basis as long as state employees are not directly involved in providing religious instruction.

D. Ralph will not prevail because the testing is presumably impersonal in nature, and children are then simply reimbursed for a function required by Utopia.

3. The Aarp religion has, as one of its tenets, the principle that its members should be prepared to defend themselves at all times. As a consequence, members of this religious group are taught to conceal weapons such as handguns, knives, and brass knuckles on their persons.

   The state of Utopia recently enacted legislation that makes it illegal, except in the case of persons who typically carry substantial amounts of money or jewelry because of their occupations, to carry a concealed weapon of any type. The term "weapon" is defined in the statute to cover the items referred to above. The legislative history of this law indicates that the legislators were concerned with the expanded tendency of private citizens to arm themselves.

   A member of the Aarp religion who ordinarily carries one or more of the items described above challenges this statute as being violative of the Establishment Clause.

   Based on the foregoing, it is most likely that

   A. the law is unconstitutional if concealed weapons are a *major* tenet of the Aarp religion.

   B. the law is unconstitutional because it is violative of a tenet of the Aarp religion.

   C. the law is constitutional because it is merely a generally applicable criminal prohibition and does not appear to be the product of religiously motivated hostility or animus.

   D. the law is constitutional if, on a careful balancing of the governmental and religious interests involved, the former exceeds the latter.

4. Great Bobco Co. (Bobco) operates a garbage-disposal facility in Claremont County, Utopia. When the facility was initially commenced, the land around it was barren. However, in the last 15 years, a number of residential homes and shopping centers have "grown up" around the

facility. Although the facility is operated in accordance with applicable law, it nevertheless generates a foul odor. This situation has begun to disturb the nearby residents. They recently persuaded the Utopia legislature to pass a law that requires (1) Bobco to install equipment that will diminish the foul odor and (2) the facility's closure within a maximum period of time of five years. The equipment will cost Bobco about $75,000 over the succeeding five years to install and maintain. Bobco ordinarily earns per annum profits of $250,000 to $300,000 from the facility. After the five-year period, Bobco can use the land for any other lawful commercial (or residential) purpose.

Based on the foregoing, if Bobco contends that the law constitutes an unconstitutional "taking" under the Fifth Amendment, it is most likely that

A. it will prevail because the legislation eventually deprives Bobco of the ability to operate a garbage-disposal facility on land that it owns.

B. it will prevail because the facility was there prior to the time that the surrounding land became residential in character.

C. it will not prevail because the purported "taking" does not unduly affect Bobco's reasonable, investment-backed expectations and is a reasonable land use regulation.

D. it will not prevail because there is a rational relationship between the state interest and the regulation.

5. A federal law makes it a crime for any U.S. citizen, not specifically authorized by the president, to negotiate or otherwise communicate with a foreign government for the purpose of influencing the foreign government with respect to a dispute involving the United States. The *strongest* constitutional grounds for sustaining the validity of this law is that

A. Congress may legislate to preserve the monopoly of the federal government over the conduct of U.S. foreign affairs.

B. the president's inherent power to negotiate for the United States with foreign countries authorizes the president, even in the absence of statutory authorization, to punish citizens who engage in such negotiations without permission.

C. the law deals with foreign relations and therefore is not governed by the First Amendment.

D. federal criminal laws dealing with international affairs need not be as specific as those dealing with domestic affairs.

6. In Utopia, robbery with "a weapon" was a crime punishable by a fine and 6 to 10 years in state prison. (A "weapon" was defined as any device capable of causing serious bodily injury.) This offense was called "aggravated robbery." As this type of crime increased, the Utopia legislature passed a new statute to deal with the offense called "armed robbery," which involved robbing someone with a firearm. The jail sentence for this crime was 10 to 15 years (but no fine was applicable). Dellum robbed James at gunpoint just prior to passage of the armed robbery statute. However, when Dellum was **arrested**, the armed robbery statute had recently been passed. He was charged and convicted of armed robbery (rather than aggravated robbery) and sentenced to 12 years in prison.

Based on the foregoing, if Dellum asserts that the sentence is unconstitutional, it is most likely that

  A. Dellum will prevail because punishment was enhanced **after** the illegal act had occurred.

  B. Dellum will prevail if he had actual knowledge that aggravated robbery carried only a 6- to 10-year sentence.

  C. Dellum will not prevail because he was not arrested and charged until **after** the new criminal statute had taken effect.

  D. Dellum will not prevail because armed robbery is an entirely different (i.e., narrower) offense than aggravated robbery.

7. Recent studies available to Congress indicate that there is a close correlation between smoking and lung cancer. Although this has been known for some time, the medical evidence is now more corroborative of this conclusion. Antismoking groups successfully lobbied Congress to pass a law that precludes smoking advertisements from the Internet, television, and radio and in regularly printed literature (magazines, newspapers, and brochures). In fact, other than "word of mouth" or distributing flyers, it is now virtually impossible to advertise cigarettes. However, no similar legislation has been passed with respect to cigars. Although the evidence is not quite as strong that cigars cause lung cancer, arguably sufficient data exist to indicate this result. Several tobacco companies have recently commenced an action in U.S. district court, claiming that the statute violates their First Amendment rights and the Equal Protection Clause.

Based on the foregoing, it is most likely that

  A. the statute is unconstitutional, based on equal-protection grounds.

  B. the statute is unconstitutional, based on the First Amendment.

C. the statute is constitutional because it directly advances a substantial governmental interest.

D. the statute is constitutional because, in light of the recent medical studies, advertising cigarettes without clearly describing the likelihood of lung cancer is misleading.

8. The U.S. Congress recently passed a law that states that, two years from the date of passage of the bill, professionals (doctors, lawyers, dentists, etc.) may not use salaries paid to receptionists as business-related deductions. A "receptionist" is defined as an employee whose primary function is to answer telephonic, electronic, or "in person" inquiries or who spends at least 50 percent of her time performing such an activity. The American Physicians Association (APA) brought an action in federal court, asserting that this law was discriminatory and a deprivation of due process.

Based on the foregoing, it is most likely that

A. the APA lacks standing because the law applies to all professionals.

B. the APA lacks standing because taxpayer standing is lacking (i.e., none of the members could successfully sue).

C. the APA has standing because the act discriminates against professionals since it does not end this deduction for all other businesses.

D. the APA has standing because most individual members of the organization have suffered a direct injury.

Questions 9-10 are based on the following facts:

Kristin, Harriet, and Jenny live in the state of Euphoria. They live in the same neighborhood and are the very best of friends. They are all seven years old, but each attends a different school. Kristin attends St. Mary's Parochial School, a private school that offers religious instruction; Harriet attends Sedgewick School for Girls, a private, girls-only school that offers elementary and secondary education (but that denies admission to anyone of Hispanic origin); and Jenny attends the local public school. All of the public schools in Euphoria have been desegregated. A Euphoria law provides for the free distribution of computers to students in **all** public and private schools. Accordingly, Euphoria provides free computers to St. Mary's, Sedgewick, and the public school. Euphoria accredits all state elementary schools and certifies all teachers.

Jenny's parents, who are avowed liberals and atheists, object to Euphoria's providing free computers to St. Mary's and Sedgewick.

9. The **strongest** constitutional argument that Jenny's parents could make **against** Euphoria's distribution of computers to Sedgewick is that

A. Euphoria may not aid private schools in any way.

B. the U.S. Constitution forbids private discrimination of any kind.

C. Euphoria is promoting segregation by the distribution of computers to students attending Sedgewick.

D. the distribution of computers by Euphoria promotes no significant educational function.

10. The **strongest** argument that Jenny's parents could make **in favor of** the constitutionality of the free distribution of computers to students at St. Mary's is that

A. state-promoted instruction at private schools is constitutionally permissible.

B. Euphoria's distribution of computers is secular in nature and does not engender church-state entanglement.

C. similar treatment of students at public and private religious schools is required by the Free Exercise Clause.

D. private religious schools fulfill an important state educational function.

11. Doe is prosecuted for giving his 14-year-old daughter a glass of wine in violation of a state statute prohibiting any person from serving an alcoholic beverage to a minor. Doe defends on the ground that the state statute as applied in his case unconstitutionally interferes with the free exercise of his religion. In determining the constitutionality of the state statute as applied in this instance, the court may **not** properly

A. require Doe to bear the burden of establishing that the statute is unconstitutional as applied to him.

B. determine the reasonableness of Doe's religious beliefs.

C. ascertain whether Doe's religious beliefs require him to serve wine to his child.

D. decide whether Doe is sincere in his religious beliefs (i.e., whether he really believes them).

12. A federal law requires U.S. civil service employees ordinarily to retire at age 75. However, the statute also states that civil service employees of the armed forces must retire at age 65. Prentis, a 65-year-old civil service employee of the U.S. Army, seeks a declaratory judgment that would forbid his mandatory retirement until age 75.

The **strongest** argument that Prentis can make to invalidate the requirement that he retire at age 65 is that the law

A. denies him a privilege or immunity of national citizenship.

B. deprives him of a property right without just compensation.

C. is not within the scope of any of the enumerated powers of Congress in Article I, §8, of the U.S. Constitution.

D. invidiously discriminates against him on the basis of age in violation of the Fifth Amendment.

13. Pfeifer Madison, a wealthy eccentric living in the state of Ukiah, is an "antitax" person. He formed a new political party called "Americans Against Taxes." Pfeifer decided to run for governor and told his followers that, if he is elected, he will do everything in his power to minimize state taxes. By state statute, to run for office in Ukiah, Pfeifer must file a petition containing 20 percent of the registered voters' signatures before he can be placed on the ballot. Pfeifer and his campaign supporters worked diligently to obtain enough signatures to put his name on the ballot, but they were unsuccessful. (They obtained only 12 percent.) Thus, Pfeifer failed to get on the Ukiah state ballot as an independent candidate for governor.

Pfeifer then retained Ukiah's largest law firm to commence a suit against the appropriate state officials in U.S. district court. This firm sought an injunction against the signature requirement on the ground that it was unconstitutional and therefore invalid.

The *strongest* argument for the state statute's unconstitutionality is that

A. the statute was intended to keep candidates who lacked strong voter support off the ballot.

B. relatively few independent candidates have, in fact, ever succeeded in obtaining the requisite number of signatures.

C. there is probably a less burdensome means of accomplishing the statute's purpose.

D. all voter signature requirements are an unreasonable means of ensuring that a potential candidate has adequate popular support.

14. The state of Euphoria is located near the border between the United States and Mexico. Within the past several years, Euphoria has experienced increasing problems with illegal immigration. Unattended yard items and license plates are constantly stolen. This has resulted in anti-illegal immigrant protests. Members of the Euphoria legislature have proposed laws that prohibit the state from providing medical and

educational services to illegal immigrants, as well as English literacy requirements for voting in local, state, and federal elections.

Several minority-rights groups decide to challenge the constitutionality of these proposed laws. (Assume these entities have standing.)

The **strongest** basis for finding the English literacy voting law unconstitutional is the

A. Equal Protection Clause of the Fourteenth Amendment.

B. Due Process Clause of the Fourteenth Amendment.

C. power of Congress to exclusively determine the manner of holding elections for U.S. senators and representatives (art. I, §4).

D. constitutional provision that U.S. representatives be chosen by the people of the several states.

15. Polly Pitman is a citizen of the state of Macon. She has been lobbying her local assemblyman, Roy Hodges, to pass a law authorizing the construction of a new highway to run directly through the small rural town in which Polly owns a small business. This road would link two already existing state highways. This development would presumably result in more business for Polly. Also, Polly's husband, Bob, owns Pitman Construction Co. Roy, in fact, ultimately secured legislation that authorized funds for the new state highway. Shortly thereafter, Macon retained Pitman Construction Co. to assist with building the new road. However, when news of this legislation became widely known, the Macon legislators were criticized for failing to allocate funds to improve its existing highways. As a consequence, the legislature repealed the statute authorizing the new state highway and repealed the contract with Pitman Construction Co. Bob commenced an action to compel Macon to adhere to the agreement.

Based on the foregoing, it is most likely that the cancellation of the contract with Pitman Construction Co. is

A. invalid under the Contracts Clause.

B. invalid if Bob had relied on the original statute in a substantial manner.

C. valid because a state legislature may rescind its own laws.

D. valid because, pursuant to the Eleventh Amendment, a state is not liable to individuals.

16. Recently, Congress enacted a statute that appropriated $30 million to study the effect of acquired immunodeficiency syndrome (AIDS) on

the families of persons suffering from that disease and to determine if costs could be saved by having members of those families render medical-type assistance to the infected person. Pursuant to this legislation, the secretary of health and human services was required to "distribute all of the appropriated funds within one year" from the date on which the statute was passed.

A short time later, however, the need for a balanced budget again came to the political forefront. To demonstrate that he was doing his part, the president ordered the members of his cabinet to effectuate an across-the-board 20 percent reduction in their departmental expenditures. Based on various reports that a cure for AIDS was imminent, the president (via an executive order) instructed the secretary to spend only 50 percent of the monies allocated for this particular program. Numerous AIDS groups now contend that this action by the president is unconstitutional.

Based on the foregoing, the secretary may constitutionally expend which of the following amounts for the AIDS program?

A. $15 million if the president reasonably determined that this program had ceased to be of significant importance to the general welfare

B. $15 million because the president may exercise control over the actions of his subordinates by executive order

C. $24 million because a more drastic cut would contravene the Equal Protection Clause, as compared to the beneficiaries of other programs

D. $30 million because the president cannot impair a valid federal statute imposing a duty to spend appropriated monies

Questions 17-19 are based on the following facts:

As part of a comprehensive federal aid-to-education program, Congress included the following provisions as conditions for state receipt of federal funds: (1) whenever textbooks are reimbursed by the federal government, they must be used in classes that include no religious instruction and must be made available on the same terms to students in all public and private schools accredited by the state educational authority; (2) salary supplements can be paid to teachers in public and private schools, up to 10 percent of existing salary schedules, where present compensation is less than the average salary for persons of comparable training and experience, provided that no such supplement is paid to any teacher who instructs in religious subjects; (3) construction grants can be made toward the cost of physical structures at private colleges and universities, provided that no part of the grant is used for buildings in which instruction in religious subject matters is offered.

17. Federal taxpayer Allen challenges the provision that allows the distribution of free textbooks to students in a private school where religious instruction is included in the curriculum. On the question of the adequacy of Allen's standing to raise the constitutional question, the most likely result is that standing will be

   A. sustained because any congressional spending authorization can be challenged by a federal taxpayer.

   B. sustained because the challenge to the exercise of the congressional spending power is based on a claimed violation of the Establishment Clause.

   C. denied because there is an insufficient nexus between the taxpayer and the challenged expenditures.

   D. denied because, in the case of private schools, no state action is involved.

18. Federal taxpayer Bates also challenges the salary supplements for teachers in private schools where religious instruction is included in the curriculum. On the substantive constitutional issue, the most likely result is that the salary supplements will be

   A. sustained because the statute provides that no supplements will be made to teachers who are engaged in any religious instruction.

   B. sustained because to distinguish between private and public school teachers would violate the Religious Freedom Clause of the First Amendment.

   C. held unconstitutional because some religions would benefit disproportionately.

   D. held unconstitutional because policing the restriction would amount to an excessive entanglement with religion.

19. Federal taxpayer Bates also challenges the construction grants to church-operated, private colleges and universities. The most likely result is that the construction grants will be

   A. sustained because aid to one aspect of an institution of higher education not shown to be pervasively sectarian does not necessarily free it to spend its other resources for religious purposes.

   B. sustained because the construction of buildings does not aid religion in a way forbidden by the Establishment Clause of the First Amendment.

C. held unconstitutional because any financial aid to a church-operated school strengthens the religious purposes of that institution.

D. held unconstitutional because the grants involve an excessive entanglement with religion.

20. State X accredits both public and private schools, licenses their teachers, and supplies textbooks on secular subjects to all such schools. Country Schoolhouse, a private school that offers elementary and secondary education in state X, denies admission to all non-Caucasians. In a suit to enjoin as unconstitutional the continued racially exclusionary admissions policy of Country Schoolhouse, which of the following is the *strongest* argument *against* the school?

A. Because education is a public function, Country Schoolhouse may not discriminate on racial grounds.

B. Because the state is constitutionally obligated to eliminate segregation in all public and private educational institutions, Country Schoolhouse may not discriminate on racial grounds.

C. Each state is constitutionally obligated to eliminate segregation in all public and private educational institutions.

D. Teachers who are licensed by a state accreditation entity are forbidden to discriminate on racial grounds.

21. Ben and Sheila Wellness owned a relatively low income apartment complex in the state of Euphoria. Two months ago, one of the units in the complex became vacant. Ben and Sheila advertised in the local paper for a new tenant. A few days later, Malcolm Grant, an African American man who had become disabled because of a manufacturing accident, telephoned to request a viewing of the unit. Sheila, based on his voice, thought that Malcolm was a person of color and responded, "Sorry, the unit has already been rented." Malcolm subsequently discovered that the unit had, in fact, not been rented at the time he asked to inspect it. Malcolm retained an attorney, whose research disclosed a U.S. statute that prohibited "any denial of housing based solely on racial or ethnic grounds."

Based on the foregoing, the *most easily justifiable* basis on which Congress could have enacted this statute is the

A. Thirteenth Amendment.

B. Fourteenth Amendment.

C. General Welfare Clause of Article 1, §8.

D. Contracts Clause.

22. During her gubernatorial campaign, Melinda Duke vociferously promised the citizens of the state of Primera that she would "boost the state's sagging economy." True to her word, as soon as Duke became the governor of Primera by garnering 63 percent of the popular vote, she induced the legislature to enact a statute requiring all business entities selling goods in Primera with annual sales in excess of $1 million in any calendar year to make at least 10 percent of their purchases each year from companies doing business in Primera. Breed Corp., whose sales within Primera the prior year were in excess of $1 million, prefers to **not** comply with the new law. It retains an attorney to assert that it is unconstitutional.

Based on the foregoing, which of the following constitutional provisions represents the **strongest** basis for invalidating this statute?

A. Commerce Clause

B. Due Process Clause of the Fourteenth Amendment

C. Privileges and Immunities Clause of the Fourteenth Amendment

D. Equal Protection Clause

23. There had recently been newspaper articles and television shows about the "poaching" of animals from national parks and recreation areas (including Yosemite National Park). Animal-rights activists persuaded Congress to pass legislation that made "the taking of any type of live wildlife" by a private citizen from a federal area illegal. In fact, in addition to monetary fines, anyone convicted under this statute could be compelled to spend up to three years in a federal prison. Two days after passage of this legislation and the necessary presidential signature, Charles Winterhead was apprehended attempting to remove a live squirrel from a federal preserve. Charles claimed that he had no knowledge of the recent change in law and asserted that the federal law was unconstitutional.

Based on the foregoing, which of the following represents the **strongest** basis for sustaining the statute against constitutional attack by Charles?

A. Commerce Clause of Article I, §8

B. Privileges and Immunities Clause of Article IV, §2

C. Enforcement Clause of the Fourteenth Amendment

D. Property Clause of Article IV, §3

24. A recent federal study titled "Car Thefts in the United States" concluded that approximately 22 percent of all stolen vehicles were transported into adjoining states and disposed of in those states. One of the report's recommendations was that Congress enact legislation that would establish a national vehicle registry. This would, according to the report, make it easier for police within a state to determine if a particular vehicle had been stolen from another state.

Anxious to demonstrate its anticrime fervor to potential voters, Congress quickly passed this legislation. However, the law required each vehicle owner to complete forms containing the required information and send them, along with $18, to a federally established national registry in Oklahoma City. Of course, a few registered drivers contended that the new law infringes on their privacy. They commenced an action contending that the law is unconstitutional.

Based on the foregoing, the statute is probably

A. constitutional because Congress has the power to regulate property for the general welfare.

B. constitutional because Congress could determine that vehicle thefts affect interstate commerce.

C. unconstitutional because the study found that the vast majority of stolen vehicles remain within the state in which they are stolen.

D. unconstitutional because the registration of vehicles is a matter impliedly reserved to the states by the Tenth Amendment.

25. Medico Enterprises, a major drug manufacturer, has just announced its ability to produce a drug that, when taken by females, avoids pregnancy without any harmful side effects. The Food and Drug Administration (FDA) approved the drug one week ago. Medico now plans to distribute the drug called "Gogoco" throughout the United States. However, legislators in the state of Butah are "fearful that Gogoco would have a pernicious moral effect on the young." They pass legislation forbidding the sale or distribution of Gogoco to minors within their jurisdiction. The age of majority in Butah is 21. The American Civil Liberties Union (ACLU) and the largest retail pharmacy (eight stores) within Butah have joined in an action to declare the new law unconstitutional.

Based on the foregoing, the ***strongest*** constitutional argument that could be asserted for invalidating this statute is that it

A. constitutes an undue burden on interstate commerce.

B. denies minors a fundamental right.

C. violates a privilege or immunity of national citizenship.

D. violates the First Amendment right to freedom of religion because it regulates morals.

26. Daniel Baker owned a substantial real estate development company. He decided to develop a large residential community in Springdale, Euphoria, which would showcase "Family Values: The Way America Was in the Fifties." Accordingly, Daniel's development plan includes covenants and restrictions (CCRs) that mandate that all homeowners (1) paint their houses at least once a year, using white paint only; and (2) maintain well-manicured lawns in the front of their houses. Before borrowing the necessary funds, Daniel consulted an attorney for the purpose of preparing the CCRs that would be incorporated into the deed given to each purchaser. However, she advised Daniel that legislation pending in the Euphoria legislature would make all privately imposed CCRs unenforceable. The Euphoria Land Use Board would (via zoning) have sole, exclusive control in these matters.

Based on the foregoing, if Daniel decided to challenge the proposed legislation, which of the following constitutional concepts is the *least* likely to succeed?

A. Deprivation of property rights without compensation

B. Privileges and immunities (art. IV, §2)

C. Excessive use of police power

D. Impairment of contracts

27. The state of Euphoria places a high value on computer education, which legislators believe is the "wave of the future." As a consequence, the legislature has enacted a special, state-sponsored loan program for college or graduate students majoring in computer-related studies. However, only residents of Euphoria who are U.S. citizens are eligible for this program.

William Gaung applied for a loan pursuant to this program. His application was about to be granted, when the reviewing officer noticed that he was merely a legal resident alien. As a consequence, the application was rejected. When William inquired as to why the loan program was restricted to U.S. citizens, he was advised that an 11-year-old federal study had concluded that only 36 percent of resident legal aliens still remained in the jurisdiction of their collegiate schooling within five years after their education had been concluded.

William promptly commenced an action in federal court, contending that the restriction contained in the Euphoria loan program was unconstitutional.

Based on the foregoing, it is most likely that the loan program's restriction to U.S. citizens is probably

A. constitutional because aliens are not a "discrete and insular minority."

B. constitutional because the line drawn by Euphoria was reasonably related to a legitimate state interest.

C. unconstitutional because the justification for this restriction is insufficient to overcome the burden imposed on states for alienage classification.

D. unconstitutional because the Privileges and Immunities Clause of Article IV does not permit such arbitrary classifications.

28. Alison, who works for American Bracks, Inc., is vice president of marketing. She was recently promoted. As part of her promotion, Alison had to relocate from the state of Argon to the corporate headquarters in the state of Mercer. Alison moved to Mercer in September. She planned to vote the "Republican ticket" in the upcoming local and gubernatorial elections in November. However, when Alison went to the polls in November, she was *not* permitted to vote. Alison was informed that a Mercer law provided that persons moving into the jurisdiction could *not* vote in any elections, until they had demonstrated their "*bona fide* intent" to become residents of the state by living there for six months. Because Alison had been a citizen of Mercer only slightly more than two months, she could not vote in *any* election.

Based on the foregoing, the *strongest* constitutional argument that Alison could assert to invalidate the Mercer statute is that

A. it can be legitimately presumed persons moving to a new jurisdiction intend to remain there.

B. the statute discriminates against interstate commerce.

C. there are no sufficiently compelling reasons to justify the exclusion from voting of new residents.

D. Mercer could use less restrictive means to assure that only genuine residents voted in its elections.

29. Muffy became addicted to cocaine while attending an exclusive all-girls prep school. She took the drug to maintain her weight and to stay up all night studying or writing papers. When Muffy entered an Ivy League college, she was still addicted to cocaine. To acquire money to support her habit, Muffy sold cocaine. One night, when she was 19 years old, Muffy was arrested. She was later convicted for possession and distribution of cocaine (a felony).

Muffy subsequently transferred to another college, where she met Biff. Muffy and Biff fell in love and married after graduation. They settled in Euphoria. Biff never knew of Muffy's past cocaine use or arrest. Unfortunately, Muffy soon again began using cocaine, without Biff's knowledge. Two years after their marriage, Muffy gave birth to twin daughters. However, six months later, Muffy was again arrested for possession of cocaine and convicted (her second felony).

A state of Euphoria statute requires that any adult who has been twice convicted of a drug abuse-related felony shall permanently lose custody of a minor child. Euphoria commenced an action under the statute to terminate Muffy's parental rights because of the second felony conviction. Muffy contends in rebuttal that the statute is unconstitutional as applied to her in this situation.

Based on the foregoing, it is most likely that the burden of persuasion in this matter is on

A. Muffy, to show that the statute is *not* rationally related to a legitimate state interest.

B. Euphoria, to show that the statute as applied to Muffy is rationally related to a legitimate state interest.

C. Euphoria, to show the statute satisfies a compelling state interest.

D. Muffy, to show that no substantial state interest is furthered by the statute.

30. In the state of Wissola, a recent spate of accidents has involved commercial trucks and vans. Apparently, as drivers seek to impress their employers with the expeditious manner in which their tasks can be accomplished, they occasionally exceed the speed limit or take unnecessary chances. Believing that accidents could be lessened if the drivers of these vehicles wore harness-type (rather than simply waist-type) seat belts, Wissola enacted a law requiring the former in all "commercially used trucks and vans." Private trucks and vans were *not* affected.

BUPS, a national entity that delivers packages in Wissola and 22 other states, objects to this law. Some of the BUPS trucks that operate in Wissola also deliver packages in adjoining states that do *not* require this type of seat belt. BUPS estimates that it would incur substantial costs to install harness-type seat belts in all of its trucks that constantly or occasionally operate in Wissola. Also, several of its drivers have expressed unhappiness with the new law.

Based on the foregoing, the **best** constitutional basis for invalidating the new Wissola law is the

A. Due Process Clause.

B. Equal Protection Clause.

C. Dormant Commerce Clause.

D. Contracts Clause.

31. The state of Euphoria has recently experienced an increase in violent crime. Local citizen groups are demanding that the government provide additional police to better protect law-abiding citizen-taxpayers. The particularly vociferous "Tired of Being Victims" group, along with local police unions and the governor of Euphoria, petitioned the federal government for greater police protection.

   After much lobbying, Congress passed (and the president signed) a law requiring state and local police departments that receive federal funds to hire sufficient patrol officers. The law provides that each city of 50,000 or more residents must have at least two police officers for every 500 citizens. Cities with less than 50,000 inhabitants are not expressly covered by this legislation.

   The **strongest** constitutional basis for validating the enactment of the statute is the

   A. war and defense powers.

   B. Tenth Amendment.

   C. Privileges and Immunities Clause of the Fourteenth Amendment.

   D. power to tax and spend for the general welfare.

32. Martha, a citizen of the state of Spud, is an ardent disciple of Reverend Richquick, who tells his followers that the more money they contribute to his church, the higher will be their place in heaven. Martha is very concerned that her place in heaven is questionable. As a consequence, she takes up selling Tupperware to enhance her contributions to Richquick's church. Martha does not have a commercial license to sell Tupperware, even though "persons engaged in retail sales" are required to have one. However, persons engaged in the retail sale of items for "religious purposes" are exempt from the license requirement.

   One day, Martha sold Tupperware to Kathryn, an undercover police officer. When Kathryn asked Martha for a copy of her commercial license for retail sales, Martha admitted she didn't have one. Martha was then arrested and charged with violating this law. Martha's attorney, hired for her by Reverend Richquick, asserts that her sales were for "religious purposes" and thus exempt from the statute in question.

Based on the foregoing, it is most likely that, under the statute in question, Martha is

A. not guilty if Martha's religious beliefs are sincerely held.

B. not guilty because, under the First Amendment, a state may not criminalize *bona fide* religious tenets.

C. guilty because a generally applicable criminal prohibition may infringe on religious activities.

D. guilty if the fact finder concludes that Martha's religious beliefs are clearly erroneous.

33. State X passed a law requiring all single-family dwellings whose composition is more than 60 percent stucco to be reinforced with metal slats within two years. This process would ordinarily cost approximately $1,200. The law was passed after a report pertaining to potential damage in the event of an earthquake indicated that loss of life and property would be diminished as a result of such metal reinforcement. However, statistics indicate that 64 percent of all single-family dwellings in state X that have a composition of more than 60 percent stucco are owned by Hispanic individuals.

Is state X's law unconstitutional?

A. No, because there is a rational basis for the law

B. Yes, because the strict-scrutiny standard is not satisfied in this instance

C. Yes, because the law has a disproportionately negative racial impact

D. Yes, because the $1,200 fee necessary to reinforce the homes violates due process

34. A state legislative committee wants you to draft legislation to make all restrictions on land use imposed by deeds (now or hereafter recorded) unenforceable, so that public planning through zoning will have exclusive control in matters of land use. Which of the following is *least* likely to be a consideration in drafting such legislation?

A. Compensation for property rights taken by public authority

B. Impairment of Contracts Clause (art. I, §10, cl. 1)

C. Privileges and Immunities Clause (art. IV, §2)

D. Tenth Amendment

35. Gasoline prices recently have increased dramatically. This development has incensed many citizens and engendered numerous groups whose stated purpose is to "throw out" their present legislators. Fearful of such a voter reaction, Congress hurriedly enacted a statute that allows the secretary of energy to "set" the retail price of gasoline that is produced in the United States or brought into the United States from a foreign country. Numerous large oil companies have asserted that this law is unconstitutional.

Based on the foregoing, the ***strongest*** argument for upholding this statute is the power of Congress to

A. enact laws for the general welfare.

B. regulate the sale of products or goods that are manufactured or produced in the United States.

C. regulate the importation of foreign goods and products brought into the United States from abroad.

D. regulate interstate and foreign commerce.

Questions 36-37 are based on the following facts:

Legislators in the state of Euphoria were very concerned about its skyrocketing divorce rate. Divorces in this jurisdiction were occurring at almost a 70 percent rate for marriages that had occurred within the prior ten years. The legislature therefore passed a law that declared that no couple could obtain a marriage license unless and until they had paid for and received at least 15 hours of marriage and family counseling from a licensed counselor in that state. The Euphoria State Bar persuaded the legislature to include another provision, which required a couple who had applied for a marriage license to pay for and attend at least ten hours of classes given by an attorney of that state pertaining to community-property principles. In Euphoria, a couple could apply for a marriage license if the older person was at least 18 years of age and the younger one at least 16 years old.

36. Paul and Mary are 19 and 18 years old, respectively. They intend to attend college, marry, and then go to law school. They were both incensed at the new law and retained Art Smith, Esq., to represent them in having the legislation declared unconstitutional.

Based on the foregoing, Mr. Smith commenced an action on his clients' behalf in U.S. district court. In response, the Euphoria attorney general moved for dismissal.

The ***strongest*** basis for dismissal is that

A. Paul and Mary are citizens of the same state.

B. no substantial federal question is presented.

    C. the suit is not ripe.

    D. the suit presents a nonjusticiable political question.

37. Assuming that Paul and Mary's action was **not** dismissed and that the age of majority (i.e., when one can vote) in Euphoria is 21, it is most likely that the burden of proof is on

    A. the plaintiffs because Euphoria may regulate the conditions for marriage pursuant to the Tenth Amendment.

    B. the plaintiffs because an enactment by a state legislature is presumed to be constitutional.

    C. Euphoria because marriage is a fundamental right.

    D. Euphoria because legislation affecting minors is subject to strict scrutiny.

Questions 38-39 are based on the following facts:

A recently enacted state X law forbids legal aliens from owning more than 100 acres of land within the jurisdiction and directs the state attorney general to bring an action in ejectment whenever an alien owns in excess thereof. Zane, a resident legal alien, purchased 200 acres of land in state X after passage of that law. He brings an action in federal court to enjoin the state X attorney general from enforcing the statute against him. The defendant moved to dismiss the complaint.

38. The **strongest** argument for Zane is that

    A. states are forbidden by the Commerce Clause from interfering with the rights of aliens to own land.

    B. the state X statute violates the Equal Protection Clause of the Fourteenth Amendment.

    C. the state X statute adversely affects Zane's right to travel.

    D. the state X statute violates the Obligation of Contracts Clause.

39. The federal court should

    A. dismiss the action because, under the U.S. Constitution, aliens may not sue in federal court.

    B. dismiss the action because a state has the power to determine the qualifications for landholding within its boundaries.

    C. hear the action if the United Nations Charter forbids such discrimination.

    D. hear the action because a federal question is presented.

40. James, a practicing Buddhist, had dreamed of working for a governmental agency. He intended to use his Buddhist training to "humanize

big bureaucracy." One day, James heard of an opening for an adminis-trative assistant position at the state of Yodah Environmental Agency and immediately applied. Pursuant to agency policy, James was given a standardized test, which he passed. He was then interviewed by an employee of the Yodah Employment Office.

James's application was rejected one week later. There is no statute, regulation, or departmental policy that requires any explanation to rejected applicants. However, in a few instances (5 to 10 percent of the time), applicants have received personal or telephonic postinter-view discussions by Yodah Employment Office personnel as to why they were unsuccessful. These explanations are permitted by Yodah Employment Office regulations but are completely discretionary. Some of the Employment Office personnel occasionally believe that their comments might assist applicants with subsequent job inter-views. James specifically asked for a personal postinterview discussion but was refused.

Based on the foregoing, if James commenced an action to compel the employment officer to provide him with information similar to that supplied to other rejected applicants who had received postinterview feedback, it is most likely that

A. he will be unsuccessful because the employment of individuals is reserved to the states under the Tenth Amendment.

B. he will be unsuccessful because there is no protectable "property interest" in employment by a state agency.

C. he will be successful because the right to governmental employment is a protected "liberty" interest within the Due Process Clause.

D. he will be successful because James's treatment by Yodah contra-venes the Equal Protection Clause.

41. At night, Angela works as a part-time singer in a local nightclub. During the day, she is employed as a file clerk by the city of Trigera (where she has been employed for just over five years). According to a Trigera ordinance, Angela cannot acquire tenure until she has been employed by the municipality for ten consecutive years. Until now, Angela's one-year contract has been renewed in a timely manner. Recently, how-ever, Trigera experienced a recession. As a consequence, there were job cutbacks, and Angela was informed that her one-year contract would not be renewed. Although Angela (1) asked for a written statement as to why she was not being rehired and (2) requested an opportunity

for a hearing, she was refused. Trigera officials cited state law and city department rules that do not require either a statement of reasons or a hearing. Angela seeks to compel Trigera to furnish her with a statement of its reasons for failing to rehire her.

Based on the foregoing, the situation that would probably provide the **strongest** constitutional argument that Angela could assert is

A. in the expectation of continued employment based on renewal of her contract for five years, Angela had just purchased a home in close physical proximity to her job.

B. the contracts of only a relatively few file clerks were not renewed that year.

C. Angela had rejected another job offer after being verbally assured of continued reemployment by the city of Trigera officer for whom she worked.

D. no evidence exists that any of the file clerks retained by the city of Trigera are more qualified than Angela.

42. The state of Euphoria operates a large parking lot near the state capitol. Within the parking lot structure is a restaurant that has operated in a highly profitable manner for more than three years. Euphoria has entered into a lease for this space with the owner of this facility for ten years. Several persons of Hispanic origin have recently complained that they have been denied service by the restaurant. However, the restaurant owner contends that they were denied service only after they had acted in a loud, overbearing manner. One of the aggrieved persons commenced an action in U.S. district court, contending that the restaurant's discrimination against him violated the Equal Protection Clause of the Fourteenth Amendment. He alleged that operation of the restaurant constituted "state action."

Based on the foregoing, the district court will most likely

A. hear the case on the merits because a federal claim is presented.

B. hear the case on the merits because Euphoria is a defendant.

C. abstain from jurisdiction because any alleged constitutional issues should first be heard in a state court.

D. dismiss the case for lack of jurisdiction if the plaintiff and restaurant owner are both citizens of Euphoria.

43. The state of Euphoria accredits both public and private schools, licenses their teachers, and supplies textbooks pertaining to secular subjects to all of its educational institutions. Euphoria also supplies athletic

gear to the various varsity teams in its high schools and corresponding grade levels at private schools. The Bastion is a private school in Euphoria that offers secondary education. It has a well-established policy of denying admission applications from persons whose parents are registered members of the Republican Party or prominently espouse the views of that entity. The principals of the Bastion sincerely believe that the "ideas" promoted by this organization are extremely dangerous to society.

In a suit to enjoin as unconstitutional the exclusionary admissions policy of the Bastion, which of the following is the *strongest* argument *against* that school?

A. Education is a public function, and so the Bastion may not discriminate.

B. A state is constitutionally obligated to eliminate unconstitutional discrimination in public educational institutions.

C. A state is constitutionally obligated to eliminate discrimination in public and private educational institutions.

D. Schools that are licensed by a state accreditation entity are forbidden to discriminate.

44. The city of Littletown recently enacted an ordinance that prohibits parades or demonstrations between the hours of 4:00 P.M. and 6:30 P.M. The purpose of the ordinance was to preclude such events during rush hour, when traffic might become ensnarled and motorists might become violent if obliged to remain in nonmoving vehicles for an extended period of time. However, to avoid any challenges that streets are "public forums" and that such "speech activities" as parades and demonstrations could not be precluded in public forums, exceptions to this prohibition could be made by the Littletown Police Department commissioner. If the commissioner were presented with a waiver application at least 72 hours before a planned event, he could approve it. The police commissioner was instructed to give "prompt" attention to such applications and to determine all applications in an "even-handed manner."

Based on the foregoing, if the statute is constitutionally challenged, it most likely will be found

A. unconstitutional because traditional public forums must be made reasonably available for speech activities without condition.

B. unconstitutional because the statute vests too much discretion in the Littletown police commissioner.

C. constitutional because the restrictions are narrowly tailored to promote a significant governmental purpose.

D. constitutional because the Littletown police commissioner is required to give waiver applications his "prompt" attention and decide them in an "even-handed manner."

Questions 45-46 are based on the following facts:

Congress recently enacted legislation that provides monetary grants to public schools and integrated religious schools for the purchase of computers. These grants were based solely on the number of students at each institution. The purpose of this legislation was to make certain that America did not fall behind in the technological arena. This legislation also provided for hiring technology teachers, who were expressly prohibited from providing any type of religious instruction at either public or private schools.

45. Based on the foregoing, if Anna, an avowed atheist and federal taxpayer, challenges the statute, it is most likely that

A. she lacks standing if she has no children in either public or private school.

B. she lacks standing because the legislation in question is a general funding measure.

C. she has standing because the statute arguably contravenes the Establishment Clause.

D. she has standing if the expenditure in question was made pursuant to the General Welfare Clause.

46. Assuming Anna has standing, the portion of the statute providing for the funding of technology teachers probably is

A. constitutional because the statute applies equally to public and private religious schools.

B. constitutional because, given the prohibition against any type of religious instruction, there is insufficient governmental-religious entanglement.

C. unconstitutional because this portion of the statute might result in excessive governmental-religious entanglement.

D. unconstitutional because private, nonreligious schools are **not** included within the statute.

47. Clarence had worked as a federal public defender for almost 20 years. He was about to celebrate his sixtieth birthday. A U.S. law, however, requires federal public defenders to retire at age 60. Accordingly, when Clarence returned to his office the day before he became 60, there was

a letter on his desk. This letter explained that retirement was mandatory and instructed him to "clean out his desk" by the close of the following day.

Clarence called a friend of his, Melvin, who had worked at the Federal Bureau of Investigation (FBI) for 12 years. Melvin advised Clarence that FBI agents did not have to retire until they had reached age 70. Clarence, who is currently working on a number of interesting cases, decides to seek a declaratory judgment that would extend his mandatory retirement until age 70.

Based on the foregoing, the *strongest* argument that Clarence could make to invalidate the present law is that this legislation

A. discriminates against him in violation of the Fifth Amendment.

B. violates the Fifth Amendment's Due Process Clause because employment is a property right.

C. violates the Privileges and Immunities Clause.

D. violates the Equal Protection Clause of the Fourteenth Amendment.

Questions 48-49 are based on the following facts:

Congress decided that the application of the Uniform Consumer Credit Code (UCCC) should be the same throughout the United States. To that end, it enacted the UCCC as a federal law and made it directly applicable to all consumer credit, small loans, and retail installment sales. The law is intended to protect borrowers and buyers against unfair practices by suppliers of consumer credit.

48. Which of the following constitutional provisions may be *most easily* used to justify federal enactment of this statute?

A. Obligation of Contracts Clause

B. Privileges and Immunities Clause of the Fourteenth Amendment

C. Commerce Clause

D. Equal Protection Clause of the Fourteenth Amendment

49. A particular religious organization, pursuant to the tenets of its faith, makes loans throughout the country for the construction of churches. The federal UCCC would substantially interfere with the organization's objective of expanding religious institutions. The organization seeks to obtain a declaratory judgment that the federal law may not be applied to its lending activities. Which of the following best describes the burden that must be sustained?

A. The federal government must demonstrate that the governmental interest outweighs the interference with the organization's lending activities.

B. The federal government must demonstrate that it rationally believed that the UCCC helps to achieve a legitimate national interest when applied to both religious and secular lending activities.

C. The organization must demonstrate that no reasonable legislator could believe that application of the UCCC to this organization would be helpful in accomplishing a legitimate governmental objective.

D. The organization must demonstrate a specific congressional purpose to inhibit the accomplishment of the organization's religious objectives.

Questions 50-51 are based on the following facts:

The state of Caldonia is in the midst of a severe recession. As a result, foreign investors have purchased many businesses and a substantial amount of real estate. Martha Winston, the governor of Caldonia, is running for reelection. As part of her gubernatorial campaign, Winston promises that, if reelected, she will "prevent foreigners from buying up our state." She is reelected by a landslide vote and promptly prevails upon the Caldonia legislature to pass a law that forbids aliens from owning a "controlling" interest in any company incorporated in Caldonia. She directs the Caldonia attorney general to commence a criminal action to vigorously enforce the new enactment.

Schmidt, a wealthy German businessman, who was unaware of the new law, purchased 60 percent of the shares of Walco, Inc. (a private company incorporated in Caldonia), for $50,000. Schmidt had reached a verbal agreement for the purchase of the shares before the law was passed, but the transaction was not closed until one week after the law became effective. Schmidt is a legal alien. Just before the Caldonia attorney general files a criminal action against Schmidt pursuant to the new law, Schmidt commences an action in federal court to enjoin enforcement of the statute and dismiss the criminal complaint against him.

50. Based on the foregoing, it is most likely that the federal court will

   A. dismiss the action because aliens may not sue in federal court.

   B. dismiss the action because a state may determine the qualifications for the ownership of assets within its boundaries.

   C. hear the action because a state is defendant.

   D. hear the action because a federal question is presented.

51. Based on the foregoing, Schmidt's *strongest* argument to have the new Caldonia law declared unconstitutional is that it

A. violates the Impairment of Contracts Clause.

B. violates the Equal Protection Clause.

C. violates the Privileges and Immunities Clause of Art. IV, § 2.

D. violates the Interstate Commerce Clause.

Questions 52-53 are based on the following facts:

State X College (College) is engaged in an important microbiological research project under a grant from the U.S. Army. This research requires the use of several hundred monkeys, which College has already purchased. Recently, the state X legislature enacted a law that forbids the use of various animals (including monkeys) for research purposes. Using a special procedure whereby its case could be heard by the state X Supreme Court, College asserted that the act was unconstitutional. The state X Supreme Court held in favor of College.

52. State X now seeks review in the U.S. Supreme Court. The U.S. Supreme Court will probably

    A. refuse to hear the case because the U.S. Army is the only party with standing to contest the state X law.

    B. refuse to hear the case unless it grants state X's petition for certiorari.

    C. hear the case because state X has an automatic right of appeal.

    D. hear the case because a federal question has been resolved by a state court.

53. Which of the following theories represents the *weakest* argument by College for invalidation of the act?

    A. The act violates the Takings Clause.

    B. The act contravenes the Commerce Clause.

    C. The act is invalid under the Supremacy Clause.

    D. The act contravenes the Impairment of Contracts Clause.

54. Martin and Dorothy lived together in the state of Euphoria, but were unmarried. Dorothy became pregnant with Martin's child. Martin, who had always been very insecure, accused Dorothy of "cheating on him" and told her that he doubted the child belonged to him. The couple's baby girl, whom Dorothy named Patricia, was born shortly thereafter. One month after Patricia's birth, Martin ordered Dorothy and the baby "out" and cut off all contact with them.

One year after Patricia's birth, Martin bought a winning $10 million lottery ticket. However, on the way to collect his prize, Martin was struck and killed by a bus. Martin was survived by one sister, one brother, and both of his parents. He had no other living relatives.

When Dorothy read about Martin's death in the newspaper, she filed a claim with the appropriate state court seeking intestacy benefits for Patricia (because Martin, who died intestate, was the father). Euphoria state law, however, prohibited unacknowledged children born out to unmarried biological parents from inheriting through their father. Intestacy principles, exclusive of the unacknowledged child born out of wedlock, were applicable. After Patricia's claim was rejected, Dorothy filed suit in federal court, alleging that the Euphoria statute was invalid.

Based on the foregoing, Patricia's **strongest** argument for invalidating the statute on constitutional grounds is that it

A. denies Patricia procedural due process because it doesn't give her an opportunity to prove paternity.

B. is not substantially related to an important governmental interest and therefore violates the Equal Protection Clause.

C. violates the Privileges and Immunities Clause of the Fourteenth Amendment.

D. deprives Patricia of her fundamental right to inherit property.

55. The state of Butah has a statute that requires all public employees to swear or affirm that they will "oppose anyone seeking to overthrow the state or federal government by force, violence, or any other unlawful means." Janet Jones passed all of the physical and written tests necessary to become a firefighter in the city of Amityville (in the state of Butah). However, she adamantly refused to take the oath described immediately above and was not hired. Jones retained an attorney, who filed a complaint in the appropriate U.S. district court. The complaint alleged that the statute was unconstitutional and sought to enjoin its application.

Based on the foregoing, the **strongest** argument for **sustaining** the statute against constitutional attack is that

A. governmental employment is not a "right" and therefore may be conditioned on an oath or affirmation.

B. the Tenth Amendment permits a state to determine the qualifications of those employed by it.

C. the oath in this situation is merely a commitment to abide by legal procedures.

D. a state is entitled to refuse employment to potentially disloyal persons.

56. Mirza fled Iran with his family to escape religious and political persecution. In Iran, Mirza had worked at the government motor pool. Since legally arriving in the United States, she has lived in the state of Trent. Mirza has been learning English and is able to communicate fairly well. She recently applied for a job as a mechanic at the State Motor Pool's main garage. However, Mirza was informed that she is prohibited from obtaining the job because of a Trent law that provides that the state may employ only U.S. citizens. Mirza's attorney commenced an action in U.S. district court, challenging the statute's constitutionality.

Based on the foregoing, which of the following statements concerning the burden of proof is most likely correct?

A. Trent must prove that the citizenship requirement promotes a compelling state interest that cannot be satisfied by any less burdensome means.

B. Trent must prove that there is a rational relationship between the citizenship requirement and a legitimate state interest.

C. Mirza must prove that the citizenship requirement fails to advance an "important" state interest.

D. Mirza must prove that there is no rational relationship between the citizenship requirement and any legitimate state interest.

Questions 57-58 are based on the following facts:

Marvin was transferred recently by his company from the state of Facia to the state of Libertania. Marvin has one son, age 15, who began attending the local public high school. One night at dinner, Marvin asked his son, Steve, "What did you learn at school today?" Steve excitedly told Marvin that part of his sex education course was about "safe sex." To Marvin's horror, Steve told him that at the end of the class, the teacher had distributed free condoms.

Marvin was so outraged that the following day, at 1:00 P.M., he went to the school superintendent's office. However, the school superintendent refused to see Marvin. Marvin then spontaneously staged a one-man demonstration. He began yelling and shouting on the steps of the building: "The school administration is run by sex perverts and child molesters, who are utterly destroying our children. I'll kill those SOBs." The school superintendent eventually appeared and asked Marvin to leave. Marvin refused, continued his diatribe, and advised the school superintendent that he was a "filthy, SOB pervert" that he (Marvin) should kill "in a slow manner."

There are two pertinent statutes. The first one prohibits "all speeches or demonstrations in front of any public school or government building during usual school or business hours." The second imposes sanctions on any person "who shall, with or without, provocation, use toward another, and in his presence, opprobrious words or abusive language tending to cause a breach of the peace." These ordinances have not yet been the subject of judicial interpretation. Marvin is prosecuted under both statutes, but asserts that they are unconstitutional.

57. With respect to the first statute, the applicable burden of proof is which one of the following?

    A. Libertania must prove that the statute advanced an important governmental interest and was narrowly tailored to accomplish this objective.

    B. Libertania must prove that it had a rational basis for enacting the statute.

    C. Marvin must prove that Libertania failed to have a compelling interest or a less restrictive means by which it could satisfy the statute's purpose.

    D. Marvin must prove that Libertania did not have a rational basis for the statute.

58. Which of the following is the **strongest** constitutional argument for invalidating the second statute?

    A. Prior restraints cannot be imposed on speech in public places.

    B. Regulation of speech or expressive activity may not be unduly vague.

    C. Regulation of speech may not be content oriented.

    D. The First Amendment right of speech or expressive activity is assured by the Fourteenth Amendment.

59. The state of Araho wanted to promote its domestic insurance companies. Those companies had recently suffered economic difficulties as a consequence of a state requirement that they offer earthquake insurance. The Araho legislature passed a law that taxed the profits of out-of-state insurance companies at a higher rate than that of local companies. Congress had previously passed the McCarran-Ferguson Act, which insulates state regulation of the insurance industry from the Commerce Clause. Gamco, an out-of-state insurance company doing business in Araho, commenced an action to invalidate the new law.

Based on the foregoing, it is most likely that the statute would be held to be

    A. unconstitutional because it violates the Equal Protection Clause.

    B. unconstitutional because it discriminates against interstate commerce.

C. unconstitutional under the Supremacy Clause.

D. constitutional because it is rationally related to a legitimate state objective.

60. North Carolina and South Carolina have similar meat verification standards, which include inspections at slaughterhouses. The city of Amityville, located in North Carolina, recently had a serious outbreak of food poisoning. The source of the problem was believed to be improperly butchered meat brought into the city from outside of the area. The Amityville City Council passed an ordinance forbidding any retail concern in that city from purchasing or selling meat that was not killed at a slaughterhouse inspected by the Amityville Department of Sanitation. This entity inspects slaughterhouses within a 50-mile radius of the city, but does not attempt to cross state lines. South Carolina has meat inspection laws somewhat similar (although not identical) to those employed by Amityville within the state of North Carolina.

    The owner of a butcher shop in South Carolina sold meat from a slaughterhouse in that state to Owen, a butcher in Amityville. Owen was charged under the above-described ordinance.

    Based on the foregoing, if Owen asserts that the charges against him should be dismissed on the grounds that the ordinance is unconstitutional, it is most likely that he is

    A. correct because the statute violates the Equal Protection Clause.

    B. correct because the statute violates the Dormant Commerce Clause.

    C. incorrect because the statute is rationally related to a legitimate governmental objective.

    D. incorrect because citizens are presumed to know the law.

61. Littleton is a small midwestern town. Its two largest, most traveled streets are Main Street and Broadway Avenue. Recently, two parades on these streets caused unusually extensive traffic jams. As a consequence, the city council of Littleton enacted a statute that forbade all parades or demonstrations on either street. The ordinance did *not* affect speech activities on any other street. Citizens Against Big Government (CABG) believes that the city council is pro-business and enacted the new statute simply to make it more difficult for citizens to bring complaints to the public's attention. CABG decided to stage a demonstration on Main Street, but was advised by its legal counsel to first seek to have the law declared unconstitutional.

Based on the foregoing, if CABG asserts that the Littleton statute is unconstitutional, it is most likely that a court would rule that it is

A. constitutional because it is content neutral.

B. constitutional because it merely excludes speech from two specific places.

C. unconstitutional because streets are traditional "public forums."

D. unconstitutional because it is insufficiently narrowly tailored to serve a significant governmental interest.

62. The town of Amityville has an ordinance that provides: "No demonstration or parade involving more than 20 persons shall take place on the town's streets without the prior issuance of a permit." The permit was to be issued by the police commissioner if he concluded that "the proposed activity would not be detrimental to the overall community, giving due consideration to factors such as the time, place, and manner of the parade or demonstration." Tricia, a member of a women's rights organization called "WAR" (Women's Amityville Rights) ignored the ordinance and held a demonstration involving 30 of her adherents on an Amityville street without seeking a permit. She was arrested and charged with violating the ordinance.

Based on the foregoing, if Tricia contends that she cannot be successfully prosecuted under the foregoing statute, it is most likely that

A. she is correct because the statute is overly broad.

B. she is correct because the statute attempts to regulate speech activity in a traditional public forum.

C. she is incorrect because she failed to obtain a declaratory judgment prior to violating the statute.

D. she is incorrect because the statute permits a procedure for obtaining a waiver of the 20-person limit.

63. Two years ago, Hobson was appointed to a tribunal established pursuant to an act of Congress. The tribunal's duties were to review claims made by veterans and to make recommendations on their merits to the Department of Veterans Affairs. Congress later abolished the tribunal and established a different format for review of such claims. Hobson was offered a federal administrative position in the same bureau at a lesser salary. He thereupon sued the government on the ground that Congress may not (1) remove a federal judge from office during good behavior or (2) diminish his compensation during continuance in

office. Government attorneys filed a motion to dismiss the action. The court should

   A. deny the motion because the independence of the federal judiciary is constitutionally guaranteed by Article III.

   B. deny the motion because Hobson has established a property right to federal employment on the tribunal.

   C. grant the motion because Hobson lacked standing to raise the question.

   D. grant the motion because Hobson was not a judge under Article III and therefore was not entitled to life tenure.

Questions 64-65 are based on the following facts:

Bosco is an importer and distributor of goods from South America. His head-quarters (and only place of business) is in state Orange. In June of last year, Bosco received a large shipment of vases from a manufacturer in Peru. The items that Bosco purchases are ordinarily stored in his warehouse until a purchaser is located. In December of last year, Rudy, a citizen of state Blue, called Bosco to inquire about the vases. Bosco sent Bando, one of his employees, to show Rudy a sample of the vases and to negotiate a possible agreement. A sale for 1,000 of the vases was negotiated by Bando, subject to Bosco's acceptance. Bando and Rudy then drove to Bosco's headquarters, where Bosco (after insisting upon an additional $1 per item) approved the deal. Rudy presented a check to Bosco for the proper amount. One of Bosco's drivers then delivered the vases to Rudy in state Blue.

State Orange imposes an *ad valorem* tax on all personal property physically located within the jurisdiction on July 31. State Blue imposes a sales tax of 6 percent on all purchases made by its residents. State Orange has a 3 percent sales tax.

  64. If Bosco contends that the state Orange *ad valorem* tax on the vases is invalid, which of the following statements is ***most*** accurate?

    A. Bosco is correct because the vases were sold later that same year.

    B. Bosco is correct because the vases were still "imports."

    C. Bosco is correct if the tax was simply a means of reimbursing state Orange for its inspection of imported goods.

    D. Bosco is incorrect because the Import-Export Clause applies only to taxes on goods that are in transit.

  65. If state Blue assessed a sales tax on Bosco with respect to the vases purchased by Rudy, it would probably be

    A. constitutional because the transaction was negotiated in state Blue and Rudy was a state Blue resident when he purchased the items.

B. constitutional because the items were sold and purchased with the knowledge that Rudy would resell them in state Blue.

C. unconstitutional because the sale was consummated in state Orange.

D. unconstitutional because the tax would violate the Import-Export Clause.

Questions 66-67 are based on the following facts:

A congressional subcommittee found that the wheat industry has been suffering severe price and supply fluctuations in recent years. In response, Congress enacted the following statute: "No person may cultivate in wheat more than the amount of land she cultivated in wheat in the immediately preceding year. If a farmer cultivates more than the allotted land, (1) she may not sell wheat grown on excess acreage in interstate commerce; and (2) a tax of $3 per bushel will be imposed on wheat grown on the excess acreage, whether grown for sale on the open market or for home consumption, seed, or livestock feed." Weedy planted 20 acres, which was 10 acres over his allotment. On these 10 acres, he harvested 120 bushels. A tax of $360 was assessed against him, and he was enjoined from selling his wheat to a buyer in another state.

66. Weedy challenged the tax on wheat he grew for home consumption on the ground that Congress exceeded its authority under the Commerce Clause. Which of the following statements is the ***most accurate*** regarding Weedy's claim?

    A. Weedy is correct because the statute regulates the local production and consumption of wheat and is therefore beyond the reach of congressional power under the Commerce Clause.

    B. Weedy is correct because wheat planted and harvested for home consumption has only an indirect effect on interstate commerce.

    C. Weedy is incorrect because Congress could rationally find that wheat grown for home consumption, in the aggregate, constitutes economic activity that affects the national wheat market.

    D. Weedy is incorrect because the statute is a proper regulation of a product after interstate commerce has ended.

67. Assuming, rightly or wrongly, that Congress has no authority under the Commerce Clause to enact the statute, which statement, if true, is ***least relevant*** to Weedy's claim that the tax is unconstitutional?

    A. The tax provision is enforced and collected by the Department of Agriculture.

    B. The jurisdiction in which Weedy has his farm also taxes wheat grown in excess of an allotment set by a state statute.

C. The $3 per bushel tax amounts to 60 percent of the average selling price of each bushel (an amount that effectively discourages all but a very few farmers, such as Weedy, from overproducing).

D. All monies collected under the tax provision are to be spent on a grant to one wheat-producing company to study how that company could maximize its profits.

Questions 68-70 are based on the following facts:

Fisheries, Inc., leased from the state of X, for a five-year period, 200 acres of state-owned natural oyster beds. The lease granted Fisheries "complete rights" to farm the beds and sell all oysters extracted from them. Shortly thereafter, an industrial accident resulted in an unusual accumulation of waste materials in X's offshore waters. This pollution discolored over 70 percent of the oysters in the natural beds. The discolored oysters could be eaten without physical illness, but the pollution gave them a slightly bitter taste. Fearful that public consumption of the discolored oysters would permanently injure the market for X's oysters, the state of X adopted legislation prohibiting the sale of the discolored oysters. Also, to protect local interests dependent on the oyster market, it prohibited any fishery from selling unaffected oysters to out-of-state entities if local purchasers were willing to purchase the items on terms similar to those of the prospective out-of-state buyers.

After harvesting a large quantity of oysters, Fisheries contracted to sell a quantity of discolored oysters to Aldo and a quantity of normal oysters to Bart. Both Aldo and Bart are out-of-state purchasers who offered a higher price than any local buyer. State X brought suit under the statute to enjoin both sales.

68. What is the *most accurate* statement regarding Fisheries' claim that the statute violates the Obligation of Contracts Clause of the U.S. Constitution?

A. Fisheries is correct because all of its rights under the contract with state X have been impaired.

B. Fisheries is incorrect because the statute affects only a peripheral part of the contract (i.e., the right to sell normal oysters to local buyers is unaffected).

C. Fisheries is incorrect because the constitutional provision applies only to contracts between individuals, not between a state and an individual.

D. Fisheries is correct because a court will probably find against the validity of the statute.

69. What is the ***most accurate*** statement regarding Fisheries' claim that the statute constitutes a taking of private property without just compensation?

A. The statute constitutes a taking because the restriction applies to oysters that are concededly not physically harmful to the public.

B. The statute constitutes a taking because it results in a reduction in the value of Fisheries' lease; upsets Fisheries' reasonable, investment-backed expectations; and is fundamentally unfair.

C. The statute constitutes a taking because there is no public benefit (i.e., only the oyster industry would benefit from the ban on the sale of discolored oysters).

D. The statute probably does ***not*** constitute a taking because the sale of discolored oysters could adversely affect future oyster sales by state X vendors.

70. What is the ***most accurate*** statement regarding Fisheries' claim that the injunction against the sale of normal oysters to Bart violates the Interstate Commerce Clause of the U.S. Constitution?

A. Fisheries is correct because the statute discriminates against out-of-state buyers.

B. Fisheries is incorrect because out-of-state buyers may make purchases from local oyster sellers when no local buyer is willing to do so.

C. Fisheries is incorrect because, although the statute discriminates against out-of-state buyers, it has a valid health, safety, and welfare purpose.

D. Fisheries is incorrect because the statute seeks to conserve oysters (a local natural resource).

Questions 71-74 are based on the following facts:

The town of Smallberg is in state X. It has a municipal ordinance that reads: "No parade or public procession shall be held without first obtaining written permission from the town licensing commission." It is a misdemeanor to parade without having obtained a license.

The Midwest Socialist League (MSL) planned a march down Smallberg's main street for July 4. On June 25, the MSL applied to the town licensing commission for a parade permit but was refused. On June 27, the MSL announced that it would hold its march, despite the denial of the permit. On July 4, when members of the MSL began to march, the police moved in and ordered them to disperse. When they refused, several members of the MSL were arrested.

71. Which is the ***most correct*** statement regarding whether the U.S. Supreme Court would declare the Smallberg ordinance unconstitutional?

    A. The statute is unconstitutionally vague.

    B. The statute is unconstitutionally overbroad.

    C. The statute is both unconstitutionally vague and overbroad.

    D. The statute is neither vague nor overbroad.

72. Assume that (1) MSL members were convicted of parading without a permit, and (2) the conviction was affirmed without opinion by the state X Supreme Court. What is the ***most accurate*** statement regarding the disposition of the case before the U.S. Supreme Court?

    A. The MSL was correct in disobeying the statute because, although it is valid on its face, the denial of the permit by the licensing board was done arbitrarily.

    B. The MSL was correct in disobeying the statute because it was void on its face.

    C. The MSL was incorrect in disobeying the statute because it was valid on its face (and therefore the MSL was required to seek redress through proper judicial channels).

    D. The MSL was incorrect in disobeying the statute because, although it is void on its face, the MSL was required to contest the denial of the permit through proper judicial channels.

73. Assume instead that, on affirming the convictions of the MSL members, the state X Supreme Court interpreted the licensing statute as "not vesting unbridled discretion in the commission, but requiring it to give consideration, without unfair discrimination, to time, place, and manner in relation to other proper uses of the streets." Assume further that the U.S. Supreme Court would hold denial of the permit to be arbitrary and without authority. What is the ***most accurate*** statement regarding the disposition of the case before the U.S. Supreme Court?

    A. The conviction of MSL members will be affirmed because the state X Supreme Court subsequently gave the statute a constitutional construction.

    B. The conviction of MSL members will be reversed because the statute, although not void on its face, was incorrectly applied.

    C. The conviction of MSL members will be affirmed if members of the MSL had reason to anticipate such a curative construction by the state X Supreme Court.

D. The conviction of MSL members will be affirmed because the SSL could have applied for its permit months earlier and thus had time to make a proper appeal of the denial of the permit.

74. Assume that after the MSL had (on June 27) proclaimed its intention to proceed with the march despite the denial of a permit, the licensing commission (1) sought and obtained an *ex parte* injunction prohibiting this activity on July 3 and (2) served the injunction on MSL members later that day. Assume further that the U.S. Supreme Court would hold denial of the permit to be arbitrary and without authority. Members of the MSL proceeded with the march on July 4 and were held in contempt for violating the injunction.

Which statement is least relevant to the U.S. Supreme Court in deciding whether to affirm or reverse the convictions of the MSL members for contempt because they violated the injunction?

A. The injunction was granted on July 3, the day before the scheduled march.

B. The denial of the permit violated the constitutional rights of MSL members.

C. The court that issued the injunction had subject-matter jurisdiction.

D. The MSL did not attempt to appeal the injunction before attempting the parade.

Questions 75-76 are based on the following facts:

Article 7.6 of the state Z constitution provides that: "Every person shall have the right to publicly express his views in any manner that does not unreasonably interfere with the privacy or lawful activities of others." On July 4, the supreme court of Z held that Article 7.6 "precludes the owner of a shopping center from enforcing a complete ban upon sign carrying on the premises against persons who pose no threat of actual and substantial disruption of the normal activities of the shopping center."

This ruling was handed down in the case of *Ray v. Orwell*, a suit for injunctive relief brought by a student, Ray, who had been ejected from the Orwell Plaza shopping mall for peaceably walking up and down the interior of the mall carrying a sign saying, "Detente—no! National security—yes!" The security guards had told Ray that all sign carrying was banned at the mall and that if he returned he would be criminally prosecuted. In affirming the trial court's issuance of an injunction prohibiting enforcement of the ban by Orwell against Ray, the state Z supreme court reasoned as follows:

Article 7.6 imposes an obligation on every person to respect every other person's right to publicly express himself in a reasonable manner. That obligation does not cease to exist merely because a person holds legal title to the premises on which the other chooses to exercise his right to express his views, especially where, as here, the so-called "private property" is open to the public.

75. Ray, the plaintiff in *Ray v. Orwell*, did **not** base his claim for relief on the U.S. Constitution. Which essential element of a federal claim was missing?

   A. There has to be actual interference with the exercise of his claimed right of free speech.

   B. The state action interferes with the exercise of his claimed right of free speech.

   C. An actual controversy had **not** arisen because no criminal prosecution had occurred.

   D. Sign carrying is not a protected mode of expression.

76. The U.S. Supreme Court denied Orwell's petition for certiorari by a vote of 6 to 3, despite Orwell's claim that his due-process rights had been violated. Which of the following statements is the most accurate description of the significance of the action taken by the U.S. Supreme Court?

   A. Six members of the U.S. Supreme Court believed that the decision of the supreme court of Z was correct.

   B. Three members of the U.S. Supreme Court believed that the decision of the supreme court of Z was not correct.

   C. Six members of the U.S. Supreme Court believed that the case involved no federal question.

   D. Three members of the U.S. Supreme Court believed that the case should be reviewed.

Questions 77-78 are based on the following facts:

California imposed a tax on goods sold by a Nevada company to a California resident. The Nevada company has no office, plant, or place of business within California. Orders are telephoned by the seller's traveling salespersons in California to the home office in Nevada for approval. The goods are then shipped from Nevada. Title passes on delivery of the goods to the carrier in Nevada.

77. What kind of tax can California constitutionally impose on the goods?

   A. Either a sales tax or a use tax

   B. A sales tax only

C. A use tax only

D. Neither a sales nor a use tax

78. Assume, rightly or wrongly, that California can impose a use tax on the goods. Can California collect the tax directly from the Nevada company?

   A. Yes, because the tax is a sales tax

   B. Yes, because adequate contacts exist to satisfy the Due Process Clause

   C. No, because adequate contacts do not exist to satisfy the Due Process Clause

   D. No, because a use tax may only be collected from the purchaser

79. A newly enacted state criminal statute provides, in its entirety, "No person shall utter to another person in a public place any annoying, disturbing, or unwelcome language." Smith followed an elderly woman for three blocks down a public street, yelling offensive four-letter words in her ear. The woman repeatedly asked Smith to leave her alone, but he refused. In the subsequent prosecution, the first under this statute, Smith

   A. can be convicted.

   A. cannot be convicted because speech of the sort described in this instance is protected by the First and Fourteenth Amendments.

   C. cannot be convicted because, although this type of speech may be punished by the state, the state may not do so under this statute.

   D. cannot be convicted because the average user of a public street would think Smith's speech/action was amusing and ridiculous, rather than "annoying."

80. Congress passed a law that makes it a crime for a member of the Communist Party to serve as an officer of a labor union. The purpose of the law is to protect the national economy by minimizing the danger of political strikes. Is the law an unconstitutional bill of attainder?

   A. Yes

   B. No, because it does not list individuals, but rather defines a class

   C. No, because the purpose of the law is preventive, rather than retributive

   D. No, because Congress may make the determination that Communists are more likely than others to instigate a political strike

81. In response to a U.S. district court order to produce confidential presidential communications, the president invokes the claim of executive privilege. What rule of law is most likely to be applicable?

   A. In the absence of an asserted need to protect military, diplomatic, or national security secrets, the privilege is not absolute.

   B. The executive privilege is always subordinate to the need for evidence in a criminal trial.

   C. There is no executive privilege.

   D. The executive privilege is absolute in all proceedings.

82. Flyright Airlines is incorporated and has its principal place of business in New York. Flyright does not own any property in Virginia, but its airplanes regularly stop in Virginia as part of a system of interstate air commerce. Flyright's airplanes stop at Virginia airports about 20 times per day. However, the same airplane does not land every day, and none of Flyright's aircraft is continuously in Virginia. Some of Flyright's airplanes are *never* in Virginia. Which state can constitutionally levy a tax on the airplanes as personal property?

   A. New York only

   B. Virginia only

   C. New York and Virginia

   D. Neither

Questions 83-85 are based on the following facts:

A state X law requires that persons who desire to run for municipal office must (1) have been a resident of that city for at least six months, (2) pay a "ballot" fee in the amount of $100 to defray the cost involved in adding their name to the ballot, and (3) have taken the SAT and achieved a score that placed them in at least the fiftieth percentile of that particular examination. Recently, Congress enacted a statute that precludes states from requiring a filing fee or literacy test as prerequisites to running for public office. Malcolm wanted to run for mayor of a small town in X. When he applied to place his name on the ballot on June 30, he was informed about the SAT-score requirement. Malcolm was a successful businessman, but had never gone to college. As a consequence, he had never taken the SAT examination. The test was not given again until late September, and those results would not be available until the middle of December (well after the election, which was to be held on November 4). Malcolm properly filed suit in the state X Supreme Court, seeking declaratory relief.

83. If the state X Supreme Court ruled that, based on the Supremacy Clause, the state statute was unconstitutional,

   A. review by the U.S. Supreme Court is precluded by the "adequate and independent state grounds" doctrine.

   B. review may be sought by a petition for a writ of certiorari to the U.S. Supreme Court.

   C. review by the U.S. Supreme Court is precluded by the abstention doctrine.

   D. review by the U.S. Supreme Court is precluded because there are no unresolved federal issues.

84. If the state X Supreme Court held on November 8 that the statute was valid, the U.S. Supreme Court would probably

   A. refuse to hear the case because it is now moot.

   B. refuse to hear the case because Malcolm can take the SAT and run for mayor at the next election.

   C. hear the case despite the mootness doctrine.

   D. hear the case because First Amendment rights are involved.

85. With respect to the merits of this case, the state X Supreme Court would probably rule that the state X statute is

   A. valid as a proper exercise of the Tenth Amendment.

   B. valid because the federal statute was passed subsequent to the state X law.

   C. invalid because the provisions of the state X law are in conflict with a valid federal statute.

   D. invalid as to the ballot-fee and SAT-score provisions.

Questions 86-87 are based on the following facts:

State X has enacted a law that reads: "Any student who engages in demonstrations or activities on a high school or college campus that are detrimental to the U.S. government will forthwith cease to be eligible for state financial aid." Arthur, a student at X State University, was involved in a demonstration to keep the Central Intelligence Agency (CIA) off the campus. The protest was held on the X State University football field and was conducted in a peaceful manner. As a result of his participation, Arthur's state scholarship was withdrawn.

86. If the state X statute was deemed to be facially invalid because it was too vague, Arthur

   A. would be entitled to reinstatement of his scholarship.

B. would not be entitled to reinstatement of his scholarship because financial aid is not a constitutionally guaranteed right.

D. would not be entitled to reinstatement of his scholarship because the statute does not pertain to criminal behavior.

E. would not be entitled to reinstatement of his scholarship because the state X law is rationally related to a legitimate governmental purpose.

87. Arthur's claim that his First Amendment rights have been violated by X State University's action will probably be

   A. successful because demonstrations in a traditional public forum cannot serve as the basis for adverse governmental action.

   B. successful because Arthur was penalized for engaging in protected speech activity.

   C. unsuccessful because X State University, rather than state X, withdrew the grant.

   D. unsuccessful because the state X scholarship was merely a privilege (and so could be withdrawn at will).

Questions 88-89 are based on the following facts:

State X has a statute that awards college scholarships to its residents who have attained a minimum SAT score and attend a state university. If a state X resident desires to major in geology, the scholarship is extended to out-of-state universities. Joe, a state X resident, applied for a scholarship to attend a state Y college, even though he was not majoring in geology. However, his application was rejected. Mike, another state X resident, was denied a scholarship because his SAT score was one point below the minimum-score requirement.

88. Which of the following statements is *most* correct?

   A. State X's refusal to grant Joe a scholarship is an unconstitutional infringement of his right to travel.

   B. State X's refusal to grant Joe a scholarship constitutes a denial of equal protection because the "in state, out of state" classification is irrational.

   C. State X's refusal to grant Joe's scholarship will be sustained.

   D. State X's refusal to grant Joe a scholarship violates the Privileges and Immunities Clause contained in Article IV.

89. Which of the following statements is *most* correct?

   A. State X's refusal to grant Mike a scholarship violates the Privileges and Immunities Clause of the Fourteenth Amendment.

B. State X's refusal to grant Mike a scholarship constitutes a deprivation of substantive due process because students who achieve low SAT scores may otherwise be financially unable to attend college.

C. State X's refusal to grant Mike a scholarship violates equal protection because SAT scores are not rationally related to the governmental purpose of helping state X residents to attend college.

D. State X's refusal to grant Mike a scholarship is valid.

90. John sought dissolution of his marriage to Mary in a state X court. However, because of his indigence, he could not pay the required court fee of $75. The state court refused to grant him a divorce. If John commenced an action claiming that his constitutional rights were violated, what is the ***most likely*** result?

   A. The state court's action is constitutional because it satisfies the traditional equal-protection test.

   B. The state court's action is constitutional because it satisfies the strict-scrutiny test.

   C. The state court's action is constitutional because the discrimination is *de facto* instead of *de jure*.

   D. The state court's action is unconstitutional because it does not satisfy the strict-scrutiny test.

91. State X passes a law barring the sale of motor vehicles to males under 21 and to females under 18. Which of the following propositions of law is the ***most likely*** to be applied in determining if the law violates the Equal Protection Clause of the Fourteenth Amendment?

   A. The law is presumptively valid because gender is not a suspect class.

   B. Absent a compelling state interest, classifications based on gender are invalid.

   C. Unless substantially related to an important governmental objective, classifications based on gender are invalid.

   D. Statutes favoring women are valid, as long as there is a rational basis for the classification.

92. Congress passes a law limiting federal welfare benefits to those persons who are U.S. citizens. On appeal to the U.S. Supreme Court, which of the following is the probable result?

   A. The law violates the Equal Protection Clause of the U.S. Constitution because aliens are a suspect class and there is no compelling governmental interest.

B. The law violates the Due Process Clause because welfare benefits are a fundamental right.

C. The statute is constitutional because aliens are not entitled to due process.

D. The statute is constitutional because preferring U.S. citizens over aliens in the distribution of limited resources such as welfare benefits is not arbitrary or irrational.

93. The *Daily Times* published an editorial in which the newspaper accused Joe Smith, who was running for a seat in the state senate, with violation of a state law that required seekers of public office to report all campaign contributions. In a lawsuit by filed by Smith against the *Daily Times* for libel, the ***most accurate*** statement of the newspaper's defense is

A. the *Daily Times* has an absolute privilege because the First Amendment protects freedom of the press.

B. Smith must prove falsity and actual malice.

C. Smith must prove falsity.

D. Smith must prove falsity and show that the *Daily Times* failed to act reasonably.

94. State X enacted a law that gave "bonus points" in the determination of who should receive jobs offered by state X to persons who had served in the armed forces. The legislative history of the act indicates that its purpose is to reward patriotism and compensate persons who had voluntarily taken themselves out of the job market to serve their country. The legislative history also suggests that persons who had served in the armed forces had acquired a discipline and an ability to precisely follow instructions superior to comparable persons in civilian life. However, a women's group has recently produced a methodologically valid study that shows that only 15 percent of veterans are women. This group has now brought suit, claiming that the act is unconstitutional. Assuming the standing requisite is satisfied, the act is constitutional as long as

A. it is rationally related to a legitimate governmental interest.

B. it is substantially related to an important governmental objective.

C. it satisfies a compelling state interest, and there is no less burdensome means of accomplishing that objective.

D. the plaintiff can show that the legislators actually desired to give a hiring preference to males.

Questions 95-96 are based on the following facts:

On January 1, the governor of the state of Anxiety signed into law Penal Code §96, popularly referred to as the Obscene Movie Act. The statute contains the following provisions:

(A) As used in subsections B and C, the term "obscene movie" means a motion picture that, judged as a whole by an average person, depicts sexual acts in a manner that is patently offensive, appeals to the prurient interest in sex, and utterly lacks redeeming social value.

(B) It shall be unlawful to sell or exhibit an obscene movie to another person in exchange for payment or other consideration.

(C) It shall be unlawful to possess an obscene movie for the purpose of selling or exhibiting such obscene movie to another person in exchange for payment or other consideration.

95. In June, Doug was convicted of violating §96 based on evidence that he showed obscene movies at his Eros Movie Theater and charged a $10 per person admission fee. The appellate court affirmed the conviction, notwithstanding the fact that the trial court refused to permit Doug to introduce evidence concerning various efforts made by him to prevent admission by minors and persons who might not have understood that the movies being shown were sexually explicit. Which of the following decisions supports the trial court's exclusion of Doug's evidence?

    A. *California v. La Rue*

    B. *Stanley v. Georgia*

    C. *Paris Adult Theatre I v. Slaton*

    D. *Ernoznik v. City of Jacksonville*

96. In July, Dolly was indicted for violating §96(C), after police officers, acting pursuant to a valid search warrant, discovered a large cache of obscene movies in her home, which she candidly admitted constituted the inventory of a mail-order film business that she operated. Prior to trial, Dolly moved to quash the indictment on the ground that "*Stanley v. Georgia* precludes prosecution for possession of obscene material in the home." The trial court denied the motion, and Dolly appealed. How should the appellate court rule?

    A. Reverse, because of the holding in *United States v. Reidel*

    B. Reverse, because *Stanley* recognized a constitutional right to possess obscene material in the home for any purpose

    C. Affirm, because *Stanley* recognized a constitutional right to possess obscene material in the home for personal use, but did not recognize a constitutional right to possess obscene material in the home for commercial use

D. Affirm, because *Stanley* recognized a constitutional right to possess obscene material in the home for commercial use

97. In the absence of explicit consent by the applicable jurisdiction, which of the following statements is correct with respect to the Eleventh Amendment?

   A. It prevents a citizen of one state from obtaining a monetary judgment against individuals of another jurisdiction who were acting under color of that state's law.

   B. It prevents a citizen of one state from obtaining a monetary judgment against a county or city of another state.

   C. It prevents a citizen of one state from obtaining a monetary judgment against the state in which she resides.

   D. It prevents a citizen of a state from obtaining injunctive relief against officials of that state, even though the latter have acted in contravention of a federal law or the U.S. Constitution.

Questions 98-99 are based on the following facts:

Through a study based on information from the major industries in the jurisdiction, the legislature of state Yellow determined that (1) absenteeism during night shifts was higher among women than among men, and (2) much productivity was lost as a consequence of female absenteeism. The study showed that the reason for the higher rate of absenteeism among women was their need to be home with their children during periods of illness. Therefore, a state law was passed forbidding employers to hire women for night-shift work and assessing fines for violation thereof.

Jane Doe was denied employment with ABC Co. because of the state law. She filed suit against the appropriate state administrative officer, alleging that the act was unconstitutional.

98. State Yellow brought a motion to dismiss the complaint on the grounds that Jane had no standing to sue. How should the court rule?

   A. Jane has no standing because ABC is not being prosecuted by state Yellow under the act.

   B. Jane has no standing because she was not terminated from existing employment.

   C. Jane has standing because she has suffered pecuniary loss as the result of the act.

   D. Jane has standing only if she can show that similar employment in the area could not be found.

99. Jane claims that the act violates her right to equal protection under the law. How should the court rule on this claim?

   A. The act is constitutional if the state can demonstrate a rational basis for it.

   B. The act is unconstitutional unless the state can demonstrate that the legislation is substantially related to an important governmental objective.

   C. The act is unconstitutional because women are a suspect classification.

   D. The act is constitutional because there is no fundamental right to employment in a desired occupation.

100. John, a state senator in the state of X, is running for a new term of office. His opponent, James, owns the only local newspaper and radio station in John's hometown of Crossroads. The only local newspaper in Crossroads, the *Gazette*, published statements that were extremely derogatory of John's performance. Upon John's request for an opportunity to rebut the assertions contained in the *Gazette*, James refused. John has now commenced an action in the appropriate federal court, asserting that James's refusal to publish his rebuttal violated John's First Amendment rights. Which of the following statements is ***most accurate?***

   A. Where a political issue is involved, mass-media entities must offer equal access to opposing points of view.

   B. Newspapers are not required to give equal access to opposing points of view.

   C. Newspapers must give equal access to opposing points of view where a personal attack or political editorial has been printed.

   D. There is no rule requiring equal access with respect to mass-media entities.

101. Arthur Klubinski was a Bosnian Croat who visited the United States to raise money for the people in his country. He obtained a permit to speak at a public park. His speech was attended by about 200 Bosnian Croat immigrants to the United States and about 10 Muslim Americans. Klubinski made various derogatory comments, such as "All Muslims are liars" and "Muslims control the U.S. press." Suddenly, four of the Muslims in the crowd began to shake their fists angrily and advance toward Klubinski. There were 15 police officers at this event who had ringed Klubinski and the speaking podium.

Sensing a confrontation, the police asked Klubinski to discontinue his speech. When he refused, they arrested him pursuant to the local "breach of the peace" ordinance. (You may assume that this law was adequately drafted.) However, Klubinski now contends that his First Amendment rights had been violated, and so no prosecution can occur. Based on the foregoing, it is most likely that Klubinski

A. can be successfully convicted under the "fighting words" doctrine.

B. can be successfully convicted because his words were calculated to engender a violent response.

C. cannot be convicted because Klubinski was merely expressing an opinion (rather than making a statement that was factual in nature).

D. cannot be convicted because there were an adequate number of police present to restrain the persons moving toward the podium.

102. Amityville is normally a quiet Midwestern town. However, about 50 protesters recently picketed the town's abortion clinic. Although they refrained from blocking access to, or egress from, the clinic, members of the group waved "Murderer" and "Baby Killer" signs at the clinic staff, patrons, and passersby. A local ordinance forbids "the making of any public statement that is calculated to be offensive to the person addressed." In addition to the "Baby Killer" signs, the protesters also screamed "Killer" and "Murderer" at persons entering or leaving the clinic. Finally, several of the protesters were arrested and prosecuted under the above-mentioned ordinance.

Based on the foregoing, it is most likely that the arrested protesters

A. cannot be successfully prosecuted because the term "offensive" is too vague.

B. cannot be successfully prosecuted if they sincerely believed that the statements that they made were factually true.

C. can be successfully prosecuted because their conduct would be offensive to a reasonable person.

D. can be successfully prosecuted if the demonstrators intended their speech to offend the listener.

103. Bob Bilton, a citizen of the state of Euphoria, was fired from his job as a teacher at a public school. He subsequently asserted that his termination violated both Euphoria's state constitution and the Fourteenth

Amendment's Due Process Clause. He commenced an action in a Euphoria state court and requested a nonjury trial. The court ruled that each of Bob's assertions was correct and that he should be reinstated immediately. Euphoria then appealed the case to the state's supreme court, but the lower court's judgment was affirmed in all respects.

Euphoria now seeks review of the decision by the U.S. Supreme Court. Its writ of certiorari will probably be

A. rejected because it rests on independent and adequate state law grounds.

B. rejected because there is no U.S. Supreme Court review of state court decisions.

C. heard if the Supreme Court, in its discretion, decides to hear the case.

D. heard because there was a federal claim.

104. As a consequence of the "litigation explosion," federal district courts have become terribly clogged. In an effort to break this logjam, Congress enacted a law that eliminates diversity-of-citizenship jurisdiction completely.

Based on the foregoing, it is most likely that this statute is

A. unconstitutional because it violates the Equal Protection Clause.

B. unconstitutional because the U.S. Constitution specifically provides for cases between citizens of different states.

C. constitutional by virtue of the powers given to Congress in Article III, §1.

D. constitutional because cases between citizens of different states can be litigated in state courts.

105. Recently, a great deal of litigation has concerned breast implants. Many manufacturers have been obliged to seek protection under the bankruptcy laws because of these unforeseen lawsuits. Additionally, there are numerous studies that suggest that, even when successful, the breast implant process may have numerous harmful side effects. In response to this situation, Congress enacted a $3,000 tax on any breast implant procedure, to be paid by the operating surgeon prior to the implantation. The legislative history shows that the principal purpose of Congress in enacting this law was to discourage such implants and that a relatively small amount of revenue would be generated from it. In its first year, the legislation produced only about $1 million in collections.

Amy, a woman who seeks a breast implant, commenced an action to have the statute declared unconstitutional.

Based on the foregoing, it is most likely that the statute is

A. unconstitutional because it infringes on Amy's right of privacy.

B. unconstitutional because the statute's purpose was regulatory, rather than revenue-raising, in nature.

C. constitutional under Congress's power to "levy and collect taxes" as articulated in Article I, §8.

D. constitutional under Congress's power to legislate for the general welfare.

Questions 106-107 are based on the following facts:

Recently, several studies have indicated that highway accidents often resulted when drivers spilled liquids that they were drinking onto their laps. As a consequence, Congress enacted a statute requiring all cars to have cup or container holders. The federal statute also gave the minimum dimensions of each cup or container holder. Additionally, the act provided that states that prohibited the drinking of any type of liquid while driving would receive a specific amount of federal funds (based on the population of that jurisdiction) as a "safe driving" jurisdiction. In response to the federal statute, the state of Drunkaria passed a law that prohibited the drinking of any substance while driving. Ralph, who liked to drink his morning coffee while driving to work, has asserted that the federal statute is unconstitutional.

106. Based on the foregoing, the *strongest* basis for upholding the constitutionality of the federal law is that

A. the "no drinking" objective promotes highway safety and benefits the public welfare.

B. surveys throughout the country indicated that a vast majority of the people favored the "no drinking while driving" law.

C. when the states accepted federal monies to finance their highways, they ceded authority over these roads to the federal government.

D. assuming the federal government paid for a portion of the construction costs, it can regulate the use of state highways.

107. Based on the foregoing, the portion of the federal statute that predicates the disbursement of "bonus" highway funds on a prohibition against driving while drinking is most likely

A. constitutional only on the basis of the Commerce Clause.

B. constitutional only on the basis of the spending power.

    C. constitutional on the basis of both the Commerce Clause and the spending power.

    D. unconstitutional because it is an infringement on states' rights under the Tenth Amendment.

108. Citizens of the state of Euphoria have recently been complaining that most lawyers practicing in the state are extremely unethical. Several legislators have contended that the Euphoria attorneys who attended out-of-state law schools were exposed to professors who advocated overly liberal ideas and viewpoints, which was the primary cause for the moral deterioration of this group. As a consequence, the Euphoria legislature passed a law restricting admission to the bar in that jurisdiction to persons who had been educated at an in-state college and law school. Amy, a Euphoria citizen who attended college in Euphoria but law school in New York, believes that this statute is unconstitutional.

Based on the foregoing, it is most likely that the Euphoria statute is

    A. unconstitutional as an undue burden on interstate commerce.

    B. unconstitutional as a violation of the Privileges and Immunities Clause of the Fourteenth Amendment.

    C. constitutional because a state could reasonably believe that the quality of out-of-state law schools is inferior.

    D. constitutional because practicing law is a privilege (not a right) that states may bestow in any manner that they deem reasonable.

109. The city of Amityville has recently received numerous complaints about its police department. Many of its citizens contended that the police fail to enforce the laws adequately, often advising lawbreakers to "get out of town" rather than arresting them. A newspaper story concluded that approximately 60 percent of the Amityville police officers live outside of the city. In fact, many of the Amityville police officers live across a nearby river in the state of Peddle. As a consequence, the Amityville city council passed a law that required all new police officers to live within the city limits. The present members of the police force were given a three-year "grace" period to move into Amityville.

Based on the foregoing, the ***strongest*** argument that the Amityville law is unconstitutional would be under the

    A. Privileges and Immunities Clause of the Fourteenth Amendment.

    B. Due Process Clause of the Fourteenth Amendment.

C. Privileges and Immunities Clause of Article IV, §2.

D. Obligation of Contracts Clause.

110. The U.S. Senate was conducting hearings into organized crime. As part of its investigation, Al "Biggy" Boone was subpoenaed to testify before the appropriate committee. Although he was duly served, Boone failed to appear. A U.S. statute authorizes the U.S. attorney general to prosecute contempts of Congress. The Senate directed the U.S. attorney general to begin criminal contempt proceedings against Boone. However, the U.S. attorney general refused to commence any type of legal proceeding against him.

Based on the foregoing, the U.S. attorney general's nonaction is most likely

A. improper because the U.S. attorney general must prosecute if directed to do so by the Senate.

B. improper because the U.S. attorney general's primary function is to prosecute those who violate federal law.

C. proper because the U.S. attorney general decides, independently, which cases to prosecute.

D. proper because the decision to prosecute is exclusively an executive one.

111. Robert Anthracite was the U.S. ambassador to Slumberland. Unfortunately for Anthracite, a local newspaper reporter photographed the ambassador holding a famous model snugly in an intimate embrace. The picture was reprinted in numerous U.S. newspapers, which caused an uproar and demands for Anthracite's dismissal. Anthracite was subpoenaed by a House committee to appear before and testify about this incident. However, he refused to answer any questions posed to him that directly pertained to this incident. He did **not**, however, "take the Fifth."

Based on the foregoing, the **strongest** argument that Anthracite could assert as a defense is that

A. the questions were unrelated to matters on which Congress may legislate.

B. House committees may ask only about matters pertaining to the expenditure of funds.

C. because it was the body that confirmed his appointment, only the Senate may question Anthracite about matters that relate to his duties.

D. neither members of the U.S. House of Representatives nor members of the U.S. Senate may question the performance of duties by an executive officer.

112. The state of Euphoria has a 911 emergency phone line. Mary Smythe is an English citizen who moved to the United States three years ago. Mary has permanent resident status, but is not yet a U.S. citizen. Euphoria has a Public Utilities Commission (PUC) rule that only U.S. citizens can be 911 emergency operators. This rule was promulgated to make certain that persons answering the phone would understand and respond to the caller. Mary applied for a position as a 911 operator. Although otherwise completely qualified, her application was rejected because she is not a U.S. citizen. There is no question that Mary flawlessly speaks the "Queen's English."

Based on the foregoing, if Mary asserts that the Euphoria regulation is unconstitutional as applied to her, it is most likely that she

A. will prevail because the regulation has a rational basis.

B. will prevail because she is completely qualified to assume the position in question.

C. will not prevail because the regulation is rationally related to a legitimate governmental purpose.

D. will not prevail because the regulation satisfies an important governmental interest and is narrowly tailored to achieve that objective.

113. Shocked by recent studies that disclosed chronic jail overcrowding and the fact that criminals serve only about 25 percent of their prescribed time, Congress enacted legislation that would establish a nine-member Jail Reform Commission (JRC). The purpose of the JRC was to (1) investigate the reasons for jail overcrowding and early dismissal of convicts, (2) promulgate rules pertaining to the operation and functioning of jails to make them more efficient, and (3) establish a quasi-judicial system to prosecute any person or entity that failed to follow the rules that the JRC would issue. To ensure a nonpartisan response to the JRC, the chairperson was to be appointed by the vice president, four members were to be selected by the president pro tempore of the Senate, and four members by the Speaker of the House. (You may assume that standing exists.)

Based on the foregoing, the ***strongest*** argument that could be made to invalidate the legislation described above is that

A. legislative functions may not be delegated by Congress to an agency without clear, precise guidelines.

B. Congress had no constitutional basis to enact legislation dealing with these issues.

C. the legislation provides no opportunity for persons affected by the rules to contest them.

D. the JRC is unlawful because the president did not appoint its members.

114. Recently, there has been a spate of complaints to local and federal legislators by persons who found that mortgages had been unknowingly placed on their homes as part of a program to encourage borrowing for substantial improvements to their dwellings. These complainants have contended that, in many instances, the improvements were inadequately made. Besides, it took the homeowners several years to remove the mortgages, which impaired their ability to obtain credit. The actions commenced in state court to remove the mortgages often took two or more years to conclude. As a consequence, Congress enacted a federal law that required full disclosure by the home improvement entity and allowed for an action to be brought by a complainant in the U.S. district court whose jurisdiction included the site of the subject home.

    Several lending institutions objected to the federal law. They brought an action contending that the statute was unconstitutional.

    Based on the foregoing, the ***strongest*** basis for sustaining the validity of this statute is the

    A. Obligation of Contracts Clause.

    B. Commerce Clause.

    C. Equal Protection Clause of the Fourteenth Amendment.

    D. Privileges and Immunities Clause of the Fourteenth Amendment.

115. The U.S. government was extremely concerned about germ warfare. The CIA had developed information that certain foreign subversive groups might use germ warfare to extort large amounts of money or punish nations that they believed were hostile to their causes. As a consequence, the CIA entered into a written contract with XYZ University in the state of Euphoria. Under this agreement, the university was to document the effects of a large-scale biological research project. The program was scheduled to last about three years and

involve about 5,000 animals (such as dogs, cats, and monkeys). XYZ University was to be paid approximately $1,000,000 for performing this research and presenting its written results to the CIA.

The Save Our Animals Society (SOAS) asserts that this program is unconstitutional and should be invalidated. The SOAS, after an expensive lobbying effort, persuaded the Euphoria legislature to pass an act that prohibited the use of domestic animals and monkeys for biological research purposes.

Based on the foregoing, which of the following represents the **least likely** basis for invalidating the Euphoria law?

A. Takings Clause

B. Commerce Clause

C. Supremacy Clause

D. Impairment of Contracts Clause

116. The state of Bootah has a statute that makes it unlawful to make a speech, picket, or demonstrate within 200 feet of any government building or of any building in which a Bootah governmental entity has an office. Mary Brighton, a former state legislator who voted against this law five years ago, would like to make a speech in front of the state Welfare Department's main office. The purpose of the speech is to contend that this entity is far too lenient with respect to welfare "cheats." Brighton is planning to run for state senator.

Based on the foregoing, which of the following situations represents the **most likely** basis on which Brighton could obtain a hearing in a federal court challenging the validity of the Bootah statute?

A. She is intending to run for office in the next election.

B. She voted against the statute when it was enacted by the Bootah state legislature.

C. She is a member of an organization that seeks to invalidate welfare funding measures that waste taxpayer monies.

D. Brighton had been a Bootah state taxpayer for the preceding three years.

117. The U.S. Congress recently enacted a law that expressed support for colleges of all types. Shortly thereafter, the Department of the Interior donated land that it owned to Armstrong College, a private religious institution. The gift did not specify, however, that no religious instruction take place within classrooms built on the donated land. Malcolm and Malena Cooper commenced an action in the

appropriate U.S. district court, contending that the gift constituted a violation of the First Amendment requirement of church-state separation. The Coopers are U.S. taxpayers and avowed atheists.

On these facts, it is most likely that

A. the gift is unconstitutional because the college made no commitment that only secular courses would be taught on the donated land.

B. the gift is unconstitutional because only Congress may convey a gift of U.S. property.

C. the gift is constitutional because this appears to be merely a one-time conveyance of U.S. property.

D. the Coopers lack standing to challenge the gift.

118. Recently, the state of Euphoria ended its local welfare system. As a consequence, numerous state legislators received death threats. The Euphoria legislature responded by enacting a statute that made it illegal to "threaten, or to incite another, to commit bodily harm upon any Euphoria public official while in the course of, or as a result of, the performance of his or her duties." Jim Blender wrote to the Euphoria legislator for his district. His letter stated, "You've hurt me more than you can imagine. You deserve to die for what you've done. You're a callous beast who should rot in hell. Die, die, you SOB."

Based on the foregoing, if the Euphoria attorney general commences an action against Blender under the statute described above, it is most likely that

A. the statute is unconstitutionally vague.

B. the statute is unconstitutionally overbroad.

C. the statute is constitutional, but cannot serve as the basis for punishment in this situation.

D. the statute is constitutional, and Blender can be punished pursuant to it.

Questions 119-120 are based on the following facts:

State X enacts a new tax on abortion services. Every abortion service provider must pay a tax of $1,000 per abortion to the general treasury of state X. Reproductive Choices (RC) operates a family-planning clinic in Capital City, the largest city in X. After the new tax goes into effect, RC brings a lawsuit in the appropriate federal district court, seeking judicial invalidation of the new tax.

119. The **strongest** argument in favor of the court invalidating the tax would be based on the

    A. Privileges and Immunities Clause of Article IV, §2.

    B. Dormant Commerce Clause.

    C. Bill of Attainder Clause.

    D. Due Process Clause of the Fourteenth Amendment.

119. The reviewing court should **not** invalidate the law unless

    A. the law rationally fails to advance a legitimate state interest.

    B. the law imposes an undue burden on access to abortion services.

    C. the law has a substantial relationship to an important governmental interest.

    D. the law directly advances a compelling state interest.

Questions 121-122 are based on the following facts:

The state of Euphoria has been encouraging the sale of locally produced wines and beers. Although alcohol sales are usually strictly regulated by the Euphoria Alcohol Control Board (ACB), the state legislature adopts a law permitting in-state wineries and breweries to ship wine and beer directly to residents of Euphoria, provided that the customer appears in person to make the initial order and the seller verifies the buyer's age to ensure compliance with Euphoria's minimum-age requirement for the sale and possession of intoxicating beverages, including wine and beer.

121. Angry at the competitive advantage Euphoria wine and beer producers will enjoy through their ability to directly ship products to Euphoria residents, a group of out-of-state wineries and breweries initiate a constitutional challenge to the new law in federal district court. The **strongest** argument in favor of finding the Euphoria direct-shipment law unconstitutional would be that

    A. it violates the Privileges and Immunities Clause of Article IV, §2.

    B. it violates the Dormant Commerce Clause.

    C. it violates the Twenty-first Amendment.

    D. it violates the Equal Protection Clause.

122. If Euphoria's legislature wished to make it more likely that a federal reviewing court would sustain the law permitting direct shipment from local wineries and breweries, it should amend the law by

    A. permitting Euphoria wineries and breweries to ship products directly to out-of-state residents.

    B. permitting Euphoria wineries and breweries to make initial sales for direct shipment on the Internet as well as in person.

C. permitting the direct shipment of hard liquor produced by in-state companies.

D. permitting out-of-state wineries and breweries to directly ship their products to residents of Euphoria, provided that the seller registers with the Euphoria ACB, the initial sale occurs in person, and the seller enforces Euphoria's minimum-age laws for the sale of wine and beer to residents of Euphoria.

123. Washington High School releases its students so they can see the local university basketball team, which recently won the national championship, participate in a victory parade. As the parade approaches the school, Jane Smith, a sophomore at Washington High School, unfurls a banner that says "SteroidHits-4-U!!!" Smith was standing on a public sidewalk adjacent to the school grounds at the time she unfurled the banner. Principal Skinner, fearing public embarrassment and disruption of the event, rips up the banner. The high school subsequently suspends Smith for two weeks as punishment for "disrupting a school event" and also for "advocating the use of unlawful drugs, in violation of official school policy against drug abuse." Suppose that Smith challenged her punishment in federal district court, alleging a violation of her First Amendment rights with respect to both the suspension and the destruction of the banner. The most likely outcome of the case would be

A. judgment for the plaintiff because the principal cannot discipline a student for conduct that occurs off school property.

B. judgment for the plaintiff because the sign related to a matter of public concern and the facts do not suggest that a disruption in the high school occurred or was likely to occur.

C. judgment for the defendant because the banner could reasonably be construed as advocacy of illegal drug use by student athletes.

D. judgment for the defendant because the principal has a right to control speech related to the high school's curriculum.

124. Incident to the execution of a valid search warrant of Congressman Swindle's home in Alexandria, Virginia, FBI agents discover $89,000 in cash in his freezer, organized in bundles of sequential $100 bills and repackaged into Swanson frozen lasagna boxes. Swindle refuses to answer any questions about the source of the money, invoking his Fifth Amendment right against self-incrimination. Believing the cash to be a bribe from agents of a foreign government, the FBI secures a second search warrant to search Congressman Swindle's

official congressional office on Capitol Hill, in the Rayburn House Office Building, located in Washington, D.C. The warrant specifically authorizes agents to examine paper and electronic records related to the alleged bribe. The FBI seizes all of Congressman Swindle's file cabinets and computers, removes them to its headquarters for examination, and refuses to permit Congressman Swindle or his staff access to either the paper files or the computers during the pendency of the criminal investigation. Based on the foregoing, if Swindle seeks to quash the warrant, suppress the evidence gathered incident to the search of his official office, and obtain the prompt return of his files and computers, the local district court will likely

A. quash the warrant, suppress the evidence gathered incident to the execution of the warrant, and order the return of the files and computers because the FBI search violated the Speech and Debate Clause of Article I, §6, cl. 1.

B. quash the warrant, suppress the evidence gathered incident to the execution of the warrant, and order the return of the files and computers because the FBI search usurped the power of each house of Congress to "determine the Rules of its Proceedings, punish its Members for disorderly Behaviour, and with the Concurrence of two thirds, expel a Member" under Article I, §5, clause 2.

C. deny the motion to quash and suppress because the search did not take place on the floor of the House of Representatives.

D. deny the motion to quash and suppress because the Supreme Court has held that the Speech and Debate Clause does not protect a member of Congress from answering criminal bribery charges related to his duties of office.

125. To prevent voter fraud and better secure the integrity of the ballot, the state legislature of New Augusta enacts a requirement that all voters must show a valid government-issued form of photographic identification at the polls. To ensure that indigent voters are not unduly burdened by this new requirement, the state will issue a free photographic voter identification card to any person who seeks such a card at any county courthouse or city hall. If challenged in federal court, this law would probably be

A. invalidated as a violation of the Fifteenth Amendment.

B. invalidated as a violation of the Equal Protection Clause of the Fourteenth Amendment.

C. sustained as a "necessary and proper" means of combating voter fraud under Article I, §8, clause 18.

D. sustained as advancing a sufficiently weighty state interest in preventing voter fraud in a narrowly tailored way that does not facially unduly restrict or abridge the fundamental right to vote.

126. Concerned about a recent spate of colleges and universities barring military recruiters from their campuses, Congress enacts and the president signs a bill that conditions receipt of "any federal funds used to support higher education, including but not limited to federal student financial aid and any grants issued by a department or agency of the federal government to support research and development programs" on the recipient institution, and "requiring all university units to afford access to military recruiters on terms no less favorable than those provided to nonmilitary private employers." State University has adopted a nondiscrimination policy that prohibits employers who discriminate on the basis of race, sex, religion, national origin, disability, marital status, or sexual orientation from recruiting at the university. At the same time, many divisions of State University receive federally funded grant money, and thousands of State University students receive various forms of federal financial aid. Based on the foregoing, if State University refuses to permit military recruiters on campus but continues to accept federal funds, the military

A. would prevail in requiring State University to provide it with equal access to the university's recruiting services because Congress may condition the receipt of federal funds on compliance with conditions of its choosing, provided that the conditions are clear, reasonably relate to the purpose of the program at issue, and the recipient is free to accept or decline the subsidy.

B. would prevail because State University's policy of denying the military access to student recruiting facilities is preempted by federal law under the Supremacy Clause.

C. would not prevail because the restriction imposes an unconstitutional condition on State University.

D. would not prevail because the restriction coerces State University to speak in favor of discrimination against gays and lesbians.

Questions 127-128 are based on the following facts:

Farm City owns and maintains City Park, a large public park, with walking paths, tennis courts, benches, and picnic tables. In 1945, at the end of World War II, the city council of Farm City voted to erect a memorial, at a prominent point in the very center of the park, to members of the armed forces who died in the conflict, as part of a war memorial grove. Since 1945, Farm City has augmented the memorial grove with additional monuments to those who served and died in the Korean Conflict, the Vietnam Conflict, the First Gulf War, and the Second Gulf War. Private veterans' organizations actually donated and placed the last three of these monuments, with the express approval of the city, which now owns the monuments and maintains them.

127. Citizens for Peace, a local civic group that advocates pacifism, upset by the placement of what its members view as a group of blatantly "pro-war" monuments in such a prominent public space, seeks permission to place a peace monument in the memorial grove. The peace monument would consist of a tasteful obelisk with the peace symbol emblazoned on all four sides and a large bronze dove holding an olive branch in its beak at the top. The city declines to accept the monument, and Citizens for Peace brings suit, seeking an injunction forcing the city to accept the monument and to place it in the memorial grove. The federal district court should rule

   A. in favor of the plaintiff because if the city accepts one monument for public display it must accept all monuments for public display in the memorial grove.

   B. in favor of the plaintiff because the city has created a limited-purpose public forum for speech related to war and the proposed monument fits within the scope of the forum.

   C. in favor of the city because the government may decide which messages it wishes to communicate on public land when the government itself is the speaker.

   D. in favor of the city because the city created a limited-purpose public forum for speech in favor of military service and the plaintiff's proposed monument opposes military service.

128. During the pendency of the litigation over its proposed monument, Citizens for Peace decides to conduct a public protest of the memorial grove in the grove itself (which is generally open to the public, just like the other parts of City Park). Members create signs and placards protesting the war memorials and arguing that military service should not be encouraged or celebrated. At the onset of the protest, city police officers insist that the demonstrators leave the memorial

grove and relocate their protest to a sidewalk on the edge of City Park, a location more than 200 yards from the memorial grove. After being threatened with arrest for disorderly conduct and breach of the peace, the protestors leave the memorial grove voluntarily and without further incident. The local chapter of the ACLU brings suit against Farm City and seeks an injunction permitting the use of the memorial grove for an antiwar protest by Citizens for Peace members. Farm City will *most likely*

- A. not prevail in limiting the protest because protestors have an unqualified right to use government property such as a park for speech activity.

- B. not prevail in limiting the protest because the police were not enforcing a content- and viewpoint-neutral reasonable time, place, and manner regulation that limits speech activity either in the park generally or in the memorial grove in particular.

- C. prevail in limiting protests proximate to the memorial grove because the protestors sought to dishonor the dead war veterans.

- D. prevail in limiting protests proximate to the memorial grove because the city may limit speech in the memorial grove to speech sympathetic to and respectful of deceased military service people.

129. The state of Alpha adopts a new statute that prohibits "protesting or otherwise attempting to disrupt a funeral or burial service." Violations of the new law are punishable by "a fine of up to $10,000 and a term of imprisonment not to exceed two years." After the enactment of this law, the members of the Eastwick Village Church (EVC) go to Centerville, a town in Alpha, and engage in a nondisruptive, peaceful protest of a funeral. At all times during their protest, EVC members remain on public streets or sidewalks and fully comply with the generally applicable regulations governing the time, place, and manner of protest on public property in Centerville. Local police officers nevertheless arrest the EVC members, and the local district attorney indicts them under the state's new anti-funeral protest law. The defendants move to dismiss the charges. The state trial could should

- A. deny the motion to dismiss because the statute is a valid time, place, or manner regulation.

- B. deny the motion to dismiss because the statute is content neutral.

C. grant the motion to dismiss because the statute is *not* content neutral.

D. grant the motion to dismiss because the statute violates the Free Exercise Clause.

130. The state of Arden enacts a law that requires all would-be purchasers of firearms to enroll in a firearms safety course prior to completing the purchase of a gun. Francis Jones (FJ), a resident of Arden, seeks to purchase a gun and does not wish to take the mandatory firearms safety course. She goes to the Acme Gun Store and attempts to purchase a gun, but the store owner refuses to sell her the gun unless FJ first presents a certificate showing that she has completed the mandatory state firearms safety course. If FJ were to bring a lawsuit in federal district court seeking invalidation of Arden's firearms safety training requirement, the **most likely** outcome is

A. the law will be invalidated based on the Privileges and Immunities Clause of the Fourteenth Amendment.

B. the law will be invalidated based on the Second Amendment.

C. FJ's suit will be dismissed because the plaintiff lacks standing.

D. the law will be sustained against FJ's constitutional challenge.

131. Church operates a religiously affiliated school in the state of Columbia. Principal John Smith fires Mary Jones, a biology teacher at the school, for allegedly holding "heretical" views. A local state law in Columbia prohibits employers who employ more than 15 persons from "discriminating on the basis of religion or religious belief." Although the law includes an exception for ministers, it does not exempt employees at church-affiliated schools, including teachers, from its scope. The school employs more than 15 persons. Jones initiates a civil action under the law against C seeking back pay and reinstatement to her job. On these facts, the most likely outcome of this litigation is

A. Church will prevail because the state law cannot constitutionally be applied to a teacher in a religiously-affiliated school.

B. Church will prevail because the government cannot regulate any church-sponsored enterprises.

C. Jones will prevail because the state has a duty to prohibit religious discrimination.

D. Jones will prevail because the state law may constitutionally be applied to prevent religious discrimination by any employers within the state.

132. The state of Valhalla (V) amends its state constitution to grant its elected governor a 20-year term of office. Jane Smith (JS), a citizen and registered voter of V, objects to such a long term for an elected state official. JS initiates litigation in the local federal district court, alleging a violation of the Guaranty Clause. V files a motion to dismiss. On these facts, the district court will **most likely**

- **A.** deny the motion to dismiss because a 20-year term of office violates the Guaranty Clause of Article IV, '4.

- **B.** deny the motion to dismiss because the 20-year term of office violates the Supremacy Clause of Article VI, cl. 2.

- **C.** grant the motion to dismiss because JS lacks standing to bring the suit.

- **D.** grant the motion to dismiss because the claim presents a nonjusticiable political question.

133. Congress, concerned about the safety and well-being of children, enacts a new law that permits the Department of Justice to seek the involuntary civil commitment of any convicted sex offenders within the federal prison system after such offenders have completed their federal prison sentence. If the power of Congress to enact this law were called into question before the Supreme Court, the **most relevant** provision of the Constitution would be

- **A.** the Commerce Clause, Art. I, §8, cl. 3.

- **B.** the Property Clause of Article IV, §3, cl. 2.

- **C.** the Necessary and Proper Clause, Art. I, §8, cl. 18.

- **D.** the Taxing and Spending Clause, Art. I, §8, cl. 1.

134. The state of Arcadia (A) adopts a law prohibiting the sale of "unduly violent video or computer games to persons under 18 years of age." Savmart (S), a large discount chain store doing business in A, sells computer games to minors, including games that arguably fall within the scope of the new state law prohibiting such sales. If S were to challenge the prohibition in a local federal court, the **most likely** outcome of the case would be

- **A.** the law will be invalidated on First Amendment grounds.

- **B.** the law will be invalidated on Equal Protection grounds.

- **C.** the law will be sustained.

- **D.** the case will be dismissed on standing grounds.

135. XYZ Corporation (XYZ) donates $50,000 to the campaign of a candidate for the U.S. Senate from the state of Avalon. Under the applicable federal campaign finance law, corporations are completely barred from making contributions to the campaigns of candidates for federal elective office. The statute provides for both civil and criminal sanctions for violations. The U.S. Attorney for Avalon seeks and obtains a criminal indictment against XYZ for violating the federal statutory ban on corporate campaign contributions to candidates for federal elective office. At a pretrial hearing, XYZ moves to quash the indictment, arguing that the federal statutory ban on corporations making campaign contributions violates XYZ's First Amendment rights. Under current Supreme Court precedents, which describes the ***most likely*** outcome of the motion to dismiss?

   A. The district court should deny the motion because Congress may constitutionally prohibit corporations from donating money to the campaigns of candidates for federal office.

   B. The district court should deny the motion because Congress may prohibit corporations from donating money under the Guaranty Clause of Article IV, §4.

   C. The district court should grant the motion based on the First Amendment.

   D. The district court should grant the motion based on the Equal Protection Clause.

136. Congress enacts a law that establishes criminal penalties for offering bribes to state or local officials "of entities that receive at least $10,000 in federal funds per year." Defendant (D) was indicated and convicted of offering a bribe to a Ruralville city council member. On appeal, D argues that the federal antibribery law is unconstitutional. In resolving this claim, which of the following constitutional provisions would be *least* relevant?

   A. The Commerce Clause

   B. The Property Clause

   C. The Spending Clause

   D. The Eleventh Amendment

137. Congress enacts amendments to the Securities and Exchange Act (Act) that authorize administrative law judges (ALJs) working for the SEC to hear and decide common law claims, provided that such claims are "integral to core proceedings arising under the Act and the regulations implementing it." ALJs are not Article III judges. Under the new statutory amendments, the SEC's jurisdiction over such common law claims does not depend on the consent of both parties but instead is mandatory. A U.S. district court may hear an appeal from an ALJ's decision involving a common law claim, but the statute provides that "it may review the ALJ's findings of fact only for clear error." Defendant objects to the adjudication of her common law contract claim in an SEC administrative adjudication before an ALJ. If the Supreme Court heard this case, it would

A. sustain the SEC's new jurisdiction over common law claims because Congress may define the jurisdiction of the lower federal courts under Article III, §2.

B. sustain the SEC's jurisdiction over common law claims because the contract claim constitutes a public right.

C. invalidate the SEC's jurisdiction over common law claims because it violates the non-delegation doctrine.

D. invalidate the SEC's jurisdiction over common law claims because it violates the separation of powers.

138. The Consumer Protection Commission (CPC) consists of five members, appointed by the president and confirmed by the Senate. The president may only remove CPC members for "good cause shown." The CPC's organic act provides that good cause findings are subject to judicial review. Congress creates a new entity within the CPC, the Credit Card Fair Marketing Committee (FMC). Members of the FMC will be appointed by the CPC to four-year terms of office and are subject to supervision by its members. FMC members may be removed prior to the expiration of their terms of office by the CPC *only* "for good cause shown" and may seek judicial review of good cause findings. The statutory provision limiting removal of FMC members to "good cause" probably

A. is unconstitutional because it violates the separation of powers doctrine.

B. is unconstitutional because it violates the nondelegation doctrine.

C. is unconstitutional because it violates the Commerce Clause.

D. is constitutional.

Multiple-Choice Answers

1. **B** A party lacks standing unless he has suffered a direct injury as a consequence of the defendant's conduct. When the plaintiff suffers a diminution of enjoyment in the performance of an activity, that diminution of enjoyment constitutes an adequate "injury" for standing purposes; the harm need not be economic in nature. *Sierra Club v. Morton.* Because Kevin has used and will continue to use the facility covered by the legislation, he has arguably been injured by the secretary of the interior's failure to perform his statutory duties. Choice **A** is incorrect because there is no *per se* right of U.S. citizens to sue a federal official for failure to perform her duties. There must be a direct injury to the plaintiff. Choice **C** is incorrect because, although the statement of law is accurate, Kevin has, in fact, suffered a direct and immediate injury. Finally, choice **D** is incorrect because the failure to incur economic loss does **not** preclude an otherwise "injured" party from maintaining an action.

2. **C** To avoid violating the Establishment Clause, governmental assistance to religious schools (1) must have a secular purpose, (2) must neither advance nor inhibit religion, and (3) must not entangle government with religion. Governmental services may ordinarily be rendered at religious schools where the activity is provided on a neutral basis and does not involve a public employee in providing religious education. *Zobrest v. Catalina Foothills School District.* The state may offer services to students attending religiously affiliated schools on a neutral basis, which is precisely what is happening here. Choice **D** is incorrect because services rendered by public employees at religiously affiliated schools need not be limited to those involving a brief, impersonal visit. Choice **A** is incorrect because the fact that governmental services are provided at the religious institution does not make the activity *per se* unconstitutional. The rendering of such services must, however, ordinarily be on a neutral basis. Finally, choice **B** is incorrect because reimbursement to religious schools or their students for the cost of complying with state-mandated activities is ordinarily valid. *Committee for Public Education v. Regan.*

3. **C** Generally applicable criminal statutes whose purpose is not to burden a particular religious belief are constitutional, regardless of the extent to which a religious tenet is burdened by the legislation. *Employment Division v. Smith.* In addition, no balancing of the state's interest in its prohibition against the burden on the individual's beliefs need be carried out provided that the ban is generally applicable and not motivated by government animus, or prejudice, toward a particular

religion or group of religionists. Because the criminal legislation (1) is generally applicable and (2) was not intended to hinder the Aarp religion, it is constitutional. Choice **D** is incorrect because no judicial "weighing" is required in this situation. Finally, choices **A** and **B** are incorrect because it is irrelevant whether the religious tenet involved is a major or minor one. In either event, the law appears to be constitutional in this situation.

4. **C** A "taking" of property occurs where (1) the owner of land is basically deprived of any economically viable use of her property; or (2) the owner's reasonable, investment-backed expectations are upset by an unreasonable governmental action that substantially affects the property's value. *Lingle v. Chevron U.S.A., Inc.* Bobco is **not** being deprived of **any** viable use of its land, and the present activity is allowed to continue for five more years. In addition, the effect on the property's value might actually be positive, the government is abating a nuisance, and Bobco has not suffered a significant harm to its *reasonable*, investment-backed expectations. Thus, no "taking" will be deemed to have occurred. Choice **A** is incorrect because an owner has no *per se* right to operate land in any manner she would like to do so. Choice **B** is incorrect because the fact that Bobco's facility preceded the surrounding residential nature of the area does **not** preclude the enactment of legislation limiting Bobco's use of the land. (Note that the Due Process Clause of the Fifth Amendment is applicable to the states via the Fourteenth Amendment.) Finally, choice **D** is incorrect because the taking must unreasonably affect the landowner's ownership interest; the abstract reasonableness of the land use regulation is irrelevant to the Takings Clause analysis.

5. **A** Under the doctrine of inherent sovereign powers, Congress is empowered to enact legislation pertaining to external affairs. Under the doctrine of inherent sovereign powers, the sovereign (i.e., the federal government) has the inherent power to legislate in those areas traditionally occupied by a central government (whether or not specifically recognized in the U.S. Constitution). *United States v. Curtiss-Wright Export Corp.* Thus, Congress would have the right to make it a crime for any citizen to negotiate with a foreign government. Choice **B** is incorrect because whatever inherent power the president might have to negotiate on behalf of the United States with foreign countries, it could **not** serve as a basis for the enactment of federal legislation by Congress. Choice **C** is incorrect because there is no proposition of law that legislation pertaining to foreign relations is exempted from

the First Amendment. Finally, choice **D** is legally incorrect because criminal laws pertaining to international affairs must be as specific as those dealing with domestic matters.

6. **A** Under the U.S. Constitution, states are prohibited from enacting *ex post facto* laws. U.S. Const. art. I, §10. An *ex post facto* law is one that retroactively (1) makes particular conduct illegal, (2) increases the severity in the definition of criminal conduct, (3) increases the punishment for a crime, or (4) alters the rules of evidence for a particular act. *Collins v. Youngblood.* The applicable statute was ***not*** in effect when the crime was committed. Thus, Dellum's actions were defined more severely retroactively (and the prohibition against *ex post facto* laws violated). Choice **B** is incorrect because Dellum's knowledge (or lack of knowledge) of the possible sentence for aggravated robbery has no effect on his right to assert the *ex post facto* defense. Choice **C** is incorrect because the moment at which Dellum was actually charged is irrelevant. The severity of punishment for a criminal act cannot be enhanced retroactively to the date of the act. Finally, choice **D** is factually incorrect (similar conduct constituted ***both*** aggravated robbery and armed robbery). As discussed above, the *ex post facto* prohibition is operative.

7. **B** Commercial speech may be restricted, even though it involves a lawful activity and is not misleading, if the restriction (1) directly promotes a substantial governmental interest and (2) is no more extensive than necessary to effectuate the governmental interest. However, the government may not restrict commercial speech when a more direct means exists to advance the government's interests. *Greater New Orleans Broadcasting Assn. v. United States.* Here, increased taxes or a direct ban on cigarette sales would be more direct means available to the government to advance its interest in promoting health. Accordingly, the law is unconstitutional on free-speech grounds. Choice **D** is incorrect because it does not state the grounds for upholding the statute and because advertising is ***not*** "misleading" merely because it fails to disclose negative information about the product. Choice **A** is incorrect because there is no colorable equal-protection difficulty with the statute. It applies to everyone and is rationally related to a legitimate governmental interest. Finally, choice **C** is incorrect because, as discussed above, the legislation uses a ban on commercial speech, rather than direct regulations such as new taxes or a ban on cigarette sales.

8. D An organization has standing if it can show that (1) the legislation in question causes an injury in fact to its members, who would thereby have a right to sue on their own behalf; (2) the injury is related to the organization's purpose; and (3) the nature of the lawsuit does **not** require the participation of the individual members. *Hunt v. Washington Apple Advertising Commission.* Presumably, most doctors have receptionists at their offices; accordingly, there has been a measurable injury to the individual members of the APA. Choice **C** is incorrect because it merely asserts a substantive basis for negating the law without addressing the issue of standing. (This assertion is dubious anyway because the statute is probably rationally related to a legitimate governmental purpose—enhancing federal revenues from a group capable of absorbing the loss of this deduction.) Choice **A** is incorrect because the statute's application to all professionals does not destroy standing by the physicians' organization, one of the professional groups affected. Finally, choice **B** is incorrect because the APA does not lack standing; at least some of its individual members are adversely affected by the law.

9. C In *Norwood v. Harrison*, the U.S. Supreme Court held that a program in which textbooks were purchased by the state and loaned to students in private schools that practiced racial discrimination was unconstitutional. The decision stated that a state could not constitutionally give "significant aid to institutions that practice racial or other invidious discrimination." Because in this case the computers are being given to a school that denies admission to Hispanics, the program to distribute computers is unconstitutional. Choice **D** is incorrect because, although the distribution of computers may promote a significant educational function, the distribution may not be used to favor one racial group over another. Choice **B** is incorrect because it is overly broad. The Constitution does not forbid private discrimination of any kind. Finally, choice **A** is incorrect because states may assist private schools, provided the help is secular and does not involve undue governmental entanglement with religion.

10. B The Establishment Clause of the First Amendment is **not** violated where a governmental activity (1) has a secular purpose, (2) has a secular effect, and (3) does not promote excessive governmental entanglement with religion. Euphoria's purpose in distributing computers to its students is presumably to enhance the computer literacy of its citizens. In *Mitchell v. Helms*, the Supreme Court sustained a state program that provided computers to religiously affiliated schools to implement "secular, neutral, and nonideological" school programs. Thus, absent facts not provided, St. Mary's could probably successfully contend that the distribution of computers to it causes no impermissible state-church entanglement. Choice **A** is incorrect because its proposition is stated too broadly. Not all state-promoted instruction at private schools *is permissible*; state-promoted instruction at a religious private school is constitutionally ***impermissible*** if it promotes state-church entanglement (i.e., if Euphoria sent religion class teachers to religious schools, this action would be patently unconstitutional). Choice **D** is incorrect because state action may not violate the Establishment Clause, even if the educational function promoted is an important one. Finally, choice **C** states an incorrect proposition of law. The Free Exercise Clause does ***not*** mandate similar treatment of public and religious private schools.

11. **B** Under the Free Exercise Clause of the First Amendment (applicable to the states via the Fourteenth Amendment), a generally applicable law burdening religious practices is constitutional, provided that it was not enacted or maintained based on *animus* toward a particular sect. *Employment Division v. Smith.* Even though religious practices may be regulated incident to general laws, "free exercise means, first and foremost, the right to believe and profess whatever religious doctrine one desires." Hence, even if the law might be constitutional as applied to Doe, the reviewing court cannot second-guess the plausibility of his religious beliefs. In determining whether the Free Exercise Clause has been violated, a court may ***not*** look into the reasonableness of the religious belief asserted. Choice **C** is incorrect because a court may determine if the conduct asserted by the plaintiff is truly required by the tenets and beliefs of the person's religion. Choice **D** is incorrect because a court may determine if the party is sincere in the exercise of her religious beliefs. *United States v. Ballard.* Finally, choice **A** is incorrect because, under *Smith*, the burden of establishing that a statute infringes "free exercise" rights is ordinarily on the challenger.

12. **D** Classifications based on age are ordinarily reviewed under the rational-basis test (i.e., the statute is valid if there is a reasonable relationship between a legitimate governmental objective and the legislative means selected to accomplish that purpose). Because the rational-relationship test is applicable, Prentis would have to argue that the statute invidiously discriminates against him (i.e., there is

no rational relationship between the classification made by the statute and the purpose that it seeks to achieve). Choice **B** is incorrect because, in the absence of a legitimate expectation to the contrary, there is no property right to permanent public employment. *Bishop v. Wood*. Choice **A** is incorrect because the Privileges and Immunities Clause contained in the Fourteenth Amendment has been construed as precluding *a state* from impairing "national" rights (i.e., the right to travel from state to state, the right to petition Congress for grievances, the right to vote for national officers, the right to assemble and communicate with respect to national legislation, etc.). Finally, choice **C** is incorrect because the legislation in question would be within the specific grant of congressional power to "raise and support armies"; Article I, §8.

13. **C** The ability to compete for political office is ordinarily judged by the application of strict scrutiny. The governmental restriction must further "vital state objectives" that could not be accomplished by "significantly less burdensome" means. *American Party of Texas v. White*. Although a state has a legitimate interest in limiting ballot placement to viable candidates, this could presumably still be accomplished by requiring a lower percentage of voters' signatures and/or an adequate amount of financial assets. An excessive requirement in the number of registered voters' signatures arguably keeps potentially viable candidates off the ballot. Choice **D** is incorrect because a voters' signature requirement is not, *per se*, unreasonable. The Supreme Court has upheld a "5 percent of voters in the previous election" requirement. Choice **B** is incorrect because, although it may be the fact that relatively few candidates have succeeded in meeting the voters' signature requirement, that does not justify a system that effectively prevents unpopular candidates from getting on the ballot. Finally, choice **A** is incorrect because, although a state does have an interest in keeping the number of candidates from becoming confusingly large, the requirement for support among 20 percent of ***all*** registered voters is probably too difficult.

14. **A** The right to vote has been determined to be a fundamental right for purposes of applying the Fourteenth Amendment's Equal Protection Clause. *Harper v. Virginia Board of Elections*. Thus, the statute is constitutional only if it accomplishes a compelling governmental interest and there is no less burdensome means of accomplishing this objective. Although there is certainly a governmental interest in requiring voters to be literate, there is probably no "compelling" interest in

making certain that they have this ability in the English language only. A voter could arguably be adequately informed about the issues and candidates through reading material in Spanish and through the other media or conversations with other persons. Because the statute imposes a restrictive classification among otherwise equally eligible voters, the statute violates the Equal Protection Clause. Choice **D** is incorrect because Article I, §2, of the Constitution does not prevent the states from enforcing the same requirements for voting in congressional elections as they do in state elections. Choice **B** is incorrect because, although the right to vote is a fundamental one under the Due Process Clause, the Equal Protection Clause constitutes a stronger argument because this statute imposes a restrictive *classification* among otherwise equally eligible voters. Finally, choice **C** is incorrect because Article I, §4, of the Constitution does not give the federal government exclusive control of voters' rights in federal elections. The states may impose the same limitations on voters in federal elections as they do in state elections.

15. **A** The Contracts Clause of the U.S. Constitution prohibits the impairment of contractual rights, unless necessary to achieve a "significant public purpose." *Energy Reserves Group v. Kansas Power & Light Co.* Although the improvement of existing highways is a legitimate state function, there are no facts that indicate that the necessity for these repairs had reached emergency proportions. Moreover, the federal courts scrutinize a state government's decision to invalidate contracts to which it is a party with particular care. *United States Trust Co. v. New Jersey.* Here, Macon is voiding a contract to which it is a party. Thus, rescission of the construction contract is probably constitutionally invalid. Choice **D** is incorrect because the Eleventh Amendment provides only that states may not be sued for **monetary** relief in federal court and imposes no limits on the enforcement of federal constitutional claims in the state's own courts. Bob's action does not seek monetary damages. Choice **C** is incorrect because there is no general legal proposition that a state legislature may rescind its laws with impunity. Finally, choice **B** is incorrect because there is no general legal proposition that a state is precluded from rescinding legislation whenever estoppel-type circumstances are present.

16. **D** Pursuant to Article I, §8, of the U.S. Constitution, Congress alone has the power to tax and/or spend for the general welfare. The president (whose duty is to execute the laws passed by Congress) is constitutionally required to spend monies allocated by an act of Congress

if **expressly** directed to do so. The president may not unilaterally impede implementation of an appropriation passed by Congress. Choice **A** is incorrect because it overstates the powers of the president. Choice **B** is incorrect because the question doesn't deal with the president's control over his subordinates. Choice **C** is incorrect because the question does not deal with issues arising under the Equal Protection Clause.

17. **B** A U.S. taxpayer has standing to challenge a federal spending measure where it is alleged that the expenditure (1) violates the Establishment Clause and (2) is part of a direct federal spending program authorized by Congress (as opposed to an incidental expenditure under a regulatory statute). *Hein v. Freedom from Religion Foundation, Inc.*; *Flast v. Cohen*. Because Allen is contending that the distribution of textbooks to students in a private religious school violates the First Amendment (applicable to the states via the Fourteenth Amendment), he would probably have standing to challenge the statute. Choice **A** is incorrect because, unless the legal standard set forth above is satisfied, the nexus between the payment of taxes and a congressional expenditure is ordinarily deemed too tenuous to support standing. Choice **C** is incorrect because taxpayer standing with respect to a federal expenditure does exist where (1) the enactment offends the Establishment Clause, and (2) the expenditure is part of a federal spending program. Finally, choice **D** is incorrect because Allen is challenging a **federal** statute (so the existence, or not, of state action is irrelevant).

18. **D** Governmental action will be deemed to violate the Establishment Clause unless (1) it has a secular purpose, (2) the primary effect of the action neither advances nor inhibits religion, and (3) it will not result in excessive entanglement with religion. The Supreme Court has held that salary supplements for teachers of secular subjects in religious schools involve excessive governmental entanglement (i.e., the governmental entity would have to constantly monitor the teacher to make certain that he is not injecting religious theories into his subjects). *Lemon v. Kurtzman*. Choice **C** is incorrect because a statute that is otherwise valid under the Establishment Clause is not unconstitutional merely because a particular private institution may benefit more than others. Choice **A** is incorrect because it does not address the issue raised. The issue is not whether supplements are paid to teachers of religion, but whether salary supplements may be paid to **all** teachers, public or private, as long as

they do not teach religion. Finally, choice **B** is incorrect because the Establishment Clause is not violated if the tripartite test described above is satisfied.

19. **A** Governmental action will be deemed to violate the Establishment Clause unless (1) it has a secular purpose, (2) the primary effect of the action neither advances nor inhibits religion, and (3) it will not result in excessive entanglement with religion. In *Tilton v. Richardson*, the U.S. Supreme Court held that a federal construction grant for buildings to be used for strictly secular activities at private colleges (including those operated by religious entities) was constitutional. The Court stated that although religious education might take place at other facilities at the college, there was no First Amendment infringement. The Court noted that universities are not involved in educating impressionable young people. Choice **B** is incorrect because the construction of buildings could violate the First Amendment if the structures were to be used for religious instruction. Choice **C** is legally incorrect (financial aid to a church-operated college does not necessarily "advance" the religious purposes of the institution). *Tilton.* Finally, choice **D** is incorrect because the U.S. Supreme Court has stated that a one-time disbursement of construction aid for a building in which secular courses are to be taught does not entail substantial governmental surveillance. *Tilton.*

20. **B** Where a governmental entity is involved with a private entity in a significant manner, the latter's conduct may be deemed "state action." The strongest argument ***against*** Country Schoolhouse is that, as a consequence of the state accrediting, licensing, and supplying it with textbooks, the institution has become so entwined with the governmental authorities that operation of the school could be deemed state action. *Brentwood Academy v. TSSAA; Norwood v. Harrison.* Choice **A** is incorrect because operation of a private school has been deemed to ***not*** constitute a public function. *Rendell-Baker v. Kohn.* Because education has never been exclusively reserved to the government, it is unlikely that an institution that offers elementary and secondary education would automatically constitute a state actor. Choice **C** is legally incorrect (a state is ***not*** constitutionally obligated to eliminate segregation in private educational institutions). Finally, choice **D** is incorrect because licensing, although a factor in determining if a state is significantly involved with a private entity, is

insufficient, in itself, to make the latter's activities state action. *Moose Lodge No. 107 v. Irvis.*

21. **A** Under the Thirteenth Amendment, slavery and involuntary servitude are forbidden. Section 2 of the Thirteenth Amendment empowers Congress to enact appropriate legislation to accomplish this purpose, including the regulation of conduct undertaken by private individuals. The purpose sought to be achieved by the Thirteenth Amendment was to erase the "badges and incidents" of slavery, including racial discrimination in real estate transactions. Because the statute in question lessens discrimination against African Americans, arguably a legacy of the practice of human slavery in the United States, it probably provides the "most easily justifiable" constitutional basis for the law. *Jones v. Alfred H. Mayer Co.* Choice **B** is incorrect because the Fourteenth Amendment prohibits discriminatory actions by states and *state actors*, not private, nongovernmental entities. The statute in question addresses the conduct of private individuals. Choice **C** is incorrect because the General Welfare Clause is limited to the congressional power to *tax* and *spend* for the general welfare, not to legislate in the name of general welfare. *United States v. Butler.* Finally, choice **D** is incorrect because the Contracts Clause is a restriction on a state's power to repudiate outstanding agreements. It is ***not*** a basis for enactment of federal legislation.

22. **A** State action or legislation that discriminates against interstate commerce is ordinarily unconstitutional. A state statute that requires a business entity to make purchases within that state is ordinarily viewed as discriminating against interstate commerce. (There are exceptions to this rule, such as where the government is acting as a market participant.) Because the Primera statute requires local entities, at least to some extent, to eschew interstate commerce, the legislation is arguably unconstitutional. Although Primera has an interest in improving its economy, it probably ***cannot*** show that requiring certain businesses to purchase a percentage of their goods within that state will have a significant impact on the economy. The fact pattern is very similar to the facts in a U.S. Supreme Court decision that struck down an Oklahoma statute that forced privately owned in-state power plants to purchase and burn locally produced coal. *Wyoming v. Oklahoma.* Choice **D** is incorrect because, although there is a plausible argument that the Equal Protection Clause is violated by the fact that Primera businesses grossing *less* than $1

million in any calendar year are not required to purchase goods within that state, economic legislation is ordinarily judged only by the "rational relationship" test. Because improving the Primera economy is a legitimate state purpose and a legitimate objective can be accomplished "one step at a time," the statute meets the rational-relationship test. Choice **C** is incorrect because the Privileges and Immunities Clause of the Fourteenth Amendment (1) applies only to real persons (who can be "citizens"), not to corporations (which, as fictional "persons," are not and cannot be "citizens"); and (2) prevents states from impairing the rights of national citizenship (i.e., the right to move from state to state, the right to petition Congress, the right to vote for national officers, etc.); neither condition is met on the facts presented. Accordingly, the clause is simply not applicable. Finally, choice **B** is incorrect because the Due Process Clause is not violated if a state pursues a legitimate state objective by rational means.

23. **D** Article IV, §3, of the U.S. Constitution provides that Congress shall have the power to "make all needful rules and regulations respecting the territory or other property belonging to the United States." Because the act in question pertains to "national parks and recreation areas," choice **D** represents the strongest means of sustaining this law. Choice **A** is incorrect because, although the legislation *might* be sustainable under the Commerce Clause (i.e., interstate commerce would arguably be diminished by a law that prevents the removal of wildlife from federally owned land), it is a less direct means of sustaining the statute than a specific enumerated power that pertains to the subject matter of the enactment. *Graham v. Connor.* Choice **C** is incorrect because the Enforcement Clause of the Fourteenth Amendment only empowers Congress to implement the constraints on state action described in that provision. Finally, choice **B** is incorrect because the Privileges and Immunities Clause of Article IV, §2, precludes states from discriminating against U.S. citizens from other jurisdictions. It does not constitute a basis on which federal legislation can be enacted.

24. **B** Under the Commerce Clause, Congress may regulate any activity (even though primarily intrastate) that, in the aggregate, could have a significant impact on the movement of persons, information, or items across state lines. Because motor vehicles can be moved easily across state lines and obviously are instruments of interstate commerce, the legislation could be premised on the Commerce Clause.

Choice **A** is incorrect because Congress's power to regulate for the general welfare applies only to matters of taxation and spending. Choice **C** is incorrect because, even if most vehicles remained within the particular state in which they were stolen, Congress could have reasonably concluded that the movement of stolen cars across state lines would adversely affect interstate commerce (i.e., if her car is stolen, the owner cannot travel to another state to purchase items or work). Finally, choice **D** is incorrect because the Tenth Amendment merely reserves to the states whatever powers cannot be exercised by Congress under the U.S. Constitution. It is not a basis for nullifying Congress's right to legislate.

25. **B** Governmental action that infringes on a fundamental right violates substantive due process, unless there is a compelling interest involved and there is no less burdensome means of accomplishing that objective. The right to use contraceptive devices has been held to be a fundamental right (*Griswold v. Connecticut*) and has been extended to apply to unmarried persons (*Eisenstadt v. Baird*) and also to minors (*Carey v. Population Services International*). Thus, the law in question arguably violates the Due Process Clause of the Fourteenth Amendment. Choice **A** is incorrect because there is no indication that the statute in question constitutes an undue burden on interstate commerce; the impact of the legislation on interstate commerce is minimal compared to the state objective sought to be achieved by the act. In fact, the legislation would probably have a rather minor effect on interstate commerce. Choice **C** is incorrect because the Fourteenth Amendment has been interpreted to protect only a very limited number of national citizenship rights (e.g., moving freely from state to state, petitioning Congress, voting for national officers, advocating national legislation, etc.), which do not include the right to contraceptives. Finally, choice **D** is incorrect because a law that arguably regulates moral conduct is ***not***, *ipso facto*, a violation of the freedom of religion.

26. **B** The Privileges and Immunities Clause contained in Article IV, §2, of the U.S. Constitution precludes a state from discriminating against the citizens of other states with respect to the exercise of rights that are "fundamental to national unity," such as the right to be employed, the right to practice one's profession, and the right to engage in business. Because the legislation in question applies to all persons within or without Euphoria and to all property in Euphoria (i.e., parcels owned by citizens of Euphoria, as well as those owned by

persons residing outside of the state), the Privileges and Immunities Clause is probably the **least** applicable doctrine mentioned. Choice **C** is incorrect because the constitutional basis for this legislation is the police power (reserved to the states in the Tenth Amendment). Choice **A** is incorrect because the proposed legislation might arguably constitute an unconstitutional deprivation of property under the Fourteenth Amendment. This is because restrictions placed in deeds can often increase the value of real property. Finally, choice **D** is incorrect because the CCRs in deeds are typically a significant part of a transaction involving the sale of land, and the legislation in question might impair existing and prospective contractual relationships.

27. **C** Under the Equal Protection Clause of the Fourteenth Amendment, state legislation (as opposed to *federal* legislation) pertaining to legal aliens is ordinarily subject to strict scrutiny (i.e., there must be a compelling state interest and no less burdensome means of accomplishing that objective). The Supreme Court has rested this rule on the Equal Protection Clause itself, as well as the idea that regulation of lawfully resident aliens is a special concern of the federal government. *Mathews v. Diaz.* However, where the classification affects an area that involves the "execution of broad public policy," such as a law preventing aliens from becoming state troopers, the "mere rationality" test is used. *Foley v. Connelie.* Because the Euphoria legislation impairs the general rights of legal aliens, it must meet the strict-scrutiny test. Euphoria's objective in enacting this legislation was probably to extend the disbursement of funds only to persons who would remain in its jurisdiction and thus strengthen the state's technology base. Even so, there is probably no compelling state interest in limiting computer training to U.S. citizens, and there are less burdensome means of accomplishing this objective (e.g., require students to become U.S. citizens during their training period). Thus, the alienage restriction is probably unconstitutional. Choice **D** is incorrect because the Privileges and Immunities Clause of Article IV, §2, does **not** apply to aliens. They are not "citizens of a state" within the meaning of that provision. Choice **B** is incorrect because, even if the line drawn by the state was reasonably related to a legitimate governmental interest, the strict-scrutiny standard, which is more demanding, is not satisfied. Finally, choice **A** is incorrect because legal aliens *are* viewed as a "discrete and insular minority," at least with respect to discriminatory *state* or *local* legislation.

28. D Requirements that voters have resided within the state for more than a certain time prior to election day are strictly scrutinized. *Dunn v. Blumstein.* Such requirements have been struck down on the grounds that they interfere with the fundamental right to vote and the right to travel. Although a state might have a compelling interest in verifying that only *bona fide* residents (i.e., those living and intending to remain within the jurisdiction) can vote, the legislation in question precludes new residents from voting, even if they intend to remain in the state. A less strict means of assuring that only *bona fide* residents vote would be to require an affidavit from them, stating that they intend to continue residing in the jurisdiction. Choice **C** is incorrect because a state may limit the franchise to **bona fide** residents. Thus, nonresidents may be precluded from voting in local elections. Choice **A** is incorrect because persons moving into a new jurisdiction can constitutionally be precluded from voting for officials in that area, if they did **not** intend to remain there and there is no legal presumption that persons residing in a state at a given moment intend to remain there. Finally, choice **B** is incorrect because the statute arguably does not constitute an undue burden on interstate commerce (i.e., persons would probably **not** be dissuaded from moving to another state simply because they could not vote in the next local election).

29. C The Supreme Court has held that each person has a fundamental right to live with members of her family. *Moore v. City of East Cleveland.* Thus, the governmental entity has the burden of proving that any action affecting this right is necessary to achieve a compelling governmental interest and that there are no less burdensome means available. Choice **B** is incorrect because it understates the state's burden of justification for the law. Again, where a fundamental right is infringed, a state must show that a *compelling* governmental interest is advanced, not merely a *legitimate* one. Choice **D** incorrectly places the burden of persuasion on Muffy. Once a plaintiff establishes that her claim implicates a fundamental liberty interest, the burden of proof is on the governmental entity. Finally, choice **A** is incorrect because it (1) places the burden of persuasion on Muffy and (2) understates the measure of proof required. When a fundamental right is infringed on, the governmental entity must show that a "compelling" interest is involved.

30. C A state law is invalid on Dormant Commerce Clause grounds if it results in an undue burden on interstate commerce (i.e., the local interest sought to be protected by the legislation is outweighed by the burden that it places on the movement of persons, things, or information across state lines). If BUPS can show that (1) other jurisdictions in which it operates do not require the seat belts in question, and (2) substantial cost and inconvenience will be incurred by it in complying with the law, the statute will probably be declared unconstitutional. *Bibb v. Navajo Freight Lines, Inc.* Choice **B** is incorrect because, under these facts, all common carriers are equally affected. The fact that not all vehicles are covered by the statute is immaterial. A governmental entity may address a health or safety problem "one step at a time," and, because the evil complained of is confined to commercial vehicles, the line of demarcation is not unreasonable. Choice **A** is incorrect because no fundamental right is involved, and the statute would be tested by the rational-relationship test. Because the seat belts prescribed by the statute probably enhance the safety of persons on highways within Wissola, this test is satisfied. Finally, choice **D** is incorrect because the facts do not give rise to a Contracts Clause issue.

31. **D** Under Article I, §8, of the U.S. Constitution, Congress has the power to tax and spend for the general welfare. The general welfare is arguably served by providing federal funds for the hiring of police officers by the states and cities. Although Congress may not exercise the spending power in violation of specific constitutional provisions (i.e., the Establishment Clause), restricting federal aid to cities of a prescribed size would not run afoul of this principle. Choice **B** is incorrect because the Tenth Amendment is the basis of the states' police power (rather than a source of *federal* spending authority). Choice **A** is incorrect because the relationship of the power to make war and provide for the national defense and the statute in question is more tenuous than the relationship of the taxing and spending powers. Finally, choice **C** is incorrect because the Privileges and Immunities Clause of the Fourteenth Amendment does not confer any power on Congress. Rather, it precludes the states from hindering the exercise of rights inherent in national citizenship (i.e., the right to travel from state to state, the right to petition representatives of Congress, etc.).

32. **A** A generally applicable criminal law is enforceable, regardless of the burden that it imposes on an individual's religious beliefs. *Employment Division v. Smith.* The state need not balance its interests against the burden on the individual's beliefs, as long as the law

is generally applicable and not motivated by animus or discriminatory purpose against a particular religion or group of religionists.
In this case, however, the statute specifically exempts sales activities
undertaken for a "religious purpose." As long as Martha sincerely
believed that her sales were for a "religious purpose," she would
(under the applicable statute) be exempt from the licensing requirement. Choice **B** is incorrect because the statute is not attempting to
criminalize religious beliefs. Choice **C** is incorrect because, although
the legal proposition is correctly stated, persons engaging in sales
for a "religious purpose" are exempted under the applicable statute.
Finally, choice **D** is incorrect because the fact finder's conclusion that
the religious belief in question is erroneous is irrelevant. As long as
Martha's beliefs were sincerely held, she is exempt from the statute.

33. **A** Where there is a lack of intentional discrimination, state laws are
ordinarily reviewed under the rational-relationship test (i.e., the legislation in question must be rationally related to a legitimate state
objective), even if they have a disparate impact on a racial minority group; generally speaking, disparate impact, standing alone, does
not trigger heightened judicial scrutiny under the Equal Protection
Clause. *Washington v. Davis.* Although the law at issue produces a
disparate impact on Latinos, there is no indication in the facts provided that the state X legislature sought or intended to discriminate
against this group. In fact, the legislature's action appears to have
been motivated by a report indicating that life and property could
be saved by the integration of metal slats into the homes in question.
Choice **B** is incorrect because strict scrutiny is **not** applicable (i.e.,
the law was not a deliberate attempt to disadvantage a particular
racial minority). Choice **C** is incorrect because the fact that a law has
a disproportionately adverse impact on a particular group does not
automatically trigger the strict-scrutiny review. The discrimination
must be purposeful in nature. Finally, choice **D** is incorrect because
the $1,200 fee necessary to comply with the law would probably **not**
constitute such an undue burden as to be violative of due process
(especially because homeowners have two years to complete the
improvement).

34. **C** The Privileges and Immunities Clause of Article IV, §2 prohibits a
state from discriminating against the citizens of other states with
respect to the exercise of national rights. Because the legislation in
question pertains to **all** deeds within the state (i.e., those parcels
owned by citizens of the jurisdiction and those that are owned by

persons residing outside of the state), the Privileges and Immunities Clause would probably be the ***least*** important doctrine mentioned. Choice **D** is incorrect because the constitutional basis for the legislation requested is the police power (reserved to the states in the Tenth Amendment). Choice **A** is incorrect because the proposed legislation might constitute an unconstitutional deprivation of property under the Fourteenth Amendment. This result would occur because, if the restrictions previously placed in deeds ceased to be effective, land owned by an individual would often become less valuable (i.e., if subdivision restrictions ceased to exist, each landowner's parcel would probably be less valuable). Finally, choice **B** is incorrect because deeds are frequently made pursuant to a contract. Thus, the legislation in question would impair existing contractual relationships (i.e., persons buying a lot within a subdivision ordinarily do so on the vendor's promise that other parcels will be subject to similar restrictions). U.S. Const. art. I, §10, cl. 1.

35. **D** Under the Commerce Clause, Congress may regulate any economic or commercial activity (even though primarily intrastate) that, aggregated across the national economy, substantially affects interstate commerce. *Wickard v. Filburn*. Congress possesses constitutional authority to enact the statute in question under the Commerce Clause. Choice **B** is incorrect because it is too broad. Purchases and sales that, aggregated across the national economy, do not have a substantial effect on interstate commerce cannot be regulated by Congress under the Commerce Clause. Also, this answer does not deal with the regulation of imported products. Choice **C** is incorrect because the fact that Congress has the authority to regulate the importation of goods from abroad is not a basis for regulating items produced within the United States. Finally, choice **A** is incorrect because Congress has no power to enact general legislation for the "general welfare." The Supreme Court has interpreted the General Welfare Clause as applying only to the taxing and spending powers and not as a more general font of legislative authority.

36. **C** Federal courts will not hear a matter until it is "ripe" (i.e., there is an actual dispute between parties having adverse legal interests). *Poe v. Ullman*. Because Paul apparently has not even proposed to Mary, nor have they applied for a marriage license, a federal court would probably conclude that the ripeness prerequisite has ***not*** been satisfied. Choice **B** is incorrect because a substantial federal question is presented (i.e., may a state attach the condition of prior counseling

to a fundamental right such as marriage?). Choice **A** is incorrect because residence is immaterial in a case involving subject-matter jurisdiction over a federal question (i.e., a claim arising under the U.S. Constitution). Finally, choice **D** is incorrect because no political question (i.e., one involving the interrelationship of coequal branches of government) is presented by this fact pattern.

37. **C** Governmental action that infringes on a fundamental right violates the Due Process Clause of the Fourteenth Amendment unless a compelling interest is involved and there is no less burdensome means of accomplishing that objective. The right to marry is a fundamental one. *Zablocki v. Redhail.* Thus, the "strict scrutiny" standard applies in this instance, and the state has the burden of proof. Choice **D** is incorrect because there is no legal principle that mandates strict scrutiny with respect to any legislation affecting minors. Choice **B** is incorrect because, although there is an initial presumption that the legislation is valid, this is overcome by evidence that a "fundamental right" is involved (the determination that a fundamental right is involved is made by the court). Finally, choice **A** is incorrect because, although the statement is true, action under the Tenth Amendment is subject to the Due Process Clause of the Fourteenth Amendment.

38. **B** Under the Equal Protection Clause of the Fourteenth Amendment, state legislation pertaining to legal aliens is subject to strict scrutiny (i.e., there must be a compelling state interest and no less burdensome means of accomplishing that objective), unless the classification affects a position that is governmental ("bound up with the operation of the state as a governmental entity") or political in nature (in which event, the legislation in question is tested by the rational-relationship standard). Because there does not appear to be a compelling reason to preclude aliens from owning more than 100 acres of land within the state, Zane could probably successfully contend that the legislation violates the Equal Protection Clause of the Fourteenth Amendment. Choice **A** is incorrect because, although there would arguably be an effect on interstate commerce (i.e., legal aliens would probably make less trips to, and purchase less land in, state X as a consequence of the enactment), the undue burden on interstate commerce necessary to invalidate state legislation would probably **not** exist. Moreover, the use of alienage as a classification is not a special concern of the Commerce Clause (but *is* a suspect classification for purposes of the equal-protection doctrine). Choice **C** is incorrect because the law does not preclude Zane from coming

into, or egressing from, state X. Finally, choice **D** is incorrect because Zane purchased the land in question *after* the passage of the pertinent statute. Thus, the legislation did not impair an outstanding contractual obligation.

39. **D** Pursuant to Article III, §1, of the U.S. Constitution, Congress has empowered U.S. district courts to hear federal questions (i.e., those involving a claim arising under the U.S. Constitution, a congressional act, or a federal treaty). Because Zane could claim that the statute violates the Equal Protection Clause of the Fourteenth Amendment, a federal claim is involved. Thus, a U.S. district court should hear the action. Choice **C** is incorrect because federal courts are empowered to hear Zane's action based on the U.S. Constitution, rather than on the United Nations Charter. Choice **B** is legally incorrect because state qualifications for landholding within the jurisdiction are subject to constitutional limitations. Finally, choice **A** is legally incorrect because the U.S. Constitution does not prohibit aliens from commencing an action in federal court.

40. **B** Generally, there is no due-process "right" to public employment. *Board of Regents v. Roth.* Thus, it is unlikely that James can successfully compel the Yodah Employment Office to furnish him with an explanation as to why his application for employment was unsuccessful. Choice **A** is incorrect because it simply restates the principle that the Tenth Amendment reserves to the states all powers not specifically assigned to the federal government. It does *not*, however, empower states to ignore the other provisions of the Constitution (i.e., the Due Process Clause, the Equal Protection Clause, etc.). Choice **C** is incorrect because, as explained above, there is no Due Process Clause right to public employment. Finally, choice **D** is incorrect. Although the Equal Protection Clause guarantees that people who are similarly situated will be treated similarly, it is reasonable to permit state employment officers discretion whether to confer with unsuccessful applicants (i.e., granting all applicants postrejection interviews might become too time consuming).

41. **C** There is ordinarily no Due Process Clause "property" interest in a government job. However, procedural due-process protections of notice and a timely hearing may attach when a governmental employee is given reason to believe that her employment is not simply "at will." *Perry v. Sinderman.* If the city officer for whom Angela worked had assured her that she would be rehired, Angela's procedural due-process right to a statement of reasons and a timely hearing would

arguably attach because she would have more than a unilateral hope of continued employment; the conversation could support a "legitimate claim of entitlement" to the position. If Angela has a legitimate claim of entitlement to the position, she has a right to procedural due process before the government terminates her employment. Choice **A** is incorrect because a city employee is not entitled to rely on the expectation of continued employment. Choice **B** is incorrect because the fact pattern fails to suggest that Angela's termination was based on her status in a protected classification (i.e., race, sex, religion, etc.). Finally, choice **D** is incorrect because there is no constitutional right to employment purely on the basis of merit.

42. **A** The Supreme Court and such inferior federal courts as are established by Congress are empowered to hear cases arising under the U.S. Constitution. U.S. Const. art. III, §2. Because the plaintiff is claiming that the restaurant's conduct violates the Equal Protection Clause of the Fourteenth Amendment, a federal claim (i.e., one arising under the U.S. Constitution) is involved. However, to support his claim, he must show that the state of Euphoria is involved because the Fourteenth Amendment—the basis of the plaintiff's claim—applies to actions by government actors and not by purely private citizens. His claim is supported by *Burton v. Wilmington Parking Authority* on the basis of the "symbiotic" relationship between the state and the "private" restaurant owner. Because the extensive contact between the state and the restaurant owner results in each party's benefiting from the other's conduct in a "symbiotic relationship," the requisite state action may exist. Therefore, a federal district court has subject-matter jurisdiction. Choice **B** is incorrect because there is no federal court jurisdiction based simply on the presence of a state as a party. Choice **C** is incorrect because a federal court will abstain only when (1) a state statute is claimed to be unconstitutional, and (2) there is a possibility that a curative interpretation might be rendered by a state court. In this instance, no state legislation is at issue. Finally, choice **D** is incorrect because citizens of the same state can sue each other in a U.S. district court if a federal claim is asserted.

43. **B** Where a state is involved with a private entity in a significant manner, the latter's conduct may be deemed "state action." The strongest argument against the Bastion is that, as a consequence of its extensive dealings with Euphoria—accreditation, licensing, and supplying textbooks—the institution has become so "entwined" with the state that the school has become a state actor. *Brentwood Academy*

v. TSSAA; Norwood v. Harrison. Thus, under the Equal Protection Clause, it cannot discriminate on the basis of party affiliation or political viewpoint. Choice **A** is incorrect because operation of a private school is **not** ordinarily an "exclusive governmental function." *Rendell-Baker v. Kohn*. Choice **C** is legally incorrect (a state is **not** constitutionally obligated to take action to eliminate discrimination in **private** educational institutions). Finally, choice **D** is incorrect because licensing—although one factor in determining if a state is so significantly involved with a private entity as to make the private entity a "state actor"—is insufficient, in itself. *Moose Lodge No. 107 v. Irvis.*

44. **B** A statute is overly broad on its face (and therefore invalid) when the governmental agency empowered to enforce it has virtually unlimited discretion. Although the Littletown police commissioner is instructed to enforce the waiver provision in an "even-handed manner," the statute permits too much discretion in the commissioner without any checks on his decisions. The statute cannot be a constitutional basis for prosecution. Choice **A** is incorrect because speech activities in traditional public forums can be subjected to viewpoint-neutral, content-neutral, and reasonable time, place, and manner restrictions. Choice **C** is incorrect because, although the restrictions are narrowly tailored, no governmental interest, however significant, can justify unconstitutional limits on free speech. Finally, choice **D** is incorrect because, despite the instruction to grant waiver permits in an "even-handed manner," the statute is still overly broad.

45. **C** A U.S. taxpayer has standing to challenge a federal spending measure if she alleges that the expenditure (1) violates the Establishment Clause by directly funding a church or religious entity and (2) is part of a federal spending program (as opposed to an incidental expenditure under a regulatory statute). *Hein v. Freedom from Religion Foundation, Inc.; Flast v. Cohen*. Because Anna is apparently contending that monetary grants for the distribution of computers to students in private religious schools violate the First Amendment, which operates as a specific limitation on Congress's taxing and spending powers, she probably has standing to challenge the statute. Choices **A** and **B** are incorrect because, as explained above, Anna has "taxpayer standing" in this particular situation. Finally, choice **D** is incorrect because it is too narrow. It is not a condition of "standing" that the citizen rely on the General Welfare Clause for her claim.

46. B Governmental action that benefits religion is deemed to violate the Establishment Clause unless (1) it has a secular purpose, (2) the primary effect of the action neither advances nor inhibits religion, and (3) it will not result in excessive entanglement with religion. In *Mitchell v. Helms*, the Supreme Court sustained a government program that provided computers to religiously affiliated primary and secondary schools, and in *Agostini v. Felton*, the Supreme Court permitted state-employed teachers to undertake limited teaching duties in religiously affiliated private schools. Both cases found that the government's support, if limited to nonreligious subjects, did not give rise to an excessive entanglement. Choice **D** is incorrect because there is not necessarily an equal-protection violation. Congress could presumably decide that private nonreligious schools as a class ordinarily have the means to purchase their own computers. Choice **A** is incorrect because the equal treatment of public and private religious schools is immaterial to the issue of excessive entanglement by Congress. Finally, choice **C** is incorrect because the Supreme Court has held that government can provide computers to religiously affiliated schools without creating an excessive entanglement. Although the Supreme Court has not yet decided a case with these exact facts, it is doubtful that a state government can provide computers but no assistance for their use. Moreover, *Agostini* suggests that computer training would be permissible.

47. A Classifications based on age are ordinarily viewed under the rational-basis test (i.e., there must be a reasonable relationship between a legitimate governmental objective and the legislative means selected to accomplish that purpose). Clarence's strongest argument from the choices offered appears to be that the statute pertaining to mandatory retirement of federal public defenders is invalid under the Fifth Amendment, which applies the requirements of due process to the federal government. The Supreme Court has held that the equal-protection principle arising under the Fifth Amendment's Due Process Clause is identical in all material respects to the Equal Protection Clause of the Fourteenth Amendment. *Adarand Constructors, Inc. v. Pena; Bolling v. Sharpe.* However, Clarence probably will **not** prevail because the Supreme Court does not view age-based classifications as intrinsically suspect. *Vance v. Bradley; Massachusetts Bd. of Retirement v. Murgia.* Choice **B** is incorrect because, in the absence of a legitimate expectation to the contrary, there is no property right to permanent public employment.

Bishop v. Wood. Choice **C** is incorrect because the Fourteenth Amendment applies only to state action, and the Privileges and Immunities Clause contained in the Fourteenth Amendment has been limited to precluding a state from impairing national rights (i.e., the right to travel from state to state, the right to petition Congress for grievances, etc.). Finally, choice **D** is incorrect because the Fourteenth Amendment applies only to the states, not the federal government.

48. **C** Under the Commerce Clause, Congress may regulate any economic or commercial activity (even though primarily intrastate) that, in the aggregate, could have a significant impact on interstate commerce. *U.S. v. Morrison.* Because legislation pertaining to consumer credit plainly constitutes economic activity that, when aggregated across the national economy, substantially affects interstate commerce, it is a perfectly valid Commerce Clause enactment. *Gonzales v. Raich.* In fact, the act is quite similar to a law that the Supreme Court previously upheld against a constitutional challenge that regulated loan sharking and predatory lending; this earlier precedent leads even further support to the conclusion that Congress in fact possessed constitutional authority to enact the statute at issue here. *Perez v. United States.* Choice **D** is incorrect because the Equal Protection Clause of the Fourteenth Amendment is a restriction on state action, not a basis for federal legislation. Choice **A** is incorrect because the Impairment of Contracts Clause is a restriction on state conduct (i.e., it precludes states from impairing obligations created under outstanding agreements), rather than a basis for the enactment of federal legislation. Finally, choice **B** is incorrect because the Privileges and Immunities Clause of the Fourteenth Amendment precludes states from impairing the exercise of rights of national citizenship (i.e., the right to travel from state to state, the right to petition representatives of the U.S. government, etc.). It is *not* a source of federal legislative power.

49. **D** Under the Free Exercise Clause of the First Amendment (applicable to the states via the Fourteenth Amendment), if a general law interferes with the exercise of an individual's religious beliefs, the reviewing court should sustain the law in the absence of evidence of religious discrimination. *Church of the Lukumi Babalu Aye v. City of Hialeah; Employment Division v. Smith.* Choice **B** is incorrect because the burden of proof rests on the challenger to establish that the law was enacted or enforced with discriminatory intent against a particular

religious sect. Choice **C** is legally incorrect because it misstates the applicable standard of review in cases presenting Free Exercise Clause challenges to neutral, generally applicable laws. Finally, choice **A** is incorrect because the burden of proof rests with the party seeking to invalidate a general law under the Free Exercise Clause.

50. D Pursuant to Article III, §1, of the U.S. Constitution, Congress has empowered U.S. district courts to hear cases involving federal questions (i.e., those involving a claim under the U.S. Constitution, a congressional act, or a federal treaty). Because Schmidt will probably assert that the Caldonia statute violates the Equal Protection Clause of the Fourteenth Amendment, this case involves a federal claim. Thus, the U.S. district court should hear the matter. Choice **A** is legally incorrect; the U.S. Constitution does *not* preclude aliens from commencing an action in federal court. Choice **C** is incorrect because the presence of a state as a party is not by itself a basis for federal court jurisdiction. Finally, choice **B** is incorrect because, although the states may legislate with respect to the ownership of property, the legislation is subject to the U.S. Constitution.

51. B Under the Equal Protection Clause of the Fourteenth Amendment, state legislation using alienage as a classification for imposing burdens or withholding benefits is ordinarily adjudged by the strict-scrutiny standard (i.e., there must be a compelling state interest and no less burdensome means of accomplishing that objective). There does not appear to be a compelling reason to preclude aliens—especially legal aliens—from owning a controlling interest in corporations located within Caldonia. When Congress chooses to admit a noncitizen to the United States, a state cannot second guess or gainsay this decision by denying her civil rights otherwise available to U.S. citizens resident in the state. Choice **A** is incorrect because it is not the *strongest* argument. The attorney general would argue that the oral contract to purchase could be voided by Schmidt under the Statute of Frauds (i.e., the contract was unenforceable until reduced to a writing signed by Schmidt because the aggregate value of the stock was "$500 or more"; UCC §2-201) and that Schmidt could have voided the agreement because one can legally void a contract that is contrary to law. Choice **D** is incorrect because, although there arguably would be an effect on interstate commerce (i.e., legal aliens would presumably make fewer trips to, and purchase fewer businesses in, Caldonia), the effect would not be "unduly burdensome," the required standard for judicial intervention. Finally, choice **C** is incorrect because the Privileges and Immunities Clause applies only to U.S. citizens.

52. **B** Since Congress repealed the generic mandatory appellate jurisdiction of the Supreme Court in 1988 (Pub. L. No. 100-352, 102 Stat. 662 (1988); codified in scattered sections of 28 U.S.C.), the Supreme Court's appellate review of cases arising in both the lower federal courts and the state court systems has been exclusively through the discretionary grant of a writ of certiorari (*see* Robert L. Stern et al., *Supreme Court Practice* 47-76 (7th ed. 1993); discussing the abolition of the Supreme Court's mandatory jurisdiction in 1988). From time to time, Congress enacts specific statutory provisions that create mandatory appellate jurisdiction in the Supreme Court (e.g., 2 U.S.C. §692 (Supp. IV 1998); providing for mandatory Supreme Court appellate review of the Line Item Veto Act's constitutionality), but the facts do not suggest the existence of any such legislation in this case. Accordingly, the Supreme Court has complete discretion to hear—or decline to hear—this appeal. Choice **A** is incorrect because (1) state X, being the party that lost below, is the only entity that is now capable of appealing the case; and (2) State X College, being a party to the grant, had standing to raise the constitutional issue below. Finally, choices **C** and **D** are incorrect because no automatic right of appeal existed in these circumstances.

53. **B** Where state legislation places an undue burden on interstate commerce (i.e., the local interest sought to be protected is outweighed by the hindrance to interstate commerce resulting from the law), the law is unconstitutional. Except for the possible consequence of fewer monkeys (if needed) being imported into state X for the purpose of completing the research, the act would have virtually no effect on interstate commerce. Choice **A** is incorrect because, as a consequence of the law, College has a number of animals that have suddenly become valueless to it. Thus, a taking without due process of law has arguably occurred in possible violation of the Fifth Amendment's Takings Clause (made applicable to the states via the Fourteenth Amendment). Choice **D** is incorrect because a grant does constitute a contract, which (as a consequence of the act) significantly hinders the workings of the federal government and is invalid under the Supremacy Clause. Because the U.S. Army has contracted with College for the research in question, the act is arguably unconstitutional as applied to the grant. Choice **C** is incorrect because it

may be possible to argue that the state's action is impeding a federal interest in the research.

54. **B** Under the Fourteenth Amendment's Equal Protection Clause, classifications based on the marital status of biological parents must be substantially related to an important state interest (middle-level scrutiny; *Clark v. Jeter*). Although Euphoria may have an interest in discouraging births to unmarried biological parents and avoiding fraudulent claims, the state cannot simply bar all unacknowledged children born to unmarried parents from having any chance to inherit. These children must be given at least some reasonable opportunity to obtain a judicial determination of paternity. Therefore, it is unlikely that the statute would withstand middle-level scrutiny. A statute that prevented acknowledged children born to unmarried biological parents from inheriting from their fathers was rejected in *Trimble v. Gordon*. A six-year statute of limitations on paternity suits was invalidated in *Clark v. Jeter*. Choice **D** is incorrect because there is no "fundamental right" to inherit property. Choice **C** is incorrect because the Privileges and Immunities Clause of the Fourteenth Amendment prevents the states from impeding the rights of national citizenship (i.e., the right to travel from state to state, the right to petition federal officials, etc.); the right to inherit from one's father is not a national right. Finally, choice **A** is incorrect because, to this point, U.S. Supreme Court decisions pertaining to the rights of children born to unmarried biological parents have been predicated on the Equal Protection Clause. Additionally, Patricia's rights are substantive rights, not procedural rights. No notice or hearing can enlarge her rights as limited by this statute.

55. **C** Although governmental oath requirements must be narrowly tailored to avoid infringement of First Amendment rights, a state may condition public employment on a positive oath to abide by constitutional, lawful processes. *Cole v. Richardson*. Butah's strongest argument for sustaining the statute would be that it merely requires individuals to pledge to avoid illegal conduct. Choice **A** is incorrect because, although governmental employment is a privilege (rather than a right), it may not be conditioned on an affirmation or oath to refrain from activities protected by the First Amendment. Choice **B** is incorrect because the Tenth Amendment is merely a recitation of the states' right to exercise powers not delegated to the federal government. It does not empower the states to affix conditions on employment that are constitutionally improper. Finally, choice **D**

is incorrect because, although a state is justified in keeping disloyal persons out of governmental positions, it cannot condition public employment on so loose a standard as "potential disloyalty" or on any oath or affirmation that violates the First Amendment rights of job applicants.

56. **A** Under the Equal Protection Clause of the Fourteenth Amendment, state or local regulations that facially discriminate against legally resident aliens (persons without U.S. citizenship) must ordinarily satisfy the strict-scrutiny test (i.e., there must be a compelling governmental interest that is promoted by the statute and no less burdensome means of accomplishing that objective). However, where an alien is applying for a position that involves a political function or public policymaking duties, as opposed to solely *economic* functions, a state need only satisfy the rational-relationship test. Under these facts, because Mirza seeks a job as a mechanic in a garage motor pool, a job with no political or policymaking elements, the strict-scrutiny standard applies. Choice **B** is incorrect because an alien applicant for a nonpolitical job is entitled to the application of the strict-scrutiny standard of review to a statute that bars him from the job. Finally, choices **C** and **D** are incorrect because, as discussed above, the burden of proof rests with the state of Trent to demonstrate that the statute withstands a strict-scrutiny analysis.

57. **A** When a statute affecting speech pertains to the time, place, or manner of expression (as opposed to the content), the governmental entity has the burden of showing that the statute supports an "important" social objective and is narrowly tailored to accomplish that result. Additionally, the governmental entity must "leave open adequate alternative channels" for communicating the information sought to be expressed. *Ward v. Rock Against Racism; Clark v. Community for Creative Non-Violence.* Because the first statute is a content-neutral, "time, place, and manner of expression" law, Libertania must satisfy the standard stated in choice **A**. Choice **B** is incorrect because, as discussed above, Libertania must satisfy a higher standard under these circumstances. Finally, choices **C** and **D** are incorrect because the state has the burden of proof.

58. **B** A statute is unduly vague (and therefore invalid under the Due Process Clause of the Fourteenth Amendment) when a person of ordinary intelligence would be unable to determine if actions that are being contemplated are proscribed by the language. The words "opprobrious" and "abusive" are probably too subjective to apprise

a person of average intelligence what words would subject him to criminal culpability. Choice **A** is legally incorrect (even public forums are subject to limitations upon time, place, and manner of communication). Choice **C** is also legally incorrect (some speech content, such as "fighting words," may be regulated in certain situations). Finally, choice **D** is incorrect because, although it expresses a general constitutional principle, a governmental entity may promulgate limitations as to time, place, and manner of communication (even with respect to public forums).

59. **A** Where state regulation promotes domestic businesses by penalizing out-of-state interests, it can violate the Equal Protection Clause of the Fourteenth Amendment. *Metropolitan Life Insurance Co. v. Ward.* Although the statute involves insurance companies (which are exempted from attack under the Commerce Clause), the U.S. Supreme Court has held that such legislation violates the Equal Protection Clause. The only purpose of the statute was to promote the business of its domestic insurers by penalizing foreign insurers who seek to do business in Araho; this is not a legitimate state purpose. Choice **B** is incorrect because the McCarran-Ferguson Act exempts state insurance regulation from attack under the Commerce Clause, not the Equal Protection Clause. Choice **C** is incorrect because the Supremacy Clause comes into play only when Congress has *preempted* an area of legislation; that was not the case in the *Metropolitan* case. Finally, choice **D** is incorrect because the Equal Protection Clause may not be circumscribed or avoided even by legislation related to a legitimate state objective.

60. **B** The Dormant Commerce Clause prevents a state or local government from placing an undue burden on interstate commerce if the national interest in promoting interstate commerce overrides the local interest in regulating its own affairs. In determining if a regulation is invalid, the court will consider whether a less burdensome alternative is available. Because Amityville could presumably inspect the incoming meat when it arrived at a local destination, its ordinance is probably unreasonable. *Dean Milk Co. v. City of Madison.* Choice **A** is incorrect because the statute does not establish any clearly improper classification. It applies to everyone bringing meat into Amityville. Of course, a local entity is not authorized to assert its authority beyond state lines. Choice **C** is incorrect because the Dormant Commerce Clause is not satisfied by a mere showing of a rational relationship to a legitimate governmental objective. Finally, choice **D** is incorrect because it is a statement of an obvious truth

that is immaterial to the issue at hand; the fact that citizens are presumed to know the law does not mean that they have to accept a law that is unconstitutional.

61. **D** Although streets are traditional public forums, speech on streets can be circumscribed if the regulation (1) is content neutral, (2) is narrowly tailored to satisfy a significant governmental interest, and (3) leaves open alternative channels for communication. *Ward v. Rock Against Racism.* The inconvenience caused by traffic on two occasions is probably an insufficient governmental interest. Also, the means chosen here are not "narrowly tailored." Presumably, the parades or demonstrations could be permitted at times other than peak traffic periods (i.e., in the early afternoon, on Sundays, etc.). A complete exclusion from the two most public areas is almost certainly too broad to survive constitutional review. Choice **C** is incorrect because some speech activity in streets can be restricted (although the limitations must be narrowly tailored). Choice **A** is incorrect because, as discussed above, although the statute is content neutral, it imposes unreasonable restrictions on the exercise of speech in a public place. Finally, choice **B** is incorrect because, as discussed above, the restrictions are too broad.

62. **A** A statute that attempts to control speech but that is overly broad *on its face* cannot serve as the basis for criminal prosecution. Because the determination whether to issue a waiver of the 20-person limitation is left to the sole discretion of the police commissioner pursuant to a vague standard of application ("not . . . detrimental to the overall community"), the Amityville statute is overly broad and therefore unconstitutional on its face. Thus, it cannot be used to prosecute Tricia. Choice **B** is incorrect because speech activities in traditional public forums can be circumscribed, provided the restrictions are narrowly tailored, promote a significant governmental interest, and leave open ample alternative channels of communication. *Ward v. Rock Against Racism.* Choice **C** is incorrect because a defendant charged with commission of a crime is not obliged to seek a declaratory judgment but may challenge the statute in her direct defense. Finally, choice **D** is incorrect because the procedure under which a waiver could be obtained was itself overly broad and left to the sole discretion of the police commissioner.

63. **D** Federal judges hold their offices during good behavior and are protected from diminution of salary. U.S. Const., art. III, §1. Pursuant to Article I, Congress may establish administrative courts for the purpose of adjudicating "public rights" or "obligations" with

respect to the U.S. government (rather than among private parties). The tenure and salary of judges of administrative tribunals are dependent on the legislation that established the tribunal. Because Hobson's position was not established pursuant to Article III of the U.S. Constitution, Hobson is not entitled to hold office during good behavior and avoid any diminution in salary. Choice **A** is incorrect because administrative agencies are established by Congress pursuant to Article I of the U.S. Constitution. Thus, although Article III guarantees the independence of the federal judiciary, Hobson was **not** a member of that group. Choice **B** is incorrect because property rights to governmental employment must arise from a source independent of the U.S. Constitution (i.e., rules or understandings indicating that employment would not be withdrawn). Because the facts fail to indicate that any such rules or understandings existed, Hobson could not claim a "property" right to continuation of his position. Finally, choice **C** is incorrect because Hobson did suffer a direct and immediate injury as a consequence of Congress's action. The law, however, does not permit recovery by Hobson in this instance.

64. **D** States are not allowed, without the consent of Congress, to tax imports or exports, except where necessary for reimbursement with respect to the execution of its inspection laws. U.S. Const. art. I, §10, cl. 2. Because the goods in question were not "in transit," they were subject to a nondiscriminatory *ad valorem* tax. *Michelin Tire Corp. v. Wages.* Choice **C** is incorrect because if the tax were necessary to reimburse state Orange for its inspection of imported items, it would be valid. Choice **B** is incorrect because the vases had lost their character as imports (i.e., they had been purchased by Bosco and would be held, indefinitely, until a purchaser for them was found). Finally, choice **A** is incorrect because the fact that the vases were sold that year does not preclude an *ad valorem* tax on items owned by and in Bosco's possession on the date (July 31) that the tax was applied.

65. **C** Under the Due Process and Commerce Clauses, a state may **not** ordinarily impose a sales tax on the out-of-state seller of an item where the transaction is consummated outside of that jurisdiction. *McCleod v. J. E. Dilworth Co.* Although the transaction was arguably initiated in state Blue, it was subject to Bosco's acceptance. This did not occur until the contract was reviewed and renegotiated by Bosco in state Orange. Thus, the transaction was consummated in state Orange, and only that jurisdiction could assess a *sales* tax. Choice **D** is incorrect because, as discussed in the answer to the preceding

question, the vases were not "in transit" when delivered to Bosco. Choices **A** and **B** are incorrect because the transaction was consummated in state Orange, and Bosco has no meaningful contacts with state Blue. Thus, both the Commerce and Due Process Clauses would preclude the levy of a sales tax on Bosco by state Blue. State Blue, however, might be able to impose a 3 percent *use* tax on Rudy with respect to the vases.

66. **C** Under the Commerce Clause, Congress may regulate any economic activity (even though primarily intrastate) that, in the aggregate, could have a significant impact on the movement of persons, information, or items across state lines. *Gonzales v. Raich.* Although the wheat in question was specifically grown for home consumption, this activity (in the aggregate) constitutes an economic activity and arguably has a negative impact on the movement of wheat across state lines (i.e., there would be a decreased need for persons in that jurisdiction to purchase out-of-state wheat). Choice **A** is incorrect because the fact that an economic activity is performed intrastate does not preclude it from having a significant impact on interstate commerce. Choice **B** is incorrect because the fact that a local economic activity has only an indirect effect on interstate commerce does not detract from the applicability of the interstate Commerce Clause (as long as the activity has, in the aggregate, a significant effect on interstate commerce). Finally, choice **D** is incorrect because the wheat in question has not been shipped or transported across state lines.

67. **B** Congress has the power to assess and collect taxes for the general welfare (but may not assess and collect taxes to accomplish a regulatory purpose regarding a matter reserved to the states). *U.S. v. Butler.* The fact that the state in which Weedy is located also taxes the particular wheat involved has no relevance in determining the constitutionality of the federal statute. Choice **A** is incorrect because the fact that the tax is collected by the Department of Agriculture (as opposed to the Treasury Department) arguably indicates that the tax has a regulatory purpose. Choice **C** is incorrect because the fact that a tax has the obvious effect of greatly enhancing the cost of an item tends to show that the purpose of the enactment was primarily regulatory in nature. Finally, choice **D** is incorrect because it indicates that the income-producing portion of the statute was aimed at benefiting a particular entity (rather than the general welfare).

68. D States may not ordinarily impair obligations created by outstanding contracts. U.S. Const. art. I, §10. An impairment of contractual obligations between a state and a private entity is constitutional only if it is reasonable and necessary to accomplish an important public purpose. *U.S. Trust Co. v. New Jersey.* Pursuant to the Tenth Amendment, a state may legislate for the safety, health, and general welfare of its citizens. The contract places no constraints on the right to sell oysters. The statute, however, precludes (1) sales of all discolored oysters and (2) sales to out-of-state purchasers where local buyers are willing to purchase the items. Although the legislation's purpose appears to be legitimate (i.e., to prevent injury to the oyster market), the legislature's fear that a diminishment of the oyster market will occur as a consequence of a slightly bitter taste probably does not constitute a sufficient "necessity" to alter the agreement. Choice **B** is incorrect because the right to sell all of the oysters harvested was presumably a central part of the agreement. Choice **C** is incorrect because the impairment of the Contracts Clause applies to agreements among private entities. Finally, choice **A** is factually incorrect because the legislation has not affected "all" of Fisheries' rights. It may still farm the oyster beds and sell nondiscolored oysters to (1) local entities for any price and (2) out-of-state buyers if local entities are unwilling to meet the price to be paid by the former group.

69. B Under the Fourteenth Amendment, states may not appropriate private property for public use without providing just compensation to the owner. When deciding whether a regulatory taking has occurred, federal courts consider the owner's reasonable, investment-backed expectations; the reduction of the property's value by virtue of the regulation; and the character of the government's action. *Lingle v. Chevron U.S.A., Inc.* In this case, Fisheries' reasonable, investment-backed expectations have been seriously frustrated; the value of the lease has declined significantly; and the government's action is a *de facto* confiscation of perfectly edible oysters. On these facts, a strong argument exists for a regulatory taking. Choice **D** is incorrect because the state government cannot force one group of property owners to shoulder a disproportionately high burden to advance a general public good. If the oysters were actually unsafe for human consumption, a much stronger argument against a regulatory taking would exist because the government may act to protect the public from unsafe foods without incurring an obligation to pay for the bad foodstuffs (i.e., the *character* of the government's action would be quite different). Choice **A** is incorrect because it focuses on an irrelevant legal consideration. A regulatory taking is measured by the regulation's effect on the property owner, not by the abstract wisdom or rationality of the regulation. *Lingle.* Finally, choice **C** is incorrect because the entire state X citizenry would arguably be financially injured if there was a significant decline in the demand for oysters originating in that state; hence, the statute advances a "public purpose."

70. **A** Where a state law discriminates against interstate commerce in favor of local interests, the state must justify the legislation by showing an overriding local benefit and the absence of any nondiscriminatory alternatives. *Hughes v. Oklahoma.* Although the preservation of an important local source of income is a legitimate state purpose, that interest could arguably be protected by requiring (1) a warning to out-of-state purchasers that the particular oysters being sold might have a slightly bitter taste or (2) potential buyers to sample the product, so that a decision could be made if their customers would be satisfied with the item. Choice **B** is incorrect because out-of-state buyers are being discriminated against (i.e., they can purchase oysters only if local buyers are unwilling to do so on similar terms). Choice **C** is incorrect because, although legitimate state interests are being served (the protection of the local economy), no overriding purpose is served in that the absence of oysters from local restaurants would probably not justify the second-class status conferred on out-of-state purchasers. *City of Philadelphia v. New Jersey.* Finally, choice **D** is incorrect because there is no *per se* right of states to protect natural resources after they have been collected or taken. Where legislation places out-of-state commerce at a disadvantage, the state must show that a substantial benefit will be derived and there is no nondiscriminatory means of achieving that goal.

71. **B** A statute is unduly vague (and therefore invalid) when a person of ordinary intelligence would be unable to determine if the actions that he is contemplating are proscribed. A statute is overly broad on its face (and therefore invalid) when the governmental entity empowered to enforce the law has virtually unlimited discretion in its determination of whether the law has been violated. Because the applicable statute appears to vest total discretion in the town licensing committee (i.e., no guidelines are provided with respect to the circumstances or conditions pursuant to which a license is to

be granted), the statute is probably overly broad. Choice **A** is incorrect because the statute is ***not*** ambiguous (i.e., it clearly states that a permit must be obtained from the licensing commission). Choice **C** is incorrect because the statute in question is overly broad, but not constitutionally infirm due to vagueness. Finally, choice **D** is incorrect because the statute is overly broad.

72. **B** A statute that is overly broad on its face cannot ordinarily serve as the basis for governmental action. *Lovell v. Griffin.* Because the statute appears to be overly broad on its face, the U.S. Supreme Court would reverse the misdemeanor conviction of MSL members. Choice **A** is incorrect because the statute was ***not*** valid on its face (i.e., absolutely no standards pursuant to which a determination as to whether a license should be granted have been provided). Choice **C** is incorrect because, the statute being invalid on its face, MSL members were ***not*** required to seek redress through appropriate judicial channels. Finally, choice **D** is incorrect because a statute that is overly broad ***on its face*** may not ordinarily serve as the basis for governmental action.

73. **C** Where persons violating a statute that is facially overbroad should have anticipated a constitutionally curative construction, the law may serve as the basis for a criminal conviction. *Shuttlesworth v. Birmingham.* If the MSL members who were convicted had reason to believe that a proper narrowing construction of the statute in question would be made by the Supreme Court, their conviction should be affirmed. Choice **B** is incorrect because if the statute in question was ***not*** facially overbroad (i.e., it was merely overly broad as applied), it could serve as the basis for a criminal prosecution (unless it was unconstitutionally applied). In such instance, the party affected by the statute would be obliged to seek redress through proper judicial channels. Choice **A** is incorrect because, despite the subsequent curative interpretation by the Supreme Court, a statute that is facially overbroad cannot serve as the basis for a criminal prosecution (assuming the defendants had no reason to anticipate a curative construction). Finally, choice **D** is incorrect because it is not necessary to obtain a judicial determination of the unconstitutionality of a facially overbroad statute prior to disobeying the enactment.

74. **B** Unless patently void on its face (i.e., issued by a court that lacked subject-matter jurisdiction), a contempt conviction for disobeying a ***judicial*** order is ordinarily valid (even if such order was improperly

issued). *Walker v. City of Birmingham.* However, where, for the purpose of frustrating the defendant's First Amendment rights, an injunction is not sought until the last possible moment, a conviction for failing to obey the injunction might be unconstitutional. The fact that the permit was unconstitutionally denied would be irrelevant because the contempt-of-court conviction is predicated on the defendants' refusal to abide by a court order (not the violation of the licensing ordinance). Even if the licensing ordinance was invalid, adherence to the court order would still ordinarily be required. Choice **C** is relevant because if the court clearly lacked subject-matter jurisdiction, its order could be disregarded. Choice **D** is relevant because a court order (even if erroneously issued) must ordinarily be challenged by appeal. It ordinarily **cannot** simply be disregarded with impunity. Finally, choice **A** is relevant because, if the commission deliberately waited until the last moment to obtain an injunction against the march (i.e., the MSL announced that it would proceed with its march despite the absence of a license on June 27, yet an injunction was not sought until July 3), a conviction for disregarding the injunction might not withstand constitutional scrutiny.

75. **B** There is no First Amendment right to express one's views on another's private property. *Hudgens v. National Labor Relations Board.* States, however, may require a private property owner to permit others to express their views on commercial private property, provided such expression poses no threat of actual and substantial disruption to the activities ordinarily conducted on such private property and does not result in a deprivation of the landowner's due-process rights. *Pruneyard Shopping Center v. Robins.* State action was not involved in the earlier lawsuit (*Ray v. Orwell*). In that case, a private shopping center owner had ejected the plaintiff from the grounds. Thus, a claim based on the U.S. Constitution did not exist. Choice **A** is factually incorrect because there was an actual interference with Ray's exercise of his purported right of free speech (i.e., he had been ejected from the shopping center). Choice **C** is incorrect because it is not necessary that a criminal prosecution be imminent for the "actual controversy" requisite of federal court jurisdiction to be operative. This condition is satisfied by an actual, outstanding dispute. Finally, choice **D** is legally incorrect because sign carrying is a protected form of First Amendment protection.

76. D A party may appeal an adverse decision to the U.S. Supreme Court when a state court decides an issue of federal law; only if the state court decision rests on "independent" and "adequate" *exclusive* state law grounds is the decision unreviewable via a petition for a writ of certiorari. *Michigan v. Long.* The state supreme court decision, restricting property rights and forcing Orwell to tolerate expression on his private property, plainly implicates cognizable federal constitutional rights arising under the First and Fifth Amendments (made applicable to the states, in relevant part, by the Fourteenth Amendment). Thus, as has been the case since Congress abolished the mandatory jurisdiction of the Supreme Court in 1988, the Supreme Court could have elected to hear this appeal, but had no statutory obligation to do so. The denial of Orwell's petition for certiorari indicates only that three members of the U.S. Supreme Court believed that the lower court's opinion should be reviewed. Choice **A** is incorrect because a refusal to grant certiorari has no precedential value whatsoever. Choice **B** is incorrect because the mere fact that a justice votes to grant certiorari does not necessarily indicate that he believed the lower court was incorrect. Rather, it suggests only that the justice believed the lower-court decision should be reviewed by the U.S. Supreme Court. Finally, choice **C** is incorrect because a refusal to grant certiorari indicates only that the members of the court voting against the petition did ***not*** believe that the action merited review by the U.S. Supreme Court at that time. A refusal to grant certiorari is not indicative of any opinion with respect to the case's merits.

77. C Under the Due Process and Commerce Clauses, a state may ***not*** ordinarily impose a sales tax on the out-of-state seller of an item where the transaction is consummated outside of that jurisdiction. *McCleod v. J. E. Dilworth Co.* A use tax may be imposed on the purchaser-user of an item where the good will be used within the state assessing the tax. A use tax may not exceed, however, the difference between (1) the sales tax imposed on such items by the state in which the good will be used and (2) any sales tax assessed against the seller by the state in which the sale was consummated. *Henneford v. Silas Mason Co.* Because the transaction was consummated in Nevada, California cannot impose a sales tax on it. However, California can impose a use tax on the buyer if the item will be used in that state. Thus, choices **A**, **B**, and **D** are incorrect.

78. **B** Under the Due Process Clause, a state may require an out-of-state seller to collect a use tax pertaining to the purchase of an item by a resident of the taxing state, if the seller physically entered the state in which the buyer is located to solicit the orders in question. *Nelson v. Sears Roebuck & Co.* Because salespersons of the Nevada entity actually entered California to solicit orders for the goods in question, contacts consistent with due process would exist to require the Nevada seller to collect the use tax for California on the item. Choice **A** is incorrect because a sales tax cannot be assessed against the Nevada seller (i.e., the sale was completed in Nevada and the vendor has no permanent employees or agents in California). Choice **C** is incorrect because contacts necessary to satisfy due process do exist by reason of the fact that the order was actually solicited by the vendor's sales personnel in California. (Note, however, that if the purchase had been solicited by telephone or mail, contacts necessary to satisfy due process would **not** exist; *National Bellas Hess, Inc. v. Illinois Department of Revenue*). Finally, choice **D** is legally incorrect (a use tax may, under appropriate circumstances, be collected directly from the seller).

79. **C** A statute is unconstitutionally vague when a person of ordinary intelligence would, even with actual knowledge of the law in question, be uncertain as to whether contemplated conduct was proscribed. Expression that is made by the speaker with the intention or likelihood of provoking a violent response (i.e., "fighting words") is punishable pursuant to a properly drawn statute. *Chaplinsky v. New Hampshire.* Although "fighting words" may be punished, the statute in question is probably too vague (i.e., the words "annoying," "disturbing," and "unwelcome" are too subjective in nature for an average person to determine if particular language is punishable). Choice **B** is incorrect because the use of "fighting words" is constitutionally punishable. Choice **A** is incorrect because the statute, as presently drawn, is probably too vague to be the basis of a criminal conviction. Finally, choice **D** is factually incorrect (i.e., the average person would probably be offended by Smith's language).

80. **A** Congress is prohibited from passing a bill of attainder (i.e., a law that inflicts punishment on particular individuals or an identifiable group of persons without a trial). U.S. Const. art. I, §9. The law in question punishes persons who are members of the Communist Party simply because such individuals are members of that group. *United States v. Brown.* There is no requirement that such persons

have the specific intent to further the illegal objectives of that organization. Choice **B** is incorrect because a definable class of individuals is within the proscription of a bill of attainder. Choice **C** is incorrect because, although Congress may have intended to protect the national economy, its classification is too overinclusive (i.e., the effect of the statute would be to punish persons who did not specifically intend to overthrow the government by illegal means). Finally, choice **D** is incorrect because Congress may not enact a law that is in conflict with the U.S. Constitution.

81. **A** In the absence of an asserted need to protect military, diplomatic, or national security secrets, in criminal cases the privilege pertaining to executive communications is qualified in nature. *United States v. Nixon.* The executive privilege is ordinarily qualified in nature (i.e., a court, *in camera*, must weigh the interest being protected against the need for the information that is sought). In the above-cited case, the U.S. Supreme Court held that the importance of a pending criminal proceeding outweighed a general claim of executive privilege. Choice **B** is incorrect because there might be situations where communications would be deemed to be privileged (i.e., they related to a matter of national security), even though the information was sought for a criminal proceeding. Choice **C** is incorrect because there is at least a qualified executive privilege pertaining to information sought in a criminal trial. Finally, choice **D** is legally incorrect (i.e., the executive privilege is qualified, rather than absolute, in nature).

82. **C** Under due process, personal property that is used in interstate commerce may be taxed by the jurisdiction that constitutes the taxpayer's principal place of business and by states in which the items have a taxable situs. Because Flyright's airplanes land in Virginia on a regular basis (about 20 times per day), that jurisdiction can probably place a personal property tax on the taxpayer's flight equipment. *Braniff Airways v. Nebraska Board of Equalization.* Although goods within the stream of interstate commerce may not ordinarily be taxed by a state, that rule does not apply to equipment that is regularly used in the transportation process. One should note, however, that New York and Virginia would be obliged to apportion the aggregate personal property tax on Flyright's aircraft in an equitable manner. Choices **A**, **B**, and **D** are incorrect because **both** Virginia and New York may assess a personal property tax against Flyright's airplanes.

83. **B** Where a state court has invalidated a state statute based on the ground that it is in conflict with a federal law, review by the U.S. Supreme Court can be accomplished only by a writ of certiorari. Because the state X Supreme Court struck down the local ordinance on the ground that it conflicted with a federal law, review could be obtained only by a favorable response to a petition for writ of certiorari. Choice **D** is incorrect because a federal issue still exists (i.e., is the state X statute unconstitutional under the Supremacy Clause?). Choice **A** is incorrect because (under the given facts) the state X Supreme Court premised its decision on the Supremacy Clause. Finally, choice **C** is incorrect because the abstention doctrine is primarily applicable to situations where the language contained in a state law might be cured by a narrowing interpretation rendered by a state court. In such event, the constitutional issue would be precluded. In this instance, however, (1) there is nothing vague about the state statute in question, and (2) the constitutional issue has already been decided by a state court. Thus, the abstention doctrine is inapplicable.

84. **C** A constitutional issue that would otherwise be rendered moot will ordinarily be heard when it is capable of repetition, yet evading review. *Roe v. Wade.* Because other persons might not learn about the SAT requirement until it was too late to take the examination, the constitutional question could continually evade review. Choice **A** is incorrect because the constitutional issue involved in this instance could continually recur, if not settled at this time. Choice **D** is factually incorrect (a First Amendment claim has not been asserted by Malcolm). Additionally, case law has not given First Amendment concerns any special consideration with respect to the mootness doctrine. Finally, choice **B** is incorrect because, although Malcolm could take the SAT examination in time for the next election, there is a possibility that he might subsequently decide to not run for mayor. In such event, the SAT requirement might avoid constitutional scrutiny until it was used again by state X to prevent someone else from running for public office. Thus, the mootness doctrine would probably ***not*** be applied in this instance.

85. **D** Congress has been empowered to enforce the provisions of the Thirteenth and Fourteenth Amendments by appropriate legislation. Thirteenth Amendment, §2, and Fourteenth Amendment, §5. Because Congress could have reasonably determined that filing fees and/or literacy tests promote racial discrimination or deny persons

equal protection, the federal statute is valid. As a consequence, state legislation that conflicts with the federal law would be unconstitutional under the Supremacy Clause. Choice **C** is incorrect because the federal statute did not invalidate residency requirements. As a consequence, *all* of the provisions of the state X law would not be unconstitutional. Choice **A** is incorrect because the Tenth Amendment only reserves to the states those powers that have not been specifically delegated to the federal government. Finally, choice **B** is incorrect because application of the Supremacy Clause is not dependent on the federal statute being in existence *prior* to any state law.

86. **A** A statute that is unconstitutionally vague cannot serve as the basis of governmental action. If the statute were unconstitutionally vague (i.e., a person of ordinary intelligence could not determine whether contemplated conduct was proscribed), the provision in question would be stricken from the enactment. Choice **B** is incorrect because, although there is no constitutionally guaranteed right to tuition assistance, unconstitutional laws cannot be used to affect an existing governmental benefit. Choice **C** is incorrect because statutes that are unconstitutionally vague on their face cannot serve as the basis for governmental action. Finally, choice **D** is incorrect because the fact that a law is rationally related to a legitimate governmental purpose (i.e., in this instance, protection of the federal government) does not insulate it from attack on constitutional grounds.

87. **B** A governmental limitation on symbolic speech (conduct that is intended to communicate a message and that the viewing audience would understand as such) is permissible if (1) it furthers a substantial interest, (2) it is unrelated to the content of the expression, and (3) the restriction on First Amendment activity is closely tailored to satisfy the governmental objective. *United States v. O'Brien.* In this instance, (1) the conduct in question is related to the content of the speech (i.e., activity detrimental to the federal government), and (2) there probably is no substantial governmental interest in precluding demonstrations critical of recruitment by the CIA on a college campus. Therefore, withdrawal of the scholarship as a result of Arthur's participation in the demonstration is probably invalid. Choice **A** is incorrect because even peaceful demonstrations are subject to reasonable limitations pertaining to time, place, and manner. Thus, under proper circumstances, such demonstrations can be the basis of civil or criminal sanctions. Choice **C** is incorrect because the actions of X State University, being a state institution,

would constitute governmental action. Finally, choice **D** is incorrect because constitutionally valid conduct (i.e., in this instance, engaging in an activity protected by the First Amendment) cannot serve as the basis for adverse governmental action.

88. **C** State legislation pertaining to the health, morals, or welfare of its citizens is usually valid if the law bears any *conceivable* rational relationship to a legitimate state interest; the state government has *no* burden of justification in such cases, and the plaintiff essentially must prove a negative. *Williamson v. Lee Optical Co.; Ferguson v. Skrupa.* Joe could contend that the state X statute is demonstrably irrational because (1) state X residents can obtain scholarships for out-of-state study if geology courses are taken in another jurisdiction, but (2) no scholarship is extended to state X residents desiring to attend college outside of the jurisdiction for any other reason. If the purpose of the statute was to ease the economic burden on state X residents who desire to attend college, it is irrational to discriminate against them on the basis of where the institution is located or their course of study. However, the state X statute plainly bears a theoretically rational relationship to a legitimate state purpose (i.e., to assist state X residents in obtaining an education) and therefore is constitutional. Note that the *actual basis* for the law is quite irrelevant to the constitutional analysis. *New Orleans v. Dukes.* The fact that the state X legislature has chosen not to extend this benefit to residents who choose to attend an out-of-state university would probably **not** cause the act to be constitutionally impermissible. The state X legislature might have legitimately decided to assist students who study at colleges in state X because those persons undoubtedly purchase more local products (i.e., food, books, etc.) than persons attending out-of-state universities. An exception for geology majors might be rationally based on the determination that persons with a background in that area would benefit the state X economy in a special manner. Choice **A** is incorrect because no significant limitation has been imposed on Joe's Fourteenth Amendment right to travel (he is merely being denied a particular potential benefit if he elects to attend college in another state). Choice **D** is incorrect because the Privileges and Immunities Clause of Article IV, §2, precludes a state from discriminating against the citizens of other jurisdictions. In this instance, state X is merely refusing to extend a particular benefit to one of its own residents. Finally, choice **B** is incorrect because,

as discussed above, the classifications drawn by the statute are not irrational.

89. D State legislation pertaining to the health, morals, or welfare of its citizens is constitutionally permissible if it bears a rational relationship to any legitimate government action. The state X legislature could have rationally determined that a specified SAT score was necessary to qualify for scholarship (i.e., those persons who have a greater probability of completing their college education successfully). Choice **A** is incorrect because the Privileges and Immunities Clause of the Fourteenth Amendment precludes a state from discriminating against out-of-state residents with respect to "fundamental" or "important" rights. It does not prevent a jurisdiction from denying privileges to its own citizens if certain preconditions are not satisfied. Choice **B** is incorrect because there is no fundamental right to a college education. Finally, choice **C** is incorrect because, as discussed above, there is a rational basis for requiring a minimum SAT score to obtain a scholarship.

90. D Where a fundamental or basic right is involved, statutes must satisfy the strict-scrutiny test (i.e., there must be a compelling state interest and the law must be narrowly tailored to achieve that compelling interest (i.e., no less burdensome means of accomplishing the government's objective can exist). The U.S. Supreme Court has held that the right to marry and divorce occupies a fundamental position in our society. Thus, a similar statute was determined to be invalid under the Due Process Clause of the Fourteenth Amendment in *Boddie v. Connecticut.* The state's desire to defray a part of the expense inherent in the divorce procedure did not rise to the level of a "compelling" interest. Choice **B** is incorrect because the strict-scrutiny test, albeit applicable, is *not* met in this instance. Choice **A** is incorrect because (1) the strict-scrutiny test would be applicable to a situation involving marital status, and (2) the requisite "compelling" state interest is *not* satisfied. Finally, choice **C** is incorrect because, although the discrimination resulting from the statute is *de facto* (rather than *de jure*) in nature, this fact alone would not save the law from being unconstitutional on due-process grounds.

91. C Under the Equal Protection Clause, classifications that are purposefully based on gender must (1) serve an important governmental interest and (2) be substantially related to the achievement of those interests. The state X law replicates the applicable principle of law. *Mississippi University for Women v. Hogan.* Choice **A** is incorrect because, although laws are ordinarily presumed to be valid, so-called "intermediate" scrutiny applies to statutes that employ gender-based classifications or that are motivated by gender-based animus and produce discriminatory effects based on sex. Choice **B** is incorrect because the state interest must merely be "important" (rather than "compelling"). Finally, choice **D** is incorrect because even legislation that is favorable to women must satisfy middle-level scrutiny. *Mississippi University for Women v. Hogan.*

92. **D** *Congressional* laws pertaining to aliens are ordinarily reviewed under the rational-relationship standard (i.e., the legislation must be rationally related to a legitimate governmental objective). *Mathews v. Diaz.* Because the act in question has been passed by Congress (rather than a state legislature), it is **not** subject to a strict-scrutiny analysis. Therefore, a law that prefers U.S. citizens over aliens with respect to federal welfare monies is probably constitutional for the reason set forth in choice **D**. Choice **A** is incorrect because no Equal Protection Clause is applicable to the federal government (i.e., the Fifth Amendment refers only to due process). Choice **B** is incorrect because there is no case law establishing welfare as a fundamental right. *Dandridge v. Williams.* Finally, choice **C** is incorrect because aliens do have due-process rights (i.e., the Fifth Amendment applies to all "persons" within the United States). However, the statute in question is valid because Congress may prefer citizens over noncitizens with respect to the receipt of federal social welfare benefits.

93. **B** Where the plaintiff in a defamation action is a public figure, he must prove that the defendant's statements were (1) false and (2) made with actual malice (i.e., either with actual knowledge of their falsehood or under circumstances that reflect "reckless indifference" to their truth or falsity).. One is a public figure when he voluntarily interjects himself into a public controversy. *Gertz v. Robert Welch, Inc.* Because Smith is probably a "public figure" by reason of his decision to run for a seat in the state senate, he would have to prove that the newspaper's statement was (1) false and (2) made with actual malice. Choice **A** is legally incorrect (there is no **absolute** privilege pertaining to mass-media entities). Choice **C** is incorrect because, where the plaintiff is a public figure, he must prove that the defendant's statement was made with actual malice. Finally, choice **D** is incorrect because the plaintiff, as a public figure, must prove that the *Daily Times* acted with actual malice (not simply unreasonably). Also note that the U.S. Supreme Court has stated that where (1) the

plaintiff is **not** a public figure, (2) the speech concerns a matter of public concern, and (3) the defendant is a mass-media entity, the latter must have acted at least negligently under the circumstances for a defamation action to be successfully asserted. *Gertz.*

94. **A** Under the Equal Protection Clause, classifications that facially incorporate gender-based classifications *or* that are the product of intentional gender based animus and that produce disparate gender-based outcomes must (1) serve an important governmental interest and (2) be substantially related to the achievement of those interests. Because the facts fail to indicate that the state X legislature intentionally sought to discriminate against women, the act would be upheld as long as the "rational basis" test was satisfied. *Personnel Administrator v. Feeney.* Choices **B** and **C** are incorrect because they embody more demanding standards of review than apply on these facts. Finally, choice **D** is incorrect because a showing by the plaintiffs that the legislature intended to discriminate against women is **not** a requisite for validation of the act. In fact, if such a situation were proven, the act would be more susceptible to attack because intermediate scrutiny would apply.

95. **C** A state government may proscribe obscene material, even though only consenting adults view it. In *Paris Adult Theatre I v. Slaton*, the U.S. Supreme Court specifically held that obscene materials exhibited only to consenting adults could be criminalized. Thus, evidence that minors or nonconsenting adults were purposefully excluded from Doug's theater would be irrelevant. Choice **A** is incorrect because *California v. La Rue* held that states have broad power under the Twenty-first Amendment to prohibit sexually oriented entertainment in establishments where alcoholic beverages are being sold. It therefore has little pertinence to the evidence excluded by the trial court in this instance. Choice **D** is incorrect because *Ernoznik v. City of Jacksonville* held only that an ordinance prohibiting drive-in movies from showing pictures with nude scenes that were not constitutionally obscene was invalid. Finally, choice **B** is incorrect because *Stanley v. Georgia* recognized the right to possess obscene material in the home for personal use only. Mailing or importing obscene materials, even for personal use, may constitutionally be prohibited or even criminalized. *United States v. Reidel; United States v. Twelve 200-Foot Reels*, respectively.

96. **C** Government constitutionally may prohibit the mailing of obscene material. The *Stanley* case recognized only the right to possess

obscene material in one's home for personal use. Mailing or importing obscene materials, even for the recipient's personal use, can be constitutionally constrained. *United States v. Twelve 200-Foot Reels.* Choice **D** is incorrect because the *Stanley* case did *not* pertain to the *commercial* sale of obscene material. Choice **A** is incorrect because the *Reidel* case constitutes a basis for upholding, rather than reversing, the trial court's decision. Finally, choice **B** is incorrect because the *Stanley* decision did *not* recognize a right to possess obscene materials in one's home "for any reason" (i.e., commercial distribution).

97. **C** In the absence of explicit consent by the applicable jurisdiction, the Eleventh Amendment bars a lawsuit in federal court by a citizen against a state that could result in a retroactive charge against the general revenues of that jurisdiction. *Edelman v. Jordan.* Although the Eleventh Amendment explicitly pertains only to suits by citizens of a state against a different state, the bar contained in this provision has been judicially extended to suits by citizens of a state against their own jurisdiction. *Alden v. Maine; Hans v. Louisiana.* Choices **A** and **B** are incorrect because the Eleventh Amendment does not preclude suits against individuals (personally) or subdivisions (i.e., counties, cities, school boards, etc.) of a state. Finally, choice **D** is incorrect because the Eleventh Amendment does not preclude injunctive suits against state officials to require them to act (1) in accordance with a federal law or (2) in a constitutional manner. *Ex parte Young.* One should note, however, that if a federal law or the U.S. Constitution were not the basis of the plaintiff's claim, the Eleventh Amendment would preclude a suit for even injunctive relief in federal court. *Pennhurst State School & Hospital v. Halderman.*

98. **C** A plaintiff must be able to show a direct, concrete, and particularized injury or loss as a consequence of the defendant's action to have Article III standing in a federal court. *Lujan v. Defenders of Wildlife.* Because Jane has been denied employment at ABC Co., she has suffered a direct injury as a consequence of the allegedly unconstitutional law. Choice **D** is incorrect because, even if she could obtain similar employment nearby, she has still sustained an immediate injury by being refused employment at ABC Co. The fact that a plaintiff's injury can be mitigated does not detract from the fact that injury has occurred. Choice **A** is incorrect because the fact that ABC Co. is not being prosecuted has no bearing on the fact that Jane has been wronged. Finally, choice **B** is incorrect because Jane suffered a direct injury by reason of the denial of employment at ABC Co.

99. **B** Under the Equal Protection Clause, classifications that facially discriminate based on gender must (1) serve an important governmental interest and (2) be substantially related to the achievement of those interests. *Mississippi University for Women v. Hogan.* Because the statute facially discriminates based on gender, state Yellow must prove that the legislation is substantially related to the achievement of an important governmental objective. It is highly unlikely that the desire to reduce absenteeism on the night shift would constitute a sufficiently "important" state interest. It is also very unlikely that a reviewing court would find the statute to be narrowly drawn (i.e., only women with young children should be proscribed from working during the evening), and the logic of this rule would also be open to serious doubt, insofar as it relies on longstanding gender-based stereotypes. *U.S. v. Virginia.* Choice **A** is incorrect because, when government uses a facially discriminatory gender-based classification, a state must prove more than a mere rational basis for the enactment. Choice **C** is incorrect because it states the fact that gender-based classifications are suspect without providing the legal standard by which courts evaluate such classifications (i.e., intermediate scrutiny). Finally, choice **D** is incorrect because, although factually true (i.e., there is no fundamental right to obtain a particular type of employment), the legislation in question probably does ***not*** satisfy the intermediate-level scrutiny to which it would be held.

100. **B** There is no First Amendment right of access to the print media. *Miami Herald Publishing Co. v. Tornillo.* In *Tornillo,* the U.S. Supreme Court struck down a Florida statute that required newspapers to print the replies of political candidates whom they had attacked. Choice **D** is incorrect because broadcasting entities may be required to grant individuals the right to reply to personal attacks and concerned parties the right to reply to the station's political editorials. *Red Lion Broadcasting Co. v. FCC.* Choice **C** is incorrect because it wrongly applies the rule for broadcasting entities to newspapers. Finally, choice **A** is incorrect because newspapers are ***not*** required to give access to opposing points of view.

101. **D** "Fighting words" are a general exception to protected categories of speech and are therefore defined very tightly. The Supreme Court has defined the term "fighting words" narrowly to encompass only words that that "by their very utterance ... tend to incite an immediate breach of the peace." However, it is not enough

that the words used make the audience angry. *Chaplinsky v. New Hampshire; Terminiello v. Chicago*. In any event, the police have the duty to control the crowd, if they can, rather than arrest the speaker. Assuming that the words in this question can be construed as "fighting words," the police apparently had the physical capability to control the crowd and should have done so instead of arresting Klubinski. *Cox v. Louisiana*. Because 15 police officers could presumably have restrained the 4 people who advanced toward the podium, Klubinski's arrest was inappropriate. Choice **C** is incorrect because mere opinion can constitute "fighting words" if the opinions are sufficiently incendiary. Choice **A** is incorrect because, whether or not Klubinki's words were "fighting words," there were enough police on hand to restrain the crowd, and they had a duty to do so. Finally, choice **B** is incorrect because, even if the words were calculated to evoke a violent response, the police had an obligation to restrain the crowd before arresting the speaker.

102. A A statute attempting to control speech is unconstitutionally vague when a reasonable person who becomes aware of its terms would have to guess at its meaning and application and would not know whether his conduct was prohibited. *Connally v. General Construction Co.* Additionally, speech may not be prohibited simply because it may be "offensive" to the hearer; to be proscribable, the speech must be obscene or classified as "fighting words." *Cohen v. California*. The term "offensive" is too vague to support a criminal prosecution. Choice **B** is incorrect because the decision whether speech is protected does not depend on the speaker's opinion as to the truth or falsity of his statements. Choice **C** is incorrect because the fact that a "reasonable" person might be offended is too vague a standard by which to judge speech. Finally, choice **D** is incorrect because intent to offend is not a standard by which the right to speak is judged; it is too vague.

103. C The U.S. Supreme Court has held that it will not review a state court decision otherwise falling within its appellate jurisdiction, if (1) that decision can be supported by an "independent and adequate" state law ground, and (2) the state court hearing the case announces its intent to decide the case on exclusively state law grounds by a plain statement *in the decision itself. Michigan v. Long*. Reliance on a state law ground must be "clear" and "express" to preclude Supreme Court review. Because the facts tell us that Bob was successful on his Euphoria state constitutional arguments *and* *also* his Fourteenth Amendment claim, and in the absence of the required plain statement, the Supreme Court of the United States *could* decide to grant a writ of certiorari in this case. Choice **A** is incorrect because the Supreme Court could choose to exercise its discretion to grant a writ of certiorari under these circumstances; the state supreme court failed to make the required "clear" and "express" plain statement announcing an intention to decide the case solely on state constitutional law grounds. Choice **D** is incorrect because there is no automatic review when a state court decision involves a federal claim, if the state court's decision can stand on other grounds. Finally, choice **B** is factually incorrect because there can be U.S. Supreme Court review of a state court decision.

104. **C** Article III, §1, of the U.S. Constitution vests federal judicial power in the Supreme Court and in "such inferior courts as Congress may from time to time ordain and establish." Section 2 extends federal judicial power to "Controversies . . . between Citizens of different States, . . . and between a State, or the Citizens thereof and foreign States, Citizens or Subjects." This language has been interpreted to mean that Congress may define and restrict those diversity-of-citizenship cases that may be heard by lower federal courts. For example, Congress has imposed an amount-in-controversy floor of $75,000 in diversity cases. Congress has the constitutional power to end federal diversity-of-citizenship jurisdiction completely (at least in the lower federal courts). Choice **D** is incorrect because, although factually accurate, it is not as good a basis for validating the statute under analysis as choice **C**. Choice **A** is incorrect because there is no equal-protection issue under these facts. The impact of the statute would be felt equally by all citizens. Finally, choice **B** is incorrect because, although Article III, §2, refers to diversity cases, federal courts have construed this section to grant Congress the authority to limit diversity cases in the lower federal courts.

105. **C** In construing Congress's Article I power of taxation, the Supreme Court has squarely held that a regulatory purpose will not invalidate a federal tax law; thus, civil tax laws on activities such as illegal gambling and the sale of illegal narcotics are perfectly constitutional, even if, in practice, they generate little (if any) government revenue. *United States v. Doremus.* As long as a federal tax could plausibly produce revenue, it is ordinarily valid. *United States v. Kahriger.* Thus, even though the principal purpose of this tax is

regulatory in nature, it is constitutional. Choice **D** is incorrect because Congress has no specific power to legislate for the general welfare. Choice **A** is incorrect because a woman's right to undergo breast implants has not been held to be a fundamental privacy right entitled to due-process protection. Finally, choice **B** is incorrect because, as discussed above, the fact that the tax had a regulatory purpose does **not** *ipso facto* cause it to be unconstitutional.

106. **A** Under its power to tax to "provide for the general welfare" (U.S. Const. art. I, §8, cl. 1), Congress has the inherent power both to disburse and not to disburse the funds it collects. The legislation in question relies on this inherent power. The legislation uses the taxing power to provide the general-welfare benefit of reducing traffic accidents. Choice **C** states an incorrect conclusion; the states did **not** cede their authority over highways to the federal government by accepting federal grants to finance the construction of their roadways. Choice **D** is incorrect because the advance of federal monies to the states does not carry with it the broad and unconditional right to regulate state highways. The federal right to regulate derives from the Commerce Clause. Finally, choice **B** is incorrect because surveys do not constitute a constitutionally recognized basis to support federal (or state) legislation.

107. **B** Congress may not generally "commandeer" a state legislature and require it to enact a particular law against its will. *New York v. United States.* Nor may Congress require state executive officers to implement a federal law. *Printz v. United States.* Here, the law requires state legislatures to enact laws and local law enforcement officers to implement the new laws; both requirements "commandeer" state government officers in violation of the Tenth Amendment. *However,* Congress may, consistent with these constitutional requirements, use its power to tax and spend for the general welfare to seek voluntary state compliance with federal regulatory mandates of this sort; federal largesse may be conditioned on changes in state law, such as an increase in the minimum drinking age. *South Dakota v. Dole.* To pass constitutional muster, the program must promote the general welfare, the condition must be clearly stated and the decision to accept or reject the federal funds voluntary and noncoercive, and the condition must reasonably relate to the purpose of the spending. Here, Congress arguably has met all three conditions. Choice **A** is incorrect because, as discussed immediately above, the Commerce Clause is *not* a source of

constitutional authority for Congress to force a state legislature to enact a law. Choice **C** is also not correct because Congress cannot use the Commerce Clause to force state legislatures to enact legislation. Finally, choice **D** is incorrect because the Tenth Amendment provides for the general reservation of powers in the states; the power of Congress to tax and spend for the general welfare does not violate the Tenth Amendment if state participation in a federal spending program is genuinely voluntary. *South Dakota v. Dole.*

108. **A** If a state statute facially discriminates against out-of-state commerce or persons, it is invalid unless the jurisdiction can show that (1) an overriding benefit will accrue to it from the legislation, and (2) there is no less discriminatory alternative to achieve that interest. *Hughes v. Oklahoma.* The requirement that lawyers be graduates of Euphoria colleges and law schools burdens interstate commerce by discouraging out-of-state college and law school graduates from relocating to Euphoria. The governmental objective apparently sought here could be accomplished in a less burdensome manner (i.e., by requiring all persons desiring to practice law to pass an appropriate ethics examination and character analysis). Choice **B** is incorrect because the Privileges and Immunities Clause of the Fourteenth Amendment has been construed to pertain only to rights of national citizenship (i.e., the right to travel from state to state, the right to petition the federal government, etc.). The Privileges and Immunities Clause contained in Article IV, §2, of the U.S. Constitution would probably afford an additional basis for invalidating the Euphoria statute (*Hicklin v. Orbeck*) because the right to practice one's calling is a fundamental civil right that the states cannot infringe; however, that option is not raised by the choices offered. Choice **C** is incorrect because, although factually possible (the quality of out-of-state law schools could be inferior, and the legislature might reasonably believe this), there are other, less discriminatory ways to deal with the skill and integrity of out-of-state lawyers than to bar them altogether (e.g., to condition licensure to practice law on passage of an examination). Finally, choice **D** is incorrect because the right to practice one's calling is a fundamental right protected by the Privileges and Immunities Clause of Article IV, §2.

109. **C** The Supreme Court has interpreted the Privileges and Immunities Clause contained in Article IV, §2, of the U.S. Constitution to preclude a state from discriminating against the citizens of other

states with respect to the exercise of rights "fundamental to national unity." Among these are the right to be employed, the right to practice one's profession, and the right to engage in business. By requiring members of the Amityville Police Department to live within that city, the city council has prevented the citizens of Peddle from working as police officers in Amityville. On these facts, there is no showing that residents of Peddle are peculiarly responsible for the complaints against the Amityville police or that there is a "substantial relationship" between Amityville's problem and the proposed solution. Choice **A** is incorrect because the Privileges and Immunities Clause of the Fourteenth Amendment applies only when a state attempts to curb a right of national citizenship (i.e., the right to travel from state to state, the right to petition federal officials, etc.). Choice **B** is incorrect because the U.S. Supreme Court has never held that there is a substantive due-process right to practice a particular profession or trade. Finally, choice **D** is essentially correct because the Contracts Clause in Article I, §10, has been narrowly applied to require that a contract can be impaired only if (1) there has been a "substantial impairment" of the contract, and (2) the impairment is "reasonable and necessary to support an important public purpose." *United States Trust Co. v. New Jersey.* There is no showing that that test is met on these facts. However, choice **C** is still the better choice because a court might hold that the three-year grace period was a justifiable concession to the contract rights of the Peddle residents.

110. **D** The determination whether to prosecute a case falls exclusively within the prerogatives of the executive branch. The U.S. attorney general is appointed by the president and is entrusted with the president's authority to "take care that the Laws be faithfully executed." U.S. Const. art. II, §3. In the exercise of his discretion, the attorney general can determine that a particular case should not be prosecuted. Choice **C** is incorrect because the attorney general is not entirely independent; he is subject to direction and removal by the president. Choice **A** is incorrect because the determination whether to prosecute particular conduct is exclusively executive in nature. The Senate cannot direct the attorney general to prosecute a particular case. Finally, choice **B** is incorrect because, although it states in general terms one of the attorney general's prime functions, it ignores the fact that he has discretion in particular cases.

111. A Under the Necessary and Proper Clause of the U.S. Constitution, Congress has the power to conduct investigations into matters with respect to which it may legislate. *McGrain v. Daugherty.* If Anthracite was questioned about matters that were clearly unrelated to an area in which Congress could legislate, he could refuse to answer. The nature of the inquiry here suggests that Congress was not interested in legislation. Choice **B** is legally incorrect because the House committee could question Anthracite about any matter that could be the subject of legislation, not just with regard to the expenditure of funds. The powers of Congress extend beyond the expenditure of funds. Choice **C** is legally incorrect; the power of confirmation is immaterial to the right to conduct investigations (both chambers of the U.S. Congress have the right to conduct investigations into areas that might be the subject of legislation). Finally, choice **D** is incorrect because Congress may ordinarily question executive officers about the performance of their duties. Such information could be helpful in determining if additional laws should be enacted. Although there is a limited executive privilege to refuse to disclose information that is confidential in nature, this privilege does not extend to all executive communications. *United States v. Nixon.*

112. C At issue in this question is the impact of the Equal Protection Clause of the Fourteenth Amendment. The PUC rule has imposed an employment classification that must meet the requirements of the clause. Although the Supreme Court's strict-scrutiny standard is usually applicable where the job involved is *not* one that is "bound up with the operation of the state as a governmental entity" or that especially required local political and cultural knowledge, the rule *in this instance* need only satisfy the rational-relationship test. Working as a public school teacher, for example, may be conditioned on U.S. citizenship because of the nature of the job. *Ambach v. Norwick.* Responding to emergency calls from the citizenry is a function that could rationally be construed as requiring the special knowledge of a U.S. citizen who would typically be more able to understand and respond to the problem described by the caller. Choice **B** is incorrect because the fact that Mary could respond adequately is irrelevant. The test is applied to the general classification, which is a reasonable one, not to the application of the classification to any individual. Choice **A** is intentionally deceptive: It constitutes a basis for validating the statute, not nullifying it. Finally, choice **D** is incorrect because it states the standards required for intermediate scrutiny, not mere rationality; as discussed above, the rational-relationship test is applicable in this instance because of the nature of the job.

113. **D** Article II, §2, of the U.S. Constitution assigns to the president, not the Congress, the power to appoint executive officials. Congress may, however, appoint persons to perform legislative functions, including congressional investigations. *Buckley v. Valeo*. The authority given to the proposed JRC is essentially executive in nature and, accordingly, Congress cannot aggrandize itself by usurping the power to appoint its members. Choice **B** is legally incorrect. The scope of this legislation suggests an area that could properly be dealt with by Congress under the Commerce Clause (i.e., criminal acts, aggregated across the national economy, substantially affect interstate commerce). Choice **A** is incorrect because the Supreme Court has permitted Congress to delegate broad regulatory and quasi-legislative powers to an administrative agency under relatively imprecise standards. Finally, choice **C** is incorrect because the facts as stated do not indicate that Congress intends to preclude citizens from attacking the proposed rules in the courts or in rulemaking administrative proceedings.

114. **B** Under the Commerce Clause, Congress may regulate any economic activity (even though primarily intrastate) that, in the aggregate, significantly affects interstate commerce. *Gonzales v. Raich*. Because transactions between lenders and borrowers are clearly "economic activity" and have an effect on the interstate movement of monies (i.e., loans are often made to home borrowers by banks in other states, and construction materials often move across state lines), this legislation is valid under the Commerce Clause. The act in question is similar to one that was approved by the Supreme Court as a proper exercise under the Commerce Clause in *Perez v. United States*. Choice **C** is incorrect because the Equal Protection Clause of the Fourteenth Amendment contains restrictions on state governments, not the federal government. Choice **A** is incorrect because the Impairment of Contracts Clause of Article I, §10, is also a restriction on state governments, not Congress (i.e., it prevents the states from impairing obligations created under outstanding agreements), rather than a basis for the enactment of federal legislation. Finally, choice **D** is incorrect because the Privileges and Immunities Clause of the Fourteenth Amendment prevents

the states from impairing the rights of national citizenship (i.e., the right to travel from state to state, the right to petition representatives of the U.S. government, etc.). It is a limitation on state power, **not** a source of federal legislative power.

115. **B** If state legislation places an undue burden on interstate commerce (i.e., the local interest sought to be protected is outweighed by the federal interest in protecting interstate commerce from unnecessary local impediments), the legislation is unconstitutional. *Pike v. Bruce Church, Inc.*; *Southern Pacific Co. v. Arizona*. Except for the possibility that fewer domestic animals and monkeys will be imported into Euphoria for research purposes, the Euphoria enactment has virtually no effect on interstate commerce. Choice **A** is incorrect because, as a consequence of the law, XYZ University has a number of animals that have suddenly become valueless to it, its interest in potentially valuable research has been terminated, and its contracts have been affected. It can be argued that its property has been taken without just compensation, in violation of the Takings Clause (which applies to the states by virtue of the Fourteenth Amendment). Choice **D** is incorrect because the parties have executed a written contract, the object of which has been frustrated by the new law. Because the CIA had contracted with XYZ for the research in question, the Euphoria statute would appear to be unconstitutional under the Contracts Clause of Article I, §10. Finally, choice **C** is incorrect because it is reasonable to argue that Euphoria's new law is impeding a federal interest in the research project and is therefore violating the principles of federal supremacy.

116. **C** A plaintiff must be able to show a direct and immediate personal injury or loss as a consequence of the state's action in order to have standing to challenge the action or its application in a federal court. *Allen v. Wright*. Or she must show that the statute in question is a "specific constitutional limitation" on taxing and spending policies. Her standing to challenge the application of this statute to her proposed speech is greatest as a member of the organization described. Choice **A** is incorrect because a politician must establish more than an *intent* to run before she has any standing as a candidate. Choice **B** is incorrect because the fact that Brighton had voted against the statute is irrelevant. No one is precluded from exercising her right to change or express his opinions. Finally, choice **D** is incorrect because the status of taxpayer does

not generally confer standing to challenge the constitutionality of legislation, except in cases alleging violations of the Establishment Clause that involve governmental financial support of churches or religious institutions.

117. **D** Federal taxpayers have standing to contest spending measures made pursuant to the Taxing and Spending Clause that infringe the Establishment Clause. *Hein v. Freedom from Religion Foundation, Inc.*; *Flast v. Cohen.* In this situation, however, (1) the facts cited do not establish that the gift of land resulted directly from the statute or from any disbursement by Congress; and (2) the gift is justified under the Property Clause (Article IV, §3), rather than the Taxing and Spending Clause. *Valley Forge College v. American United.* Choice **C** is not a likely result because the fact that federal property is conveyed on a one-time basis does not shield the transaction from constitutional scrutiny. Choice **A** is not the best answer because a court cannot reach the merits of a case unless the plaintiffs have standing. It is also uncertain if this requirement would be a mandatory condition; an argument exists that it would. *Tilton v. Richardson.* Finally, choice **B** is factually incorrect because federal agencies have the power to transfer property pursuant to the Property Clause cited above, even in the absence of a specific statutory authorization by Congress.

118. **C** A defendant may be punished for threatening violence against public officials *if* his threat is real, imminent, and unconditional, rather than an expression of political hostility, impatience, or resentment. *Watts v. United States.* Although the statute appears constitutional on its face (a person can be punished for threatening real and imminent physical injury to a public official), it probably cannot be constitutionally applied to Blender in this instance. His remarks appear to suggest that he was simply venting his great frustration and displeasure with the legislation in question (albeit in a highly hyperbolic form) and had no immediate intent of inflicting harm on his representative; thus, his remarks did not constitute a "true threat." Choice **A** is incorrect because the statute is probably not excessively vague. Choice **B** is incorrect for the same basic reason. Finally, choice **D** is incorrect because, although the statute may be constitutional, it cannot be applied to Blender because there was no genuine threat of imminent injury to the legislator.

119. **D** The Due Process Clause of the Fourteenth Amendment protects
a woman's fundamental liberty interest in deciding whether to
terminate a pregnancy prior to the viability of the fetus. *Planned
Parenthood v. Casey.* A state may not impose an "undue burden" on
a woman who wishes to terminate a pregnancy. Choice **A** is incorrect because the Privileges and Immunities Clause of Article IV, §2,
simply requires that noncitizens be afforded the same rights, with
respect to fundamental interests, as citizens. Here, the tax applies
to all abortion providers, regardless of whether they are citizens of
X. Choice **B** is incorrect because the Dormant Commerce Clause
invalidates only laws that discriminate against interstate commerce
or that place a disproportionate burden on interstate commerce.
Neither condition exists on the facts presented. Finally, choice **C**
is incorrect because the tax is not a bill of attainder; it does not
impose legislative punishment on a discrete class of persons.

120. **B** The Due Process Clause of the Fourteenth Amendment prohibits
abortion regulations that impose an "undue burden" on a woman's
decision to terminate a pregnancy. *Stenberg v. Carhart.* Choice **A**
is incorrect because abortion regulations are subject to heightened
scrutiny, not the rational-basis test. Choice **C** states the "intermediate scrutiny" standard of review; this is not the applicable standard
of review for abortion regulations. Finally, choice **D** is incorrect;
since *Stenberg*, the Supreme Court has applied the undue-burden
test, rather than strict-scrutiny test, to abortion regulations.

121. **B** In *Granholm v. Heald*, the Supreme Court held that Michigan could
not permit the direct shipment of wine produced in state while
prohibiting the direct shipment of wine produced out of state; the
justices also struck down a largely identical law from New York
State in a companion case decided at the same time. Accordingly,
Euphoria may not permit in-state producers to ship beer and wine
directly while preventing out-of-state producers from doing so.
Choice **A** is incorrect because the Privileges and Immunities Clause
of Article IV, §2, protects only actual persons, not corporations;
accordingly, it would not afford relief to an out-of-state company
disadvantaged by the law. Choice **C** is also incorrect because the
Granholm Court squarely held that the Twenty-first Amendment
does not permit a state to violate the Dormant Commerce Clause by
favoring in-state producers of alcoholic beverages, including wine
and beer. Choice **D** is a plausible answer in light of the Supreme
Court's holding in *Metropolitan Life Insurance Co. v. Ward* that

a state may not invidiously discriminate against an out-of-state company without violating the Equal Protection Clause; that said, this is not the *strongest* possible answer because *Granholm* directly addresses the point at issue and applies a form of strict scrutiny not applicable to the equal-protection claims under *Ward*.

122. **D** Under *Granholm*, a state may apply nondiscriminatory regulations to direct shipments of wine and beer in order to ensure that minors do not receive the shipments. Thus, age verification requirements, initial in-person contact rules, and the like, if applied to both in-state and out-of-state wineries and breweries, would not be discriminatory and would not trigger the rule of almost *per se* invalidity that governs facially discriminatory state laws. Choice **A** is incorrect because authorizing local wineries and breweries to ship products out of state would not address the facial discrimination, disallowed in *Granholm*, contained in the statute. Choice **B** is also incorrect because permitting direct Internet sales from only in-state producers would not address the facial discrimination against out-of-state producers. Finally, choice **C** is incorrect because broadening a facially discriminatory rule to permit in-state producers of liquor to make direct shipments to in-state residents would simply compound the scope of the discrimination against out-of-state producers, rather than eliminate it.

123. **C** This question directly implicates the splintered Supreme Court ruling in *Morse v. Frederick*, in which a plurality of the Supreme Court sustained disciplinary action against a student who displayed a banner that said "BONG HiTS 4 JESUS" at a leg of the 2002 Winter Olympics torch relay through Juneau, Alaska. The majority opinion held that a school could ban student messages that contradicted the school's antidrug policies. Justice Alito provided the fifth vote and wrote a concurring opinion stating that because of the strong and consistent school policy against the use of illegal drugs, the school principal could lawfully destroy the sign and punish the student, Joseph Frederick, for displaying the sign incident to an event sanctioned by the school, but noted that official suppression of other student messages unrelated to illegal drugs would violate the First Amendment. No good reason exists to believe that the illegal use of steroids would be any less pressing as a legitimate pedagogical concern for high school officials than suppression of a pro-marijuana message. Choice **A** is not correct because *Morse* permits a high school principal to punish a student

for behavior that technically takes place off campus, but which the school embraces as part of its program. Lower federal courts also have sustained disciplinary actions for behavior that takes place off campus, but which is intended to have—and, in fact, has—effects on the public school campus. Choice **B** states the rule applicable to governmental employees under *Pickering* and *Connick*; however, the Supreme Court does not apply this test to public schools students. Choice **D** overstates the scope of a school administrator's power to censor student speech; *Kuhlmeier* and *Fraser* hold that school officials may censor curricular speech more broadly than noncurricular speech, which is governed by *Tinker*; but neither case supports unlimited censorial power by a school official over curricular speech. *Morse* directly addresses the fact pattern and better states the governing rule of constitutional law.

124. **A** The U.S. Court of Appeals for the District of Columbia Circuit quashed, in part, a warrant for the search of Representative William Jefferson's offices in Washington, D.C., in *United States v. Rayburn House Office Building, Room 2113*. The appellate court reasoned that the Speech and Debate Clause protects legislative materials from involuntary disclosure to the executive branch, even incident to a criminal prosecution for bribery, if disclosure of the legislative materials would "disrupt" the legislative process. Under such circumstances, the Speech and Debate Clause would provide a privilege against disclosure. However, relief would likely be limited to materials privileged under the Speech and Debate Clause, most of which would probably be unrelated to the bribery charges. Choice **B** is incorrect because Congress's power to discipline its own members, including the power to expel a member, does not preclude a criminal prosecution of a sitting member of Congress for bribery. *United States v. Brewster*. Choice **C** is incorrect because the Speech and Debate Clause is not limited solely to activity on the floor of the House of Representatives or Senate; instead, it applies to any activity that is integral to the legislative process. Finally, choice **D** is incorrect because, even though a member of Congress is not immune from prosecution for acts of bribery undertaken while in office (*Brewster*), the executive branch may not unduly compromise the legislative process when investigating such charges.

125. **D** In *Crawford v. Marion County Election Board*, the Supreme Court sustained an Indiana law that required a voter to provide a valid government-issued photo ID before being permitted to vote,

against an equal-protection challenge. The Supreme Court concluded that Indiana's law was not facially discriminatory and that the state's interest in preventing voter fraud was "sufficiently weighty to justify the [voting] limitation." *Crawford*; *Burdick v. Takushi*. Choice **A** is incorrect because a photo ID requirement, on its face, does not constitute a racial restriction on voting; nothing in the facts suggests that New Augusta adopted the photo ID requirement with racially discriminatory intent, nor do the facts state that the law has a racially discriminatory impact. Choice **B** is also incorrect because the *Crawford* Court sustained such a statute against an equal-protection challenge. Finally, choice **C** is incorrect because the Necessary and Proper Clause augments the powers of the Congress under Article I, §8; it has no bearing on the scope of a state's legislative authority to regulate voting requirements.

126. **A** In *Rumsfeld v. FAIR*, the Supreme Court rejected a First Amendment objection to the Solomon Amendment, which conditioned the receipt of all federal funds for higher education on universities and colleges providing campus access to military recruiters. The Supreme Court unanimously sustained the Solomon Amendment because the law was a reasonable condition on the voluntary receipt of federal funds, did not coerce speech, and did not require the plaintiff law schools to associate involuntarily with the military; instead, the law simply conditioned receipt of federal funds on permitting military recruiters onto their campuses, despite the military's ban on openly gay and lesbian persons serving in uniform. Choice **B** is incorrect because, although the *FAIR* Court suggested that Congress could directly require colleges and universities to provide access to military recruiters, the law at issue in the question does not directly mandate access; accordingly, the Supremacy Clause is not at issue. Choice **C** is incorrect because the Supreme Court in *FAIR* specifically held that the funding limitation was **not** an unconstitutional condition. Finally, choice **D** is incorrect because the Supreme Court has held that conditional funding, available on a truly voluntary basis, is not a form of coerced expression.

127. **C** In *Pleasant Grove City v. Summum*, the Supreme Court held that a city government could erect a donated monument featuring the Ten Commandments in a public park, but could refuse to accept a monument from the religious organization Summum with the seven principles of Summum inscribed on it. According to the

Supreme Court, the city was speaking itself, rather than creating a public forum or limited-purpose public forum for the speech of third parties. By parity of reasoning, Farm City could choose to erect a war memorial without incurring an obligation to erect a peace monument in the memorial grove, regardless of whether or not private parties initially donated particular elements of the memorial grove to the city. Choice **A** is incorrect because the government, as a speaker, may choose to advance some messages, but not others; establishing a war memorial does not obligate the city to establish a colocated peace memorial. Choice **B** is also incorrect because the city itself is the speaker with respect to the memorial grove in City Park; in this instance, Farm City is not creating a forum for the speech of others, but instead is speaking itself. Finally, choice **D** is incorrect because the city has not created either a general-purpose or limited-purpose public forum—the city is itself the speaker with respect to the memorial grove in City Park.

128. **B** Although a governmental entity may not generally prohibit the use of a traditional public forum, such as a street, sidewalk, or public park, for expressive activities, it may establish and enforce content- and viewpoint-neutral, reasonable time, place, and manner restrictions that regulate use of public property for speech activity. *Ward v. Rock Against Racism.* Here, however, the facts do not state that Farm City has established such rules for the use of City Park in general or the memorial grove in particular. *Clark v. Community for Creative Non-Violence.* The police cannot arbitrarily prohibit the protest by Citizens for Peace; indeed, on the facts presented, the decision to stop the protest appears motivated by viewpoint discrimination, a presumptively invalid basis for governmental censorship of speech. Even if there is some risk of misattribution of the protest speech at the memorial grove, the city government could at most seek to dissociate itself from the offensive speech. *Capitol Square Review and Advisory Bd. v. Pinette.* Choice **A** is not the correct response because would-be protestors do not have an unqualified right of access to government-owned property for speech activity. *Ward v. Rock Against Racism.* Choice **C** is also not correct because the government may not seek to suppress speech based on its viewpoint. Finally, choice **D** is not the correct answer because the park and memorial grove are a traditional public forum, not a limited-purpose public forum. Moreover, even though a city may create a limited-purpose public forum and restrict its use based on

content, it may not limit access to a limited-purpose public forum based on viewpoint, which appears to be the case here.

129. C The Supreme Court has held that even highly offensive protest cannot be banned or be made the basis for imposing civil money damages. *Snyder v. Phelps; Texas v. Johnson.* In *Snyder*, the Supreme Court held that even highly offensive speech made incident to a protest of the funeral of a deceased U.S. Marine killed in combat could not be punished through civil money damage awards if the speakers otherwise lawfully used a traditional public forum for their speech activity and also observed all local time, place, and manner restrictions. Choice **A** is incorrect because a time, place, and manner restriction must also be "content neutral" to be valid; in this instance, a ban on "funeral or burial service protests" is *not* content neutral. *United States v. Stevens.* It is not legally sufficient to regulate the time place and manner of speech without also doing so in a content-neutral fashion. So too, choice **B** is incorrect because that law at issue *is* content based. Finally, choice **D** is incorrect because although the speakers here (EVC) are a religious group, the Free Exercise Clause does not generally prevent the government from applying neutral laws of general applicability to religious groups or organizations. *Church of the Lukumi Babalu Aye v. City of Hialeah.*

130. D On these facts, the law will *most likely* be sustained against a facial constitutional challenge. Although the Second Amendment protects a personal right to keep and bear arms for personal protection and self-defense, it does not provide an absolute or unqualified right to do so, and reasonable government regulations of firearms do not violate the Second Amendment (made applicable to the states under the Due Process Clause of the Fourteenth Amendment). *McDonald v. City of Chicago; District of Columbia v. Heller.* Although the Supreme Court has not yet articulated a clear standard of review, to date, it has invalidated only flat prohibitions against firearms traditionally possessed by private citizens, and not regulations requiring registration of firearms. A training requirement, which is not an undue burden on the right to keep and bear arms, would likely survive constitutional review. Choice **A** is incorrect because the Supreme Court has never held that ownership of guns is an intrinsic right of national citizenship, like traveling across state lines or petitioning Congress. Choice **B** also is incorrect. Although the Arden state law implicates the Second

Amendment, it does not violate the personal right to keep and bear arms. Finally, choice **C** is incorrect because FJ has suffered a concrete and particularized injury in fact that is both traceable and capable of redress in a federal court. Accordingly, FJ would have standing. *Lujan v. Defenders of Wildlife.*

131. **A** Neither the federal nor a state government may regulate the employment of persons involved in the religious or ministerial mission of a church or religious organization, even to prevent discrimination. *Hosanna-Tabor Evangelical Lutheran Church v. EEOC.* Although the facts do not specify whether Jones is involved in religious education, given that she teaches biology, which includes the question of evolution versus creationism, it seems likely that C could successfully argue that her teaching duties touch upon matters of church doctrine. Accordingly, the *most likely* outcome of the litigation is that C will prevail. Choice **B** does not accurately state the applicable rule of law; in point of fact, churches *are* generally subject to government regulation, provided that the regulations are neutral with respect to religion and of general applicability. Choice **C** is incorrect because although the government itself may not engage in religious discrimination, it is not required to prohibit such discrimination by private parties (and, in fact, many private entities, like churches, possess a constitutional privilege to discriminate in ways that the government itself may not). Choice **D** is incorrect because the Supreme Court has unanimously held that government may not generally prohibit a church from enforcing orthodoxy with respect to teachers in a church-run school.

132. **D** The Supreme Court has consistently held that the Guaranty Clause of Article IV, §4 does not give rise to justiciable rights enforceable in the federal courts. *Luther v. Borden; New York v. United States.* Accordingly, the district court should dismiss JS's lawsuit as presenting a nonjusticiable political question. Choice **A** is incorrect because no case law exists to establish that an unusually long term of office for a high-ranking state official would violate the Guaranty Clause; in fact, the Supreme Court consistently has refused to reach the merits of claims arising under the clause. Choice **B** is also incorrect because the Supremacy Clause simply states that when federal law and state law conflict, the federal law governs. In this instance, however, there is no federal law because the federal government lacks the authority to impose political structures on the states, presumably including the length of the

governor's term of office. U.S. Const., amend. X. Choice **C** is also incorrect. In cases involving Equal Protection claims, the Supreme Court has recognized voter standing to challenge unconstitutional state election rules, such as racial gerrymanders and malapportioned legislative districts. *Shaw v. Reno; Baker v. Carr.* The logic of these cases should extend to a Guaranty Clause claim, although, again, the federal courts consistently have refused to adjudicate on the merits claims arising under this clause.

133.   **C** The Supreme Court has squarely held that Congress has the power to establish and initiate involuntary civil commitment proceedings for convicted sex offenders incident to the Necessary and Proper Clause of Art. I, §8, cl. 18. *United States v. Comstock.* Choice **A** is incorrect because the involuntary commitment of someone to a mental institution by the government does not constitute economic or commercial activity, nor does it implicate the channels or instrumentalities of commerce, or goods, services, and persons using those instrumentalities. *United States v. Morrison.* Choice **B** also is incorrect because convicted sex offenders are not the property of the government; accordingly, the Property Clause has no bearing on this question. Finally, choice **D** is incorrect because involuntarily committing a person to a mental institution does not directly involve taxing and spending to support the general welfare; it is not the ***most relevant*** constitutional provision.

134.   **A** The Supreme Court has rejected the argument that violent video games, at least as to minors, should constitute a new category of unprotected speech. *Brown v. Entertainment Merchants Association.* In general, a content based regulation of speech, even as to minors, will be invalidated "unless [a state government] can demonstrate that it passes strict scrutiny—that is, unless it is justified by a compelling state interest and is narrowly drawn to serve that interest." *Brown* found that protecting minors from violent video games did not constitute a compelling government interest, holding that "the State's evidence is not compelling." Choice **B** is incorrect because classifications involving age are not generally subject to heightened scrutiny and Arcadia could probably show that the statute satisfies true rationality review. Accordingly, the Equal Protection Clause ***could not*** serve as a basis for invalidating the law. Choice **C** is incorrect because a reviewing court should not sustain the law against a First Amendment challenge. Finally, choice **D** is incorrect because S has standing to challenge the suit—as a seller of violent

video games to minors, the store suffers an injury in fact that is both traceable and redressable.

135. **A** Congress may constitutionally prohibit direct campaign contributions by corporations, although it may not, consistent with the First Amendment, prohibit corporations from making direct and uncoordinated expenditures supporting or opposing candidates for public office. *Citizens United v. FEC*; *Buckley v. Valeo*. Choice **B** is incorrect because the Guaranty Clause is not a source of judicially enforceable constitutional rights. Choice **C** is also incorrect because the First Amendment does not protect a right on the part of corporations to give direct contributions in unlimited amounts to candidates for federal elective office. Finally, Choice **D** is incorrect because the Equal Protection Clause only protects corporations against irrational and fundamentally unfair discriminatory treatment; a prohibition against making direct contributions to candidates for public office would not violate this standard. Also, strictly speaking, the Equal Protection Clause applies *only* against the state governments, and not against the federal government; the Fifth Amendment's Due Process Clause, however, incorporates an identical equal protection component.

136. **D** The Eleventh Amendment protects states from being sued against their will in the federal courts and also stands for a broader concept of state sovereign immunity. *Seminole Tribe v. Florida*. It has nothing to do with whether Congress can condition receipt of federal funds on local officials not receiving bribes and therefore represents the **least relevant** constitutional provision. Choice **A** is incorrect because the giving or taking of bribes is economic or commercial activity that, aggregated across the national economy, substantially affects it. *Gonzales v. Raich*. Choice **B** is also incorrect because Congress may make any necessary regulations regarding government property, presumably including cash grants to the states to support federal programs or initiatives Finally, choice **C** is incorrect because the Spending Clause, in conjunction with the Necessary and Proper Clause, provides the most appropriate constitutional basis for enactment of such a law. *Sabri v. United States*.

137. **D** Congress may not transfer the adjudication of core Article III cases to so-called Article I or "legislative" courts that are not staffed with Article III judges; doing so violates the separation of powers. *Stern v. Marshall*. Choice **A** is incorrect. Although it states a true

proposition of law—that Congress may shape and define the jurisdiction of the lower federal courts—in this instance this proposition is irrelevant. Congress has transferred cases falling squarely
within the judicial power of the United States to non-Article III
tribunals; it has not reassigned cases within Article III or state
courts. Choice **B** is also incorrect. A common law counter claim
is *not* a "public right." "Public rights" involve claims arising under
government benefit programs (such as Social Security), tax claims,
and the like. Finally, choice **C** is incorrect because the adjudication
of common law claims before ALJs working for the SEC simply
does not implicate the nondelegation doctrine. The nondelegation
doctrine requires Congress to articulate an "intelligible principle"
that circumscribes the president's policy making authority when it
delegates administrative authority; the doctrine has absolutely no
relevance on these facts.

138. **A** The president must have the ability to direct and even remove all
federal officers involved in executing the law; a two-tiered system
of "good cause" removal unduly attenuates the president's super-
visory powers and violates the separation of powers doctrine.
Free Enterprise Fund v. PCAOB. Choice **B** is incorrect because the
nondelegation doctrine does prohibit "good cause" removal provisions, but instead requires Congress to establish an "intelligible
principle" when it grants discretionary policy making authority to
the President. Choice **C** is also incorrect because the Commerce
Clause does not limit or otherwise constrain Congress's power to
assign adjudication of common law claims to non-Article III tribunals. Finally, choice **D** is also incorrect because the statute is *not*
constitutional; as noted above, it squarely violates the separation
of powers doctrine as explicated in *Free Enterprise Fund.*

Table of Cases

Index

References are to the number of the question raising the issue. "E" indicates an Essay Question; "M" indicates a Multiple-Choice Question.

Teacher certification, denial to members of Fascist, Nazi, or Communist Party, E26

Birth control devices, sales to minors, M25

Breach of peace

Picketing, prohibition of, E19

Vagueness, M58

Breast implant surgery, imposition of tax on, M105

Bribery, M124, M133

Cable television system, transmission of motion pictures via, E17

Campaign contributions, restrictions on, M135

Censorship, M123, M128

Children and minors

Adoption, E22

Children born to unmarried parents, inheritance by, M54

Contraceptive devices, sales to minors, M25

Drug abuse-related felony, effect on custody of children, M29

Gender discrimination, sale of motor vehicles to minors, M91

Citizens

See Aliens and citizens

Civil service employees of armed forces, mandatory retirement of, M12

Coerced speech, M126

Commerce Clause, E3, E30

Commercial speech, restriction of, M7

Commissions

Appointment of members of executive commission, M113

Delegation of authority of Congress, E21

Computers, provision by state to public and private schools, M9, M10

Concealed weapons, carrying of, M3

Conditional spending, E30, M126

Congressional appropriations, implementation by president, M16

Congressional privileges and immunities, M124

Consent to loss of citizenship, E6

Constitutional facts, appellate review, E28

Contempt of court

Generally, E5, E15

Exhaustion of state remedies, E15

Content based speech regulations, E32, M134

Contraceptive devices, generally, E31

Contraceptive devices, sales to minors, M25

Contracts, impairment of

Animal research, prohibition of, M52, M115

Beard and uniform requirements for municipal employees, E6

Emergency relief legislation, E29

Land use restrictions, M26

Motion pictures, transmission via cable television system, E17

Oysters, sale to out-of-state entities, M68

Public construction contract, rescission of, M15

Criminal laws that are generally applicable, Establishment Clause, M3